IN-SERVICE TRAINING FOR
SOCIAL AGENCY PRACTICE

# In-Service Training for

# Social Agency Practice

MARTHA
MOSCROP

University of Toronto Press

# Foreword

DR. G. F. DAVIDSON

*Deputy Minister of National Welfare*

PROBABLY there has never been a time when social agencies, public and private, have not been profoundly concerned with two main problems: staff and finances. Of the two, the problem of meeting staff requirements has proved to be even more intractable than that of obtaining needed funds. Particularly during the last two decades, money has been easier to come by than qualified, competent personnel without which the fresh breath of life can never be instilled into an agency programme, however promising it may appear on paper.

This chronic shortage of personnel to staff our social agencies is in large part, of course, the product of the higher standards and requirements that we have progressively set for ourselves. There was a time when many government agencies, and some voluntary welfare organizations, were content to fill their staff requirements with run-of-the-mill "job-seekers" who, on entering employment, became "job-holders" with no thought of initial professional qualifications or the need for effort to achieve professional improvement on the job in the years ahead. As awareness developed of the need for professional competence and standards of performance in the field of social work, and as public and private social agencies began increasingly to specify in their job requirements partial or thorough professional training and experience in all positions having some social work content, two facts emerged very clearly. In the first place, the professional social worker—the full-fledged product of the professional training offered by the North American schools of social work at university and post-graduate level—came into great demand. There has never been a time during the past quarter century in the United States and Canada when we have had half as many professional social workers available for employment as there were jobs, demanding professional qualifications, waiting to be filled. The second fact to emerge is that the employing agencies, even those which were fully committed to a policy of drawing on the schools of social work for their professional staff requirements, could not, no matter what their preference, rely upon the professional schools as their sole source of staff supply.

In order to survive and to continue operations on a normal basis, agencies have had to improvise. They have been obliged to recruit on a supplementary basis by drawing into their staff ranks persons not qualified in the full professional sense so far as social work itself is concerned—but bringing with them many of the required elements in training or experience from allied professions such as nursing, teaching, personnel work and so on. Nor could the agencies stop there. Once started on this course, the agencies have had no alternative than to embark upon difficult, expensive, time-consuming programmes of orientation, training and professional development in order to "convert" so far as possible the skills and experience of these persons into skills and experience relevant to the tasks imposed upon the social agencies.

It is this problem, which the agency faces—not because it wants to, but because it has to—in the recruiting and training of a large portion of its professional staff from outside the ranks of professional social work itself that Miss Moscrop, herself essentially an "agency" person, treats with clarity, insight and sensitivity in this present study. Drawing from her rich experience as Supervisor of Staff Training and Development Programs in the British Columbia Social Welfare Branch, Miss Moscrop has extracted therefrom principles applicable to the experience and to the needs of social welfare agencies and executives in many different settings. She has sifted out the common denominator of a doctrine that is widely applicable over the broad field of social work, and she has fashioned this out of her own intensely practical and down-to-earth experience.

She has great understanding of the need for maintaining, without any shadow of compromise, professional standards and values in the training process: more than that, she has shown a keen awareness of the limitations of the agency's role and function in this area, and of our prime dependence on our professional associations and our schools of social work for preserving and strengthening what lies at the very core of professional social work training. But, having given full recognition of these factors, Miss Moscrop insists, with the conviction born of successful first-hand experience, that the agencies must themselves do something to achieve their own salvation in the face of deepening and apparently never-ending staff shortages. Her outline of what agencies can do to contribute to the solution of their own baffling problems will be for many a harassed agency executive and social work educator a timely addition to the literature of social work.

# Contents

# IN-SERVICE TRAINING FOR
# SOCIAL AGENCY PRACTICE

# I. In-Service Training:
# A Staff Building Programme

THE TERM IN-SERVICE TRAINING, as it is used throughout this book, means that part of a social agency's total programme of staff development which prepares otherwise unprepared people to do the work for which they are employed. In-service training cannot be regarded as a substitute for professional training obtained in a school of social work. But, if it has form, employs appropriate educational methods, and has objectives of which the whole agency is aware, in-service training can achieve not only its immediate goal of maintaining the agency's services, but also the long-range goal of providing suitable candidates for the schools of social work and hence for the profession.

This book has been written to show how these aims may be successfully achieved in any agency affected by shortages of professionally qualified social workers. Though based largely on experience in one agency, comparison with other agencies' efforts with on-the-job training reveals basic similarities as well as a common concern to extract some good from the adversity of staff shortages now afflicting the majority of agencies.

The experiences of British Columbia's Social Welfare Branch with in-service training covers more than a decade. In that time, approximately one-third of those who have been given this training have obtained all or part of their professional training, that is, have completed one or two years of study at a school of social work. All except a very few of this number are still employed in the agency, and all are still engaged in social work. The remainder dropped out before acquiring school training and for the usual reasons: chiefly, marriage among the women and, among the men, salaries which were found, after trial, to be too low to meet family responsibilities. Some have left at the agency's request, having proved, after trial, that social work was not their true vocation. A very few, about 5 per cent of the total staff, each of whom is now filling a niche adequately, may never obtain professional qualifications. Any plan involving the destinies of people can never wholly succeed.

The Social Welfare Branch is essentially a rural agency, and one of the stipulations of employment is that the applicant must be willing to work wherever he may be needed in the province. This stipulation has deterred some, to be sure, but the number of people who have responded to the appeal of the more rigorous life of a rural social worker is testimony to the fact that good people, possessing genuinely altruistic motives and a keen desire to enter the field of social work, do exist and can be found. At the same time the appeal of rural practice would not be as strong were there not a goal in view for each person whose progress, measured by a continuous process of evaluation, is up to an anticipated standard. This is the goal of obtaining professional qualifications by study at a school of social work.

To some, but not to all, the agency can award a bursary to help defray the costs of school training. More money than is provided at present is needed for this purpose. (In fact, more joint thinking among agencies, schools, profession, governments and the community must be given to the problem of the high costs of education for social work, for to these costs can be attributed some of the decline in school enrolments.) Whether they can get financial help or not, however, the in-service trained people increasingly feel the need to be professionally qualified in order to do their work more adequately. If they knew more, they invariably say, they could do more to help those who seek and need more skilled services than they can give. In other words, they quickly realize the extent and gravity of the problems the agency exists to meet. They feel and are willing to share the weight of responsibility such problems exert upon the agency. This identification with the agency is a wholly valid reason for investing the agency's money in the trainee's further education.

This plan of education with its ultimate goal of achieving professional qualifications is placed before the trainee when he applies for a position. This is not done primarily for the purpose of enticing the applicant into the agency, though it often has this effect. This is a goal the agency has set for itself. From the beginning, the administrators of the Social Welfare Branch have been convinced that the "true intent, meaning and spirit" of the social legislation they are charged to administer can be best carried out by qualified social workers, and throughout the years they have endeavoured to build a staff comprised of such people.

It has been a "building" task in every sense of the word. By 1953, it was as near completion as it may ever be. At that time, 76 per cent of the staff were, in whole or in part, professionally qualified. Since 1953, that percentage has dropped to just over 50. This drop is a fair enough measure of the crisis today facing not only the majority of social agencies, but also, if less drastically, the profession and the schools of social work. Moreover, the prediction is that it will persist for at least another decade. In-service training is by no means the only solution to the problem, but it is a realistic, prudent and hopeful way to maintain present standards of services and to build for the future.

The remainder of this chapter attempts to justify that last statement by a review of some of the principal considerations underlying an in-service training programme. It would be pretentious to refer to these considerations as "principles," since the evidence of more than one agency's practice will quite obviously be required to arrive at any such general conclusions. Rather, they represent a point of view or a way of thinking about in-service training. This point of view is what is meant by the phrase appearing in the first paragraph of this chapter: ". . . objectives of which the whole agency is aware." The whole agency needs to hold this point of view, to think in this way about such a programme, in order to ensure its success as a staff building effort.

There are five general points to be considered: (1) the nature of the need the social agencies are set up to meet; (2) the selection of the people whom the agency employs and trains; (3) the scope, or more accurately, the limitations, of an agency training scheme; (4) a definitive examination of the terms "agency standards" and "agency practices"; and (5) consideration of methods other than in-service training which an agency can employ to build staff and maintain standards.

### The Nature of the Need

The agencies employing the greatest number of unqualified social workers are in the main organized by governments, and of these, perhaps the majority are concerned with the problem of destitution. Their purpose, determined by legislation, is to meet the needs of the people who are, for certain reasons recognized by law, unable to maintain a "reasonably normal and healthful existence" by their own efforts. Among these the aged comprise the majority. The agencies employing the next largest number of workers are those classified either as governmental, or quasi-governmental, and which have as their purpose the protection of children whose development is endangered by parental neglect, orphanhood, or like conditions. There has recently been a growing number of agencies dealing with juvenile and adult delinquency, for society is beginning to comprehend that delinquency and crime can be treated with some success by methods which are almost indistinguishable from those of social work. At the same time there is an increasing demand for qualified people to effect the rehabilitation of the physically handicapped, again the methods being almost identical with those of social work. The need is also acute for social work services as an adjunct of psychiatry and medicine, in clinics, hospitals and communities, to treat the social and psychological complexities which arise from and contribute to mental, chronic and acute illness. Family agencies, usually set up under voluntary auspices, may touch all or none of the above social problems as they seek to treat serious emotional difficulties which threaten the stability of individual families, and hence the stability of family life in general.

This catalogue of social agencies does not exhaust the list, by any means, but it is perhaps a sufficient indication of the serious need for competent, trained people to do these saving, healing and preventive tasks. The social workers employed by the Social Welfare Branch must, in rural and smaller urban communities, meet every one of the needs enumerated above. They are general practitioners. Half of them are qualified social workers; half are in-service trained. There can be little wonder that the latter soon feel compelled to obtain proper qualifications. What their experience proves, moreover, is that any one of the separate kinds of need the total staff tries so hard to meet requires all the knowledge and skill that professional training provides. For the effort entails, indeed the law when properly interpreted usually demands, finding a remedy wherever and whenever possible.

The nature of need any social agency is set up to meet, if it is conscious of its true purpose, entails remedial effort. There are, however, those who maintain that professional qualifications are not required in some agencies. Those set up to give financial aid to people who are threatened by destitution, are the agencies most frequently cited in this connection. British Columbia's provincial social workers would say, loudly and firmly, that here of all places the knowledge and skills of social work are especially needed. They might, if pressed, go further and say that even more knowledge and more refined skills than may be acquired now in a school of social work are needed. Destitution or poverty, social research proves, can breed multiples of a problem, which grow infinitely more difficult and more costly to treat as they progress. Without early remedial efforts, initiated on the day and at the hour help is first solicited, the outcome can be almost predicted. The numbers on the public assistance rolls, in spite of enlightened laws, have grown rather than diminished. More money is not the answer, except for those few who cannot respond to remedial treatment (who may well need more in order to preserve a better semblance of decency and dignity than is now possible). The real solution lies in the provision of professional services as well as money.

Professional services begin and end with the people who are employed to give them. It is the understanding the social workers bring to the task, their judgment and their devotion which determine the efficiency of the services. It is clearly the agency's responsibility to provide every known means to deepen this understanding, to develop these powers of judgment, and sustain and recognize this devotion. This is an ethical matter. From this responsibility derives the administrator's chief duty: to see that, ever more effectively, the remedial intent, the true meaning and spirit of the legislation or of the agency's services are carried out.

Staff development programmes are the chief means by which this obligation is discharged. Such programmes are for the whole staff, but in-service training is designed for only part of the staff, those who have been unable to begin the cultivation of understanding, judgment and devotion by means of academic study. This cultivation must for them begin in the agency. If the right people are selected, if the training provided can eventually be transplanted with ease into the broader field of academic study, then standards of service will be maintained. In simpler terms, in-service training is an introductory form of education for social work.

## THE PEOPLE EMPLOYED

The wise selection of people employed and given in-service training is the chief safeguard against the dangers which the doubting may see in such a programme. The criteria of selection used by the Social Welfare Branch are the same as those employed by the school of social work in choosing their candidates, with one significant exception. Graduation from a university, though always preferred, cannot always be insisted upon. This is partly because the educational standard of the total population of this young province is such that, as yet, there are not enough people available—that is, who are not already vocationally well placed—with a complete university education. A compromise must be made. Even more careful screening is, therefore, necessary to ensure that lack of a complete university education does not mean lack of intelligence.

The University of British Columbia's School of Social Work will accept for training each year a few students without graduate standing whom the Social Welfare Branch has employed and trained. The School quite properly demands evidence of the abilities of such people to undertake academic courses, and this is always forthcoming. For if they did not have these abilities, the agency would long ago have found this out and advised them to leave.

About 40 per cent of the in-service trained staff of the Social Welfare Branch do not have a university degree. Once they achieve some professional training—and some achieve all of it, that is, two full years—although they do not acquire a degree, to be sure, they do acquire the right to the salary of a qualified person, and the same opportunity for advancement. Promotions are made on merit, but the persons without degrees are in competition for promotion with colleagues who hold the degree of Bachelor or Master of Social Work, and as a university education seldom fails to increase merit, advancement for those without it is not frequent. Their strong sense of vocation, however, and their loyalty to the agency and the people who need their services, make them steady, responsive and responsible staff members. They reinforce the growing strength of the agency.

The majority of the people employed and trained who already have a university education are not newly graduated. The Social Welfare Branch will not in fact employ any graduate, especially the new one, until all the possibilities of his obtaining professional training first are thoroughly explored. The principal deterrent is, of course, lack of money and loss of earning power, for the great majority of these applicants have worked since graduation, and many of the men have families to support. The newly graduated applicant will be accepted only when he has been counselled by the school faculty and referred back to the agency, and then only if he is at least twenty-three years of age. People with a university degree are a special responsibility for the agency, since they are expected to make greater progress, to use more immediately and to assimilate more quickly what understanding the agency can give them of their new vocation. There is a recognition of the eventual leadership which these people may bring to the agency and to the profession. All are individuals of course, and it is with the individual talent and natural abilities and interests of each that future educational and vocational directions are plotted.

There is a natural tendency, perhaps, as administrators contemplate in-service training as a necessary thing to do, to regard the in-service trained person in the abstract. If given any physical properties at all, the time and trouble which has to be taken with him tends to give him a vexatious complexion. This attitude is utterly wrong. There is, rather, in the experience on which this book is based, room for wonder that so many splendid men and women have found their way into what is their true vocation by means of in-service training. The time and trouble which initially must be taken with them is more than compensated for in the qualities of mind and spirit they bring to the work, and social work proves its worth by its ability to attract such serious-minded, socially conscious young persons in spite of low salaries.

Education and intelligence are not, of course, the sole criteria for judging a person's suitability for this exacting profession, but they are of first importance. Motivation, which is equally important, is best when it springs from feelings guided by reason. The devotion the social worker feels to the cause he serves, in the words of Georges-Henri Levesque, o.p., "remains wise because it is lucid." Devotion and judgment, in the eyes of this great Canadian scholar and teacher, are the ideal qualities of the social worker. Their cultivation is the task of schools, profession and agencies if the common purposes of all are to be realized. This is the task of the social worker himself too, of course. It is a task that quite literally never stops.

For the majority this task is best begun in a school of social work, but the times dictate that that ideal cannot for many years be fully reached. The need for the agencies' services meanwhile increases. The agencies must, therefore, set about the business of preparing the unprepared whom they must employ for the work. They must make the necessary start in the long educational process involved. The problems become those of knowing how to make this start, how far to go in making it, using what methods, employing which people as teachers, and determining how much time, effort and money to spend in the operation.

## THE SCOPE OF THE PLAN

In-service training and staff development programme are inseparable. Without the larger programme, in-service training would not achieve its purposes. For agency training thus becomes progressive, having a cumulative effect. It is this cumulative effect which supports the contention that standards of service will not fall when such a programme exists.

Since "in-service training prepares people to do the work for which they are employed," initial training will be determined by the nature of the work the agency does, and how it does it. These things must, of course, be taught to any newly appointed member of staff, whether professionally qualified or not. Orientation and in-service training are similar, but the latter has an additional ingredient: the application of reason and reasoning to the learning that takes place. The question posed, considered and answered is "why?" All administrative operations are taught with this question uppermost, for administration should be a means to an end, not an end in itself. The means must be learned, but they must also be comprehended for what they are. Such comprehension inevitably leads to an emerging understanding of the ends to be achieved. This is a professional understanding. It is at this point that professional methods merge with administrative methods to achieve objectives which are common to both. These methods of operation are indivisible. The one cannot be taught or learned without the other, any more than one can be practised without the other.

To learn methods alone would be sterile, however, unless such learning was accompanied by efforts to understand the process of applying them. This is the professional heart of the matter. There can be no effective application without knowledge and learned and intuitive skill. The knowledge required to make methods effective is vast. Skill implies talent as well as understanding, and can only be perfected by practice and by a continual assessment of practice. Time alone dictates that in-service training can do no more than introduce these purely professional ingredients. The introduction may nevertheless be incisive enough to be immediately useful, enabling the trainee not only to function but to proceed from then on consciously to refine his skills and deepen his knowledge.

The way in which this start in learning is made is of considerable importance. Two interdependent ways are used in the Social Welfare Branch. One is to learn to do the work by doing it under capable supervision. The other way is to learn about the work by talking, and thus thinking, about it in a directed, focused fashion. The talk precedes and follows the learning-by-doing, the time interval for doing being twice that of the talking. Thus the training plan has form: a beginning, a middle part and an end. Learning, of course, does not end, when the training period is over, for the same capable supervision continues, and other devices for staff development have their sure effect. The completion of the training period is a needed punctuation mark, an interim objective attained.

This rather bold way of learning, which is not for the faint-hearted, is not without its discipline. The discipline involved is two-sided. On the one side is the trainee's full awareness of the introductory nature of in-service training. (He is never permitted to forget it. He seldom needs to be reminded. His application of the little he knows to the baffling problems he encounters is reminder enough.) He, more than anyone, realizes how little he knows, and to know more becomes a compulsion. On the other side is the agency's realization of how little he knows. The wind cannot always be tempered to this shorn lamb, but as far as possible it is, at least in the first year of employment. Though he will have to assume responsibility for a case-load, in the management of which he has had a learning experience in the training period, the agency cannot expect his services in relation to it to be given with an assurance of results or at the pace expected of his professionally trained colleagues. Though both sureness and pace increase slowly but surely, the agency must nevertheless define the degree of competence it expects the trainee to achieve.

The expense of in-service training is great. Extra dividends as well as capital gains accrue, however, in time. Those who are successful will stay, not only in the work, but more than likely in the agency that has made this investment in them. Because it is expensive, the agency may —indeed should—stipulate that a specific period of service follow the in-service training period before leave is asked to attend a school of social work. In the Social Welfare Branch this period is two years. Besides making for a much needed stability of staff, it has been found that it takes this length of time for the majority to assimilate, in the slower way they must, the full meaning of the work the agency does. Motivation and ability are well tested in this period, and those who pass this test are ready to assimilate and afterwards use, promptly and effectively, the training they obtain in the school.

All of this is a staff-building effort. No edifice, it must be remembered, can be constructed overnight. It may take as many as five or as few as three years before the strength of in-service training is felt. After that a spiral of gains sets in. In ten years, provided the materials and equipment are of the best procurable quality, and the design appropriately functional (in the architectural meaning of the word), the full effect should be abundantly apparent. Standards in fact will not only remain steady but will appreciably rise. The growing crisis in supply and demand of qualified social workers led an able researcher to conclude in an address: "It is not now a question of in-service training *or* school training, but of in-service training *and* school training, at least until supply equals demand."[1] The holding of agency standards in the vaguely defined interim depends upon the agency assuming this responsibility.

[1]Mrs. Flora Hurst (Supervisor of the Social Welfare Section, Division of Research and Statistics, Department of National Health and Welfare), who headed the study, *Survey of Supply and Demand of Social Workers in Canada*, Queen's Printer, Ottawa, 1952.

## AGENCY STANDARDS OF PRACTICE

The term "agency standards" requires definition. The word implies some form of measurement, and the first measure is the results of the work the agency does when compared with the agency's objectives. Assuming that the agency's objectives are the remedying and ameliorating of social distress, "the adjustment of the individual in the interests of society," they are thus identical with the major objectives of the profession of social work. Secondly, agency standards can be measured by the methods the agency employs to achieve these results. The criteria of this measurement are those established by the profession, and they are empirically as well as philosophically derived. The process of perfecting them which began fifty years ago has by no means stopped. Agencies have a major part to play in this process, the more exciting because social work is now ready to pursue new intellectual frontiers. The agency is the laboratory, where realism—the pragmatic thought—can test professional principles, as these are refined and deepened, to ensure that they will be applicable and appropriate. Meanwhile, the realities of agency practice, made the more pronounced by the shortage of social workers, determine whether agency standards can approach professional standards as they have evolved thus far.

The major "reality" is the volume of work the agency does. In the opinion of many, this volume is sufficient to constitute a field of special inquiry by those responsible for a nation's broad social policies. The agencies in the meantime are ethically compelled to give services in response to the demands of their communities and of those who need their help. Although agency practices and methods are tempered by the numbers to be served, and by the gravity of the problems each presents, professional methods must still be employed. Professional skill is required to determine the seriousness of the individual problems brought to the agency for solution and the kind of service which is appropriate to each of these. Agencies and profession alike have an obligation to define and develop the kind of methods which are appropriate in these circumstances.

The methods or practices of the Social Welfare Branch, for example, are geared to volume and to the nature of the needs this agency serves. The needs of the greater number who are served arise largely from external stresses: unemployment, for all its many causes; family crisis, the most prevalent being the desertion of the breadwinner; illness and incapacitation which the client cannot afford or is reluctant to have treated; ignorance of or indifference to the responsibilities and pleasures of parenthood; lack of opportunity to develop attitudes and pursuits which give positive meaning to life; the concomitants of all these—bad housing, poor nutrition, occupational misplacement, declining abilities, the sense of frustration and defeat. That strong negative feelings accompany these external stresses is to be taken for granted. That inner stresses arising from faulty nurture, inadequate endowment, and under-privilege may well bring about external stress is never overlooked. The remedying of externally derived problems depends upon being able to meet proven need promptly, and at the same time discern the degree of inner stress involved. The plan of treatment or service is determined by the social worker's assessment of both outer and inner stress, the employment of appropriate resources to lesser outer pressures, and the extending of a warmly reassuring, encouraging and understanding relationship to lessen inner pressures.

This kind of service Florence Hollis has aptly called "environmental modification" and "psychological support."[2] These terms serve admirably to define the levels or techniques of professional practice the Social Welfare Branch attempts to employ. It may not be going too far to say that these levels define the competence of the majority of social workers in the first few years of their experience. There are no more important levels of practice than these. That the practitioners must have training to be successful in their practice should need no proof. If proof is needed, this simple analogy may provide it. The knowledge and skills demanded by the majority of people when bones are broken, babies are born, or measles and mumps contracted are those of the family doctor who is a general practitioner. The family doctor treats the whole person in his family setting and uses methods and prescribes treatment appropriate to each patient's unique make-up. So the social worker does his work. Had all those who are well known to public agencies as the "chronic dependents" been given such treatment when they first brought their problems to the agency, the chances are strong that their status in life would be very different today. For environmental modification and psychological support are both remedial and preventive in their import and intention.

The realities facing most social agencies suggest that the schools should, as the majority indeed do, temper their teaching of professional methods, knowledge and skills to prepare people for practice at levels that are attainable, desirable and at the same time of proven value. Another way of putting it is to ask that the training be first for general practice. (Perhaps it could be provided in one year of study, making the second year a more specialized effort based on the talent and

[2]See Florence Hollis, "The Techniques of Casework," *Journal of Social Casework*, June 1949.

crystallized interests of the practitioner determined after a period of practice.) The generic basis of the curriculum of the University of British Columbia's School of Social Work happily complements the generalized practice of the Social Welfare Branch, each having had an effect upon the other. This foundation common to both education and practice, and the "togetherness" of objectives, have tended to achieve an even development in standards of agency practice. From this even growth, there is every indication of the development of greater understanding and skill among the professionally trained staff, a large number of whom have only one year of training on top of in-service training. Their consistent desire to add to their knowledge in order to serve with increasing competence is a complementary value the agency does well to recognize. Further education may, in fact, be planned to make the best use of recognized abilities, talents, and knowledge. The positions of supervisor and consultant are thus filled, for example, positions which are two of the most important in regard to programmes of in-service training and staff development. Supervisors and consultants are the agency's teachers, and teachers must have knowledge from which to teach.

The knowledge the social worker should possess is staggering. Critics of the profession, some within its ranks but most without, deplore its lack of scholarship in the social sciences, particularly, perhaps, its failure to hold an eclectic viewpoint on psychological theory. The youth of this profession is an excuse as, indeed, is the relative youth of the social sciences generally. The profession has kept pace with new-found theory[3] as it has come from the research of the scientists. In this decade, leaders of the profession are attempting to assess older theories and to shape into teachable form new knowledge which is applicable to practice in these modern times. This is not, in short, a static profession, but one which is intensely dynamic. The frailties of humankind—social workers are people—and the slowness of new theories to circulate account for the perpetuation of closed circuits of thought if indeed they exist at all.

Old truths which have affected behaviour and conduct over the centuries may not have had the amount of attention they deserve. Relatively few social workers have made a precise study of philosophy —ethics, morals, religion, law. Surely this is required knowledge. Social workers are, as yet, humanists first and scientists second. As humanists they are doers, for they see what is to do. They cannot tolerate suffer-

[3]See Annette Garrett, "Historical Survey of the Evolution of Social Work," *Social Casework*, June 1949.

ing, otherwise they would not be social workers. They need, by their own admission, an appreciation of the verities as well as the realities which shape man's destiny.

The identification of the social worker with his profession assists in the search for such an appreciation. For professional practice, as agency practice, has authority or influence to the extent that it derives from beliefs, from a philosophy, a system of values, ethics. A moral judgment must be made not merely on the quality of the practice, that is, on the deeds done, but also on the quality of the doer of the deeds, the practitioner. Growth in the practitioner's quality of performance is commensurate with the growth of his comprehension and acceptance of the philosophy of his profession, in which at this time humanism and liberalism seem to predominate. It is commensurate also with his adherence to the advice of the Delphic Oracle, "Know thyself." This qualitative development leads to one end: the acquisition of a true humility. No profession exists that needs that quality more than does social work.

There is pain associated with this growth, for many life and cultural forces militate against it, and it may never be complete. The schools of social work provide the best start, for time and the freedom of the setting permit growth. The agency, by its affirmation of the value of qualitative practice, and its exertion to achieve it, permits a continuation of this conscious self-development, but cannot start it. Here of all places it is clear that agency training is no substitute for school training.

In in-service training the intrinsic meaning of the term "being professional" cannot, in the very nature of things, be more than indicated, though this can be done strongly enough to make the desire to search for its meaning a life-long quest. The vast knowledge on which social work practice is based cannot be more than alluded to, though a desire to fill in the gaps by every means available can be inculcated. The methods of practice—which aim at providing support and improving the environment—can be taught in an introductory way, and the lessons strengthened by staff development, especially by capable supervision. Above all else, a respect and a desire for education develop as the trainees realize how little they know and how much more they should know.

## OTHER EFFORTS TO BUILD STAFF

The administrators of social agencies need no reminder that staffing is their most important function. The operation of any agency depends upon the staff. In this sense the staff is the agency and the agency is the staff. It is an animate thing, moreover, possessed of energies and spirit. Directing the energies of the staff and sustaining its spirit to achieve the objectives of the agency is the administrator's responsibility. The administrator must work to develop a stable staff, one whose energies are well employed and whose spirit is reflected in the quality of the work it does. This is a field of inquiry beyond the scope of this book, and now only brief allusion is made to the components of this aspect of the administrator's task.

The term "working conditions" usually connotes the physical comforts and respectabilities of the setting in which the work takes place. These are always important, of course, but they are especially so to the users of the agency's services. The natural dignity of people—staff and clients—is recognized when the setting is dignified. Good working conditions also imply the orderliness of the work and a certain reasonableness of administrative procedure. Sensible office routines ensure that there is a minimum of waste motion and of muddle, and the simplification of the "paper work" is not only more efficient, but it also frees the staff to do what they are employed to do, serve people. An intelligent delegation of responsibility is also suggested. People measure up to such responsibility when it is given to them and grow in stature as a result. The well-known "line of authority" is a component of working conditions. The channels of communication form an instrument of service when the flow of ideas is up as well as down, for responsibility for service and for improving service is thus assumed by each member of staff. It is necessary to maintain statistics. Accounting for the work done and for the work that needs to be done gives perspective to each staff member when statistics make possible a qualitative as well as quantitative analysis of that work. The use of time relates to all the above administrative components, as well as to the professional components of the agency's practices. Time needs to be budgeted as carefully as money to achieve good results.

Personnel practices are of significance in building a strong stable staff. This also is too large a subject to be more than briefly discussed here. Salaries head the list, no doubt. When it is known that the administration is trying to obtain salaries for the staff commensurate to the mental and physical energies, the knowledge and skills required to achieve results, the staff will respond appreciatively. Akin to salary schedules—and increments, superannuation and other like perquisites—are job descriptions or classifications. When the social worker knows what he is employed to do, he can apply his energies better. Akin to job descriptions are staff evaluations. If he knows how he is performing in relation to the agency's expectations of him, he will try harder to realize his fullest possibilities. Also important is the skilful placement of the staff, so that each member may occupy the niche that employs his unique talent to his own satisfaction and that of the agency. Finally, each staff member should have the assurance that he is known, appreciated and recognized for the values he brings to the agency. All of these and many immediately implied but not mentioned are architectural calculations necessary in the building task.

Education is another component of the building task. Agencies have a definite obligation—that is, one which can be precisely defined—in respect of the education of the social worker. The schools of social work use the social agency to teach the application of theories learned in classrooms. Certain standards of professional practice must, therefore, be established in the agency. As more agencies attain such standards the schools will have a wider field in which to place students, and will be able to graduate more of the qualified people the agencies so desperately need. The higher the standards of agency practice, moreover, the more young people will want to become social workers. Young people who are bent upon choosing a profession examine these standards perhaps more than is realized. High standards bestow the prestige a young person seeks in his profession. This is another spiral of gain, which begins with the agency itself. Nor can any agency afford to close its doors to field-work placements. If anything, the doors must be opened wider. An in-service training programme need not curtail this; indeed, it dare not. Ways exist or can be found to provide the necessary supervision. There is never a lack of cases.

The education of a social worker does not end with graduation from a school of social work, although in the agency it takes a different form—that of learning by an application of knowledge and method. A programme of staff development has the purpose of enabling conscious growth to take place, in order to increase the competence of the social worker and thus achieve the results desired by the agency and the community. Desired results are attained by the use of desirable methods. Methods are desirable when they are appropriate to the needs being served. As they have evolved and are evolving, the methods of social work are appropriate to these needs, and the agency must be a major force in their evolution.

For the professionally prepared staff, though not for the in-service trained people, development could take place without a specific programme. When such programmes are introduced, they are usually designed to meet special needs of the staff; and they lead eventually to the best learning situation, where learning becomes pervasive: an atmosphere created by the attitude of each individual employed, the administrator included. Each considers it his duty to learn, to deepen his understanding, to extend his knowledge and to refine his skills. That this is a pleasure as well as a duty is quickly appreciated when these objectives are attained. Though pervasive, such learning needs nevertheless to have some form so that the product is recognized and utilized. The form is usually already there: supervision, evaluations, channels of communication, statistics, the case records, the literature, staff meetings, agency and community study and action committees, to name only a few.

The administrator of the social agency has all the many things discussed in this chapter in his mind when he has to decide about launching a programme of in-service training and staff development. His decision is the firmer when it is based upon conviction. Decision and conviction are the more effective when everyone concerned in the shortage of social workers—agency, profession, schools of social work, the community—understands that the exigencies of the times dictate that the agency take an active part in preparing the unprepared for social work. Whether this need to act upon expediency will persist after the supply of professionally prepared people overtakes demand is something the future will reveal.

# II. Administrative Considerations

THERE ARE FIVE BASIC QUESTIONS which the agency's administrator must consider as he sets about constructing a training plan. First, how much will it cost? Second, what amount of time will need to be given to the plan in order to make the effort worth the money spent on it? Third, what qualifications must the in-service trained persons have, what responsibilities can they safely assume, what level of performance can they be expected to achieve, and from this, what salary should they be paid for their work? Fourth, where will this programme belong in the structure of the agency? The last question to be considered is the definitions which must be made, for teaching purposes, of agency structure and function, philosophy and practice, policies and procedures. The desirability of telling the professional association and the schools of social work about the plan, its necessity and its objectives, is a sixth matter the administrator does well to consider.

### JUSTIFICATION OF THE COSTS OF IN-SERVICE TRAINING

There are hidden as well as obvious costs in setting up and conducting an in-service training scheme. Among the hidden costs are the initial uncertainties or alarms which the present staff may experience. Every administrator knows the importance of staff morale, and the effect upon it of changes which seem to threaten the status quo. The staff has a right to know the intention of an agency training programme, and to have their questions about it answered. The relationship between the staff and the administration is strengthened when this happens; when the whole staff knows what the plan is all about, they are more likely to pull together to make it work. As the staff personnel changes all too frequently, periodic assessments of the scheme, shared with everybody, should be made.

In agencies where the staff is comprised chiefly or wholly of people who have no professional training, the problem of hidden costs, or of damaged morale, may be greater. Launching such a programme implies a change in administrative thinking about agency practices. The old methods employed by the staff have not achieved the desired results. Having examined the methods of social work, and finding them sensible and appropriate, the administrator decides to initiate them. The experienced staff will undoubtedly show some initial

19

resistance both to the change and to the idea that they need to train themselves. The fear of losing their jobs, or the fear of competing with professionally trained social workers, may give rise to open or hidden hostilities which affect their work. The administrator must let his existing staff know that he recognizes their values and engage their interest in learning and applying new methods.

The size of the agency, its growth and the turn-over of staff determine the number of people it has to employ during any one year. This in turn will determine whether a full-time training officer or teacher is needed to carry out the training programme.[1] When a training officer is not employed, teaching will take some of the supervisor's time away from his normal duties, and these duties will have to be given to someone else. The serious responsibilities which teaching imposes, and the energies, physical and mental, it requires, cannot be assumed on top of an already heavy job. This point also applies, as will be seen presently, in respect to the day-to-day supervision of the in-service trained people during and following the training period. The cost involved in strengthening the ranks of supervisors can scarcely be avoided, whether a teacher is employed or not.

Assuming that the agency's size makes the appointment of a full-time teacher a necessity, the administrator must define the responsibilities which this work entails and prepare a description of the job. From this, he determines the qualifications of the person who will carry out the work. Finally, on the basis of both the job description and the qualifications demanded, he sets a salary which is appropriate.

An agency teacher should, of course, be a qualified and experienced social worker whose specialized work as agency teacher demands a specialist's salary. Besides professional training and successful experience, this teacher needs to possess certain skills to qualify as a specialist. These are the skills of teaching and of organizing programmes. They can be learned, it is true, but the learning is easiest when a talent as well as a liking for this kind of work already exists. Although such talent may have been detected during the social worker's days as a student, usually it shows up best after he has gained some experience, preferably in the position of supervisor, where if it is present at all, it is clearly noticeable. In short, when searching for a training officer the first place to look is among the agency's own staff. The recorded evaluations of all staff, supervisors included, will help in this search.

---

[1]In a later chapter a suggestion is made regarding the employment of an agencies' teacher, or a director of training programmes, to serve a community constituency—city, province or state—both to organize and share in the conducting of training schemes among like agencies.

The responsibilities which the agency teacher must accept add to the desirability of appointing a person who knows the agency thoroughly. He will need to teach all that the agency does, and the way it does it, and as well he must inculcate something of its spirit. When the going is rough, as it often is in the hurly-burly of everyday pressures, that spirit keeps the staff steadfast. The well-tempered loyalty of the training officer makes such inculcation possible, which is further justification for paying him an adequate salary.

The possibility of obtaining a training officer—supervisor, director or whatever name is given to his office—who already has had experience in agency training may not be very great. This special field of activity in a relatively young profession has only recently been opened up. It is only in the last few years that larger agencies have budgeted money specifically for staff development programmes, and as one of the aims of such programmes is to retain staff, their directors are not easily persuaded to leave to join other agencies. Schools of social work have not had time to evolve special training courses for this work. But the agency cannot wait for time to supply the lack of experienced training officers. The training officer will himself learn by doing, and quickly; he will, that is, if his professional sensibilities are fully employed. Every teaching experience is for such a teacher a learning experience, for those taught soon convey how best they can learn, and what they need most to learn.

If a supervisor who has had no previous experience in this work is promoted to the position, the known loyalties of that person should not determine his salary. The work may seem easy when it is done with ease and enjoyment, but it is actually very heavy. As every teacher knows, organizing the subject-matter to be taught involves a great amount of thought. Constant alertness and focused thinking are required to keep pace with the responses of those taught to what is taught. Professional sensibility, character and personality are needed to create and maintain a pleasurable atmosphere of learning and to stimulate the desire to learn. The work does not end when the teaching periods are over. Evaluations of the trainees and of the effectiveness of the teaching must be made, and there remain many duties in connection with the larger aspects of staff development.

It may now be more apparent that this heavy job, the heavier when it too must be learned by doing it, calls for a salary that is close to the top of the agency's salary schedule. But when someone is promoted over others with longer service, the reason therefore should be explained if dissension is likely to result. The majority, however, will understand without explanation for few people feel themselves equal to the task.

Although the salary of the training officer is one of the largest items to be budgeted, it is not the only item. There are, as mentioned earlier, the costs involved in providing supervision of the trainee during and after the training period. The supervisor assumes the role of teacher towards all his staff members, but the teaching role must predominate in his duties to the in-service trained staff member and also to the qualified social worker who is beginning his practice. For the experienced qualified staff, this teaching function is more of a consultative relationship. The supervisor's functions invariably include administrative responsibilities, which weigh heavily upon him, but which at the same time place him in a position of some authority. This adds to his prestige as perhaps the teaching function does not. Some of the supervisors, because they wear authority well and have a talent for administration, cannot teach with pleasure and therefore cannot teach effectively. For others the reverse is true.

The obvious if sometimes unobtainable solution is to know, through evaluations, what the talents and skills of each supervisor are, and through periodic examination what the task of the supervisor is. When these factors have been thoroughly investigated, it will be abundantly clear that, with the teaching of totally uninitiated people added to the supervisor's work, some help will have to be forthcoming, which adds of course to the costs. The appointment of an assistant supervisor seems the most sensible way to help, and this will certainly make the agency structure less top-heavy administratively and less costly than would the establishment of more supervisory positions. A supervisor with teaching ability would be given an assistant who could take over the handling of the details of administration—processing vouchers, managing the office, attending to the matters which concern the clerical staff. A supervisor with administrative ability would have an assistant who could teach. The supervisors with assistants retain their authoritative and their consultative functions, but are freed to exercise both with greater efficiency and effectiveness. The assistants retain a part of their usual case-load, their schedule being altered to free them for their new duties.

Obviously, the administrative assistant must have experience in the agency. The teaching assistant, just as obviously, should be a qualified social worker. Whether the administrative assistant is or is not a professional person depends upon the availability of such people and upon their talents. In all events, the assistant's position requires definition, stated qualifications, and a salary commensurate with these. It need not be emphasized, perhaps, that not all supervisors will need an assistant. The weight of their work, the number of trainees they will teach, their experience and talent, may be such that extra teaching efforts can easily be added. What does require emphasis, however, is that the supervisor, the most important figure in a training scheme, be accorded every consideration.

The salaries to be paid to in-service trained people will be discussed later in this chapter. When those salaries are to begin should be decided at the first opportunity by the administrator. There is some virtue, though not much, in paying only a partial salary during the period set aside for training. The cost is not so great to the agency should the trainee fail to measure up to expectation and be retired. Less money may induce greater effort to succeed, but that is doubtful. Paying the salary of the grade the trainee will occupy is, in the period of training, tantamount to paying him to learn, but he works hard and earns his pay. There is no question about the serious application of his mind to the task, and if there should be question, that is reason enough to ask that person to leave the agency. The group teaching sessions occupy the hours of a full working day, and though only a little home-work is assigned, there is nothing optional about the study undertaken. The atmosphere differs from that of a college classroom. It is a new kind of learning experience, and only mature adults can stand it. The period of learning-by-doing calls for double efforts, and sometimes, if it cannot be avoided, for strain. The trainee can be fully depended upon, in short, to earn his salary from the beginning.

Transporation costs, if these are involved, must also be budgeted. If the agency is a rural one, the trainee should undertake to get himself to the office where he will do his practice work, but when he returns for further group teaching, these costs should be met by the agency. If he succeeds and stays on the job, then the agency may reimburse him for his initial travel expenses. It is not necessary, surely, for the agency to pay his living expenses on top of his salary during training. Overly preferred treatment is unwise, and few expect it.

The cost of office space and equipment must be reckoned. Regardless of how the training scheme is organized, some part of the time will be spent in group discussion, and some part, probably the bulk of it, in learning by doing. For group discussion a room will be needed which is large enough to accommodate the greatest number of people who are training at any one time. The need for comfort is mentioned here with some feeling. Air and light, cushions on chairs, tables on which to write and lean an elbow, reduce the fatigue. Proximity of this room to the agency's library is a small but significant consideration. The sight of books and periodicals, the handling if not actual reading of some of them (for reading in these early days should be carefully prescribed), and the consciousness that books exist from which to learn help to impress these new people with the idea that reading will be required and also with the stature of their new vocation.

Near this room (in it if it is big enough) should be all the paraphernalia of the office in which the trainees will eventually be working. Filing cabinets, indexes, card boxes, dictaphone, stationery, supply cupboards and the like will all be used or talked about in the group teaching periods. The training officer's office will be near by. The secretary this officer needs (another cost to be reckoned) will assist in teaching office procedures and will, therefore, take pride in making this simulated work setting as perfect an example as possible of correct procedure. This centre for group teaching provides the trainee with his first experience of order. Order learned at this time speeds the attaining of efficiency, which makes for economy.

This training centre should not be thought of as the place in which the trainee does his practice work with the training officer as his supervisor. Under such a plan, both clients and trainees suffer. If a client feels that he is being diverted to a separate part of the building and to the less sure services of a trainee, he may react adversely. He will not have these feelings if he senses that, though served by a worker-in-training, he is received and interviewed in the setting where services are normally given. The office itself—its appearance, care and atmosphere—can be conducive to co-operative responses and to allaying of the clients' feelings of apprehension.

For the trainees there is an air of unreality about the made-to-order work setting, and this at a time when reality is most important for them. The realism of in-service training marks one of the differences between it and the training given at a school of social work. Moreover, in a specially created setting, there is not the opportunity to rub shoulders with colleagues, from whom much is always learned: deportment, attitude, professional manners, agency jargon, agency legend and so on. Nor is there an opportunity for the trainee to develop that all-important and somewhat unusual relationship with the supervisor who will continue to be his teacher until he gets to a school of social work. If the agency is decentralized, the trainee will not develop the feeling of responsibility to a case-load, which is the major difference between agency and school methods of teaching. Nor will he absorb the feeling and knowledge of the community or neighbourhood in which he will work. The training centre might begin in fact to look like a school of social work, thus diminishing the desire to get to one.

The expense of such a plan is thus not confined to the original cost of the facilities required. The wrong use of time can be costly. Time spent in protected isolation defeats a basic essential of in-service training: learning by a total absorption of agency activity.

Among the costs to be considered when budgeting for in-service training are those of the tools of teaching. The agency must provide sufficient copies of each of the agency's written manuals—manuals of policy, office procedures and accounting—as well as folios containing copies of the social legislation this agency may administer; copies of all the forms in daily use; and all the equipment of office activity: paper punches, staplers, fasteners, folders, and the like. The manuals are texts from which to teach and learn and the equipment is unfamiliar if not unknown to many and names and uses often must be taught.

The provision of sufficient copies of the two or three professional textbooks that can be studied, in part, during the group sessions is necessary. The reproduction of teaching outlines, of a few articles from the periodicals, of case records and other similar material adds to the cost, though the rule of any agency regarding such things should be observed in this. That rule is that only material which is pertinent to the work, and of immediate use and of common value will be reproduced and circulated. Then its purpose, how it is to be indexed and where filed are all stated conspicuously.

Visual aids are rather more expensive than many agencies can afford. A projection machine is the most costly piece of equipment probably, but the most useful. Although one can be rented or borrowed, precious time can be wasted in fetching and carrying, putting it together and taking it down. Prints of films are also expensive, but these can be rented for small cost and little trouble. Film strips require special equipment for showing and there are not many available having immediate value. Graphs of one sort or another are helpful if they illustrate the agency's operation. Pamphlets on the agency's work are useful for recruiting purposes and public interpretation but not in teaching. By and large, visual aids are something of a luxury in teaching adults. Reading is always the most effective way of learning through the eye, though for some, skills in reading to learn may have to be re-taught.

Unfortunately, a detailed analysis of the cost to the Social Welfare Branch of its training programme does not exist. A conservative estimate, however, places obvious costs around $20,000 each year.[2]

[2]It has sometimes been suggested that this money might be better employed as training awards or bursaries to pay school fees thus making in-service training unnecessary. This cannot be done because first that money is voted for salaries of persons employed to do the work of the agency and second, the need to employ in-service trained staff arises at any time of the year and vacancies must be filled whenever they occur.

This omits the costs of the supervisors' extra efforts on behalf of the trainee during the four months of learning-by-doing which are included in the definition of the supervisor's normal work. The average number of social workers supervised is six; the maximum eight. Seldom do any of the thirty or so supervisors have more than one new trainee at a time, nor do all supervisors always have a trainee at the learning-by-doing stage. Although to many the cost will seem high, the point of view of this agency's administrators is that it is not only necessary, but also cheap considering its value.

## THE TIME INVOLVED

In-service training is a costly expediency designed to meet an emergency which has become so prolonged as to seem permanent. It is obviously not the way an agency would prefer to obtain its staff. During the first ten years that the Social Welfare Branch engaged in in-service training, each year was considered in a hopeful way to be "the last year." Following World War II when the veterans swelled the rolls of schools of social work, it looked as if the end of in-service training was in sight. For two years, only two groups with approximately twelve people in each had to be recruited. Since 1953, hopes have fallen. In three years, over one hundred people have been trained. Now the view is held that in-service training may always be needed. It may be that for some, this slower method of achieving an education for social work will prove the best. There may be some parts of the work, though this is doubtful, which can be done by people having only in-service training. In all events we know that progress towards higher standards will be slower because of the greater numbers of people who will have to be trained by the agency. All those concerned in the training plan are, therefore, determined to make it as effective as possible. The people who need the services must always be considered first in all that is done. This fact is the ever-present thought behind the agency's staff development programme, of which in-service training has become such a large part.

Budgeting enough time to achieve the maximum benefits from in-service training is a major administrative consideration. Six months is allotted to it in the Social Welfare Branch. This period has a definite beginning and a definite ending and is divided into three parts. Four weeks, starting on the day employment begins, are devoted to this group teaching, using a variety of methods but principally that of discussion. At the end of this time, the group disperses, each member going to the district office in which he will be placed permanently. Here he spends four months in learning the work by doing it. He is taught by his supervisor in a tutorial manner, which implies much guided independent study as well as close direction of his actions and discussion of his impressions and reactions. At the end of this time, the group reassembles and for four weeks talk and thought are resumed which have the effect of consolidating, amplifying and deepening the total learning each member of the group has acquired.

Six months may seem a generous amount of time to allow for this training. However, less than that would not be enough; more might suggest that the agency was encroaching upon the preserves of the schools of social work. This time, moreover, is merely the first stage in the agency's total plan for these people. The last stage is the realization of professional status after training in a school of social work. As far as the agency is concerned, the objective is the achievement of professional competence rather than the status the individual thereby achieves for himself. (Status is nevertheless important. The desire to acquire it comes as a result of association with professional colleagues. By their example, the trainee sees the values of being identified with a part of a group of professional people who use their influence outside the agency for the betterment of society.)

The leave-of-absence to attend a school should, as far as possible, be granted at the right time. The readiness of the trainee to benefit by the experience which the school provides should be determined by the feelings and attitudes, thought and skills, which his work in the agency has nurtured. These qualities are recorded by the supervisor for the administrator after frank discussion with the trainee. The latter is helped, by this kind of evaluation, to decide whether he is ready for school or not. This awareness facilitates the move into the school, when it comes, and permits the deepest kind of learning.

However, at the same time the agency must consider the cost of leave-of-absence in terms of services to its clients. Services suffer—that is, the clients suffer—when there are frequent changes in staff. Administratively such changes are to be avoided by every known means. The Social Welfare Branch, therefore, stipulates that the in-service trained staff member work for a period of not less than two years before he applies for educational leave. In the interests of holding naturally talented persons in the field, however, this rule is flexible enough to permit earlier leave-of-absence to be granted, though not, as yet, financial help. Seniority remains a criterion in this latter respect and will, no doubt, until more money for bursaries is available both within and outside the agency.

Another reason for this stipulation of a minimum of two years' service is the cost of in-service training. Since the trainee is paid a salary from the outset, the agency and the trainee too can consider this as a financial investment in him. As with all investments, some returns should accrue to the investor. These are the returns of growing competence on the job, which for the majority requires at least two years to be fully realized. The fairness of this space of time is made doubly apparent to the trainee as soon as he begins to identify himself with the agency in serving the people who crowd the waiting rooms, or who wait at the road's end and beyond for the help he can bring them.

The time that can be allowed for the final stage of education—attendance at a school—may raise difficulties for many agencies. The achievement of full professional status requires completion of two years of post-graduate training in accredited schools of social work in the United States and Canada. The Canadian schools do not operate on the semester plan which permits continuous study throughout a year, and few as yet offer courses in summer sessions. The problem of staffing the Social Welfare Branch has been such that only one year's leave can be allowed, and that only for a set number of people. The stable core of the total staff, those whose tenure has been longest, took their training before the two-year course was inaugurated. Others, since then, for their own reasons have broken their education into two parts, preferring or being forced by lack of funds to work between the two years. The agencies have employed these people largely because of their acute need for staff with some preparation, and partly because the change to a two-year course, in most localities of Canada, came quite suddenly. Agencies are not geared for sudden change; it takes time to re-schedule salaries and re-define jobs. Further, the Civil Service requires proof of the need for and competence of fully trained social workers and says in effect: show us why this extra year is needed. The administration, of course, does not deplore the two-year course, or fail to see its value. Leave is arranged each year for a few with one year of training to enrol for the second year. This return to school is, in fact, definitely encouraged among the supervisors (many of whom have only one year of training plus a minimum of three years' experience), for here is where the school training is most needed. Such a situation, if it occurs elsewhere, will probably be regarded in the same realistic fashion. The old phrase "the inevitability of gradualness" has much new meaning for social agencies these days.

Bursaries or financial help in obtaining education in a school of social work were not mentioned in the section devoted to costs of in-service training because they vary materially from agency to agency, and may even be provided by sources outside the agency. That they are necessary can scarcely be disputed. Everyone concerned, the schools, the universities of which they are a part, the profession, the agencies, governments at all levels, the segment of the public which sees clearly the need for social services, must unite in an effort to reduce the problem of the high cost of education to manageable proportions. It is vital not only to the quality of the agencies' services, but also to the survival of the profession that something be done to remove financial obstructions to education for social work.

## The Trainees' Level of Performance

In order to estimate the quality and quantity of work to be expected of an in-service trained person, the trainees' individual attributes must be taken into account. Each trainee must be helped to assess his own growth, and through this assessment to realize how to make the best use of his brain, faculties and energies to keep on growing. No standard formula, especially no formula based on competition, can ever be devised to measure performance. What has to be established, however, is the minimum rate of learning and growth which the trainee must achieve.

Six months should be sufficient to determine the rate of learning for most trainees. It could be found out earlier. However, sometimes, after a good start there will be a falling off of effort or an arresting of growth due to some unforeseen obstacle. If the obstacle is of the agency's making—a faulty placement, too many pressures, a too heavy case-load —it can be removed.[3] But if it has been created by circumstances within the trainee's personal life or by his own personality, he must

[3]Bound up in this consideration of obstacles to growth which may be of the agency's making is the more delicate consideration of the possible adverse emotional effects on the trainee of learning the rudiments of this profession and of working with clients suffering from emotional distress. Often such vulnerability is exposed in Part I of the training plan where the agency teacher is always on the watch for signs of it. If they show up, they are dealt with at once. At other times, these feelings of confusion have been revealed to the trainee's supervisor who also deals with them. The method of "dealing with them" is to give vocational counselling to help this less emotionally robust person to find work which will satisfy his desire to be of service to people without himself being harmed. The number of trainees who have needed such help in the past fourteen years is very small.

deal with it himself. Judging from his work, and from that alone, the agency must request that he go, giving him advice if he asks for it, but leaving it to him to seek help elsewhere for his problem. No more than two years should go by without decisive action being taken to deal with those whose learning is arrested for any reason. Terminating employment is usually distasteful, but is actually a charitable action.

Until the in-service trained person obtains professional training, the agency carries out, vigilantly, the process of evaluation. This is principally done for the sake of improving the agency's services, but it has much meaning for the trainee himself. During the training period he makes his first acquaintance with the process; thereafter it is carried out in the time devoted to supervision, that is, once a week, and in relation to the demands of the case-load the trainee carries, and in periodic interviews for the sole purpose of evaluation. At the end of the first year of practice, the weekly record of progress kept by the supervisor is discussed with the trainee, and he then asks about matters pertaining to his work which puzzle or distress him. When a trainee's lack of progress is too great, these interviews have to be arranged oftener. At all times evaluations include the trainee's own estimate of his work. Should employment, and thus the career he desires to follow, be threatened, he should never be able to say "I didn't know this was what you thought of me." When he makes progress in learning and thus in working effectually, he can always say "I know the things about my work I need to learn more about." Learning is consciously undertaken for the sake of the work. When he gets to school, he will have more time and greater help in cultivating an awareness of himself as the instrument of his calling.

The kind of work assigned to the trainee, as intimated earlier, may have to be determined by the staff situation in the agency. When he is to fill the shoes of a professionally prepared person, the work he does will at first be team work. The administration here must face the fact that the supervisor's time will be heavily taxed. Time and special skills are needed in supervising and teaching the professional demands of the job done by the trainee.

Here again the evaluation process is employed. There is an evaluation of what the trainee brings to the job by way of education and experience. There is an evaluation of his agency teachers' findings of him as he participated in the total training plan. Then there is an evaluation in which the trainee takes part pertaining to the work he will do. During the four months' practice part of his training he and his supervisor have together reviewed his case-load. Based on the supervisor's and the previous worker's assessment of the problems each case presents, the cases the trainee can now work on comfortably and helpfully are chosen; the cases he will have to move more slowly on are set aside for special teaching; the cases which will have to wait until he feels surer of himself are in the meantime carried by someone else. Of course, emergencies often arise to plague such an arrangement; cases in which the problem seemed relatively simple and the client relatively mature may suddenly become very complicated indeed. There can be no sure gauge of simplicity or complexity. The safeguard is the supervisor who is there to take hold when complications arise.

It is with the problems which arise from external pressures that the in-service trained person can best be entrusted. Through the use of agency and community resources he can learn how to manipulate legal and administrative tools to achieve beneficial ends. In such cases he can learn and apply the scientific method of social casework. He can experience the intellectual activity of forming judgments through reasoning which he submits to his supervisor for test. He can learn to control and use his human sympathies in a helpful and appropriate way. At every turn he will be frustrated by his lack of knowledge, and this will quicken his drive to obtain it; but he will, with the agency's and supervisor's help, see results from his labours. He will give a practical service that effects some change for the better, though at first this service may be blindly given. By observing the tangible needs of his clients, he moves from being respectful of their feelings towards an understanding of the meaning and effects of emotional discomforts. He begins to search for the causes of the needs and of the behaviour he finds. He is too busy doing to sit down and learn from his supervisors or from the literature the precise meaning, the exact cause, the predictable outcome of all that he senses as inherent in this case and that case. He is alert to but perplexed by the intricacies of human problems.

Family relationships and the problems that arise when these are faulty have not been touched on above, but they permeate the whole task. When the agency's services are directed chiefly towards correction of faulty environment, the effect of this environment on the family is a primary concern of the social worker. The welfare of children in such a setting is a chief object of the service. When the agency includes in its function direct services to families and children, or has these as its sole function, the cases to be assigned a trainee must be chosen with care. It is here that responsibility for the case is carried by the supervisor until the trainee develops sufficient understanding to handle it alone. When this transfer cannot be made, the administration must expect less effectual work. He may in the end have to re-define the agency's functions.

To sum up, the administrator can expect an in-service trained person to increase in skill and dispatch in the services which call for definite action in respect of environmental problems. He can expect a growing sensitivity to the importance and meaning of the supporting relation-ship the trainee has with the client. He can expect the trainee to learn to work within the scope and definition of the agency. By the end of a year or sooner the volume of his work will approximate that of the more experienced staff, but it will still not be done with the understanding and efficiency of a professionally prepared worker. The administrator can be sure, if the trainee is properly taught initially, that the desire to work with understanding and dispatch and assurance will lead to an almost daily improvement in his performance.

In view of these limitations, the agency can pay the in-service trained staff less than it does the professionally trained people. The trainee himself will be the first to acknowledge the validity of this, and for some it will be an added incentive towards acquiring professional status. Those with professional status will be satisfied in knowing that the difference in performance is recognized in such a tangible way, and for some trained people this could be an incentive to improve their own practices. Should the trainee be prevented by circumstances from obtaining his professional training after three years of practice, and if in that time he has demonstrated his value to the agency, an upward classification in grade and salary is wholly justified. Based on merit as reported in the supervisor's evaluation, this is not promotion as much as it is recognition.

The difference in the trainee's salary should not be so great as to undervalue his worth to the agency. The Social Welfare Branch has a difference of 10 per cent between Grade 1 social workers—the in-service trained staff—and Grade 2 social workers—the professionally trained staff. The staff has always considered this a fair spread in the salary schedule. Annual increments (for six years), however, establish differences in the reward for performance. Grade 1 social workers have a percentage increase which is less than the flat increment for Grade 2 social workers. By the end of the third year the social workers in Grade 1 have usually been re-classified as Grade 2, the majority because they have obtained professional training and a few on a basis of merit. The others will have left the agency of their own volition or by request. Those who achieve the Grade 2 status do not therefore give up their intentions to qualify themselves professionally. Except in rare instances, achieving the higher salary is not the primary motive for wanting to do so.

A word can be added here about what title the agency should give to their in-service trained staff members. The word "trainees" has been used in this book in order to identify them clearly, but that word is not in the official vocabulary of the Social Welfare Branch itself; the trainees are called "social workers." Everybody in the agency knows that they do not have professional status; better than anyone else, the trainee knows it. The clients know, and the community knows, for one of the first things the social worker learns is how to inform them of his status as trainee. It seems simpler, more dignified and even more accurate to give the trainees a title that has meaning to the community and which the holder bears and affixes after his signature with the knowledge that he is earning the right to use it. Lesser titles could carry less incentive to earn this right. The in-service trained people are not lesser men or women. They are merely beginning to achieve the place of value—nobility is not too strong a word—which the profession itself strives to achieve in society.

### FITTING THE TRAINING DIVISION INTO THE AGENCY'S STRUCTURE

The function of the training office determines its place in the agency's structure. The office may at first be devoted solely to in-service training, and certainly in-service training will always be a major part of its work at any time of the year. It must, in time, however, expand its services, because the agency must provide means whereby the trainee, after completing the formally planned training period, can continue to add to his knowledge. Such facilities are necessary for the entire staff, regardless of their training or experience or the level at which they operate. The staff after all is the agency; to develop that staff to the maximum potential of each person employed is in the agency's best interests. Staff development, in other words, is agency development. Projecting that thought forward, agency development can be regarded as community development. This is one of the primary objectives of all social agencies, and one which is not achieved when an agency is stagnant.

The broad function of the training office is therefore staff development, in which in-service training is a major part. This being so, its logical place in the agency's structure is close to the administration. It will probably constitute a department or division of the agency.

This division has no specific authority to institute or yet carry out agency policies, though it may give counsel, when this is solicited, on the formulating and changing of certain policies, largely those having to do with personnel practices. It is, in fact, most closely concerned with the administration's policies on personnel, and can be of assistance both directly as well as in a consultative way.

Interviewing and selecting applicants for positions in the agency can be undertaken by the training or staff development office as a means of directly assisting the administration. The final decision, however, should remain with the administrator in charge of personnel, where it properly belongs. The training office serves in a consultative way by offering advice to the personnel administrator, and through him to the chief administrator, in such matters as evolving methods of evaluation; assessing the educational needs of various levels of staff; planning and submitting for approval methods of meeting these needs as adequately as an agency can; granting promotions, educational leaves of absence, and bursaries; and effecting demotions or termination of employment. Decisions in all these matters rest with the chief administrator or with the personnel administrator, but none can be effected without weighing all the evidence, much of which is to be found in the training division.

The training officer is not an administrator, except in the sense that, like all social workers, he administers his own task. He is essentially a teacher. The subject he teaches, and plans and arranges to have taught, is the social agency which employs him. He thus must be in a position to know the agency in all its parts and in the sum of its parts. In a large agency, where no one person can know all the details of its operation, knowing who can teach these details (and teach them best) is sufficient. The major matters—structure and function, policies and procedures, philosophy and practice, the relation of this agency to other agencies and to the community, the viewpoint and attitudes of the administration, its vision and goals for the agency—are absorbed in the bones and sinews and bloodstream of the training officer.

This absorption can best take place when the training office is functionally attached to the administration. Immediate connections are thereby established with all levels of the organization. All communications across and down are shared with the administration; the voice of the training officer therefore is that of the administration. Staff development is pervasive. It is the will of the agency itself that the staff have the opportunity to grow.

As has been implied in the first chapter, a staff development programme seldom bursts upon the agency full blown, but rather arises out of needs as they are found. There must be a constant refinement of its methods. There is great need to gear such a programme smoothly into the agency's normal activities so as not to disrupt the everyday work, but rather to punctuate it, as the advertisements say, with the pause that refreshes. The everyday work itself, when supervision is more than merely checking the work done, can be used to induce consciousness of growth.

The gradual adoption of such a programme, moreover, engenders a regard for it that might not be obtained if it were wished upon the staff overnight. The staff at all levels, and especially the supervisory and consultant levels, usually have the function of teaching written into the definition of their jobs. These people gather up the facts of the educational situation and propose activities to fill needs as they find them. The staff development office plans and executes these proposals, adding to, co-ordinating, and timing them so as to make them of the widest value. Recording findings and giving effect to them is a further function of the office. Out of all these activities, others will suggest themselves. Some activities will be regularly constituted, and the whole programme will soon take definite shape. The agency teacher is the fulcrum.

The place the training office occupies—very near to the administration—gives it a certain merited prestige. But the entire staff will hold it in much greater regard if they feel that their ideas about education, their needs and desires are being given the serious attention that more frequently than not gets results. This programme is set up for those who need it. It will be just that much more effective when it is initiated by them, for this means that they see their own need and want to do something about it. Education is only education when it is self-motivated.

The agency with a recognized programme of staff development will attract people who want and need help in developing their skills, and very few social workers would say they did not need such help. Education for social work is tri-partite—involving the schools of social work, the agencies and the social workers. The agency's obligations in education may not have been very clearly seen in the past, but they become obvious as soon as something is done to discharge them. Not only does the morale of the staff become better, but also the quality of its work. In short, staff development is good administrative sense, as well as being a part of the long-range educational process. And it is to be remembered that it is from agency practice that professional practices can be continually refined. The social agency is the primary organism of this young profession.

## TEACHING DEFINITIONS

What is to be taught in the larger staff development programme and in the more concentrated in-service training plan is unique to each agency. All that the agency does, and how, will have to be defined. It is a living thing having authority and purpose, manner and motion. These living elements are transmitted in the teaching process, when the teacher's mind and feelings meet and move the minds and feelings of those taught. The definitions serve to focus and contain this teaching within the bounds of this agency.

Whoever prepares these definitions must do so to the satisfaction of the administration. They must be regarded as official statements, even though in form and arrangement they may not serve any other purpose than an internal one. They could, however, with slight adaptation be useful for purposes of wider interpretation and for answering the inquiries no agency escapes. They can only be useful internally and externally if they are true and accurate. (Appendix II represents an example of one such definition.) This poses the problem of what to do about parts of the operation which may as yet be imperfect. Every agency no doubt has something which it is reluctant to expose fully. This reluctance cannot be allowed in teaching. The flaws must be honestly looked at and reasonably accounted for. Sometimes this look, in the form of a definition which accounts for the shadows, is enough to get action, or at least thought which leads to action. Outside these areas of imperfection, definitions can be a source of satisfaction. They reveal accomplishment and set forth the goals still to be achieved, all of which are honourable.

The matters to be defined are the structure and functions of the agency, its policies and procedures, its practices, its philosophy and its relationships to the community. The training officer will decide in which order these matters should be introduced, for they are important in conveying the "feel" as well as the grasp of the agency's purposes. Many of these definitions will already exist. There will be charts of various kinds from which to teach structure and the chain of authority implicit in administration. Since the functions of the agency derive from the community's awareness of social need (and "the community" may be a neighbourhood or a nation) and from the moral or ethical considerations which are its philosophy, definition of function can include statements of philosophy and of community relationship. Policies and procedures should be in written manual form, indexed and cross-referenced, to facilitate the work of every staff member. (When this is done, they will more than likely be simplified. That such manuals are needed for constant reference, as well as for teaching, is apparent. No one human brain could master all the detail contained in a policy manual, although where to find the precise policy needed in any one situation can be mastered. As policies and procedures change constantly, the system used in releasing amendments and new policies must be made clear. Orderliness can be learned by such examples, as well as respect for the administrative elements of practice.)

Definition of practice may be difficult to put into words. In training, or teaching, the consultants and supervisors who do much of it are relied upon to organize their teaching material, at least in outline form, so that it can be learned easily. The training officer, for in-service training purposes, will compose the material on practice to be taught initially. These first lessons contain an approach to professional concepts; an introduction, stripped of the complicating variables which make this profession's practice more difficult than that of all professions. They are designed to provide the minimum amount of knowledge the trainee requires to perform at the level the agency expects of him. Along with the form the teaching will take, the methods appropriate to the subjects and to the ability of the people who are to learn need shaping.

### THE SCHOOL AND THE PROFESSION

The question frequently arises as to whether or not it is wise to enlist the help of the faculty of schools of social work in giving the introduction to professional concepts and methods mentioned above. Undoubtedly the teaching they could do would be effective, but whether the faculty already occupied with their heavy schedule of normal as well as extra-curricular activities, can meet this further demand upon their time and efforts is to be seriously considered. Many more than just the hours of teaching are involved always. Then, the academic note that this teaching would have, has significance. In-service training, it cannot be said too often, is no substitute for professional education. To have part of the teaching done by school faculty members could confuse the trainee and the agency on this point.[4] It may

---

[4]This statement must be interpreted within the context, which is an agency training plan. Outside this frame of reference it does not apply. When schools of social work generously offer extra-curricular courses arranged especially for practising people, the agency can do much to encourage their use by its staff. When school and agency work out on a co-operative basis ways of training staff which make in-service training unnecessary, the saving in time alone commends the enterprise. In-service training is only one way to solve the dilemma of shortages of qualified social workers.

have been noted that the terms used in discussing in-service training herein are not those of the academic halls of learning: "trainee" rather than "student," "plan" rather than "course," "group" rather than "class," and so on are used. Only the words "teaching" and "teacher" are retained.

Though the help of the schools is not enlisted, it is nevertheless wise and proper that they be made fully aware of the agency's planning. A close relationship between the agency and the school or schools of social work is always desirable, so that the latter may know for what kinds of practice they are preparing their students. The schools should be satisfied about the objectives of in-service training, and the agency's plan of achieving them, and about the content and methods of teaching. With this understanding, the agency may be certain that what it is doing is a part of a whole process of education, and an appropriate and seemly part which violates no precept of the educational institution.

The profession also, through its association, can with benefit be apprised of the objectives and plan of in-service training, although it need not examine the content and method of teaching. Satisfied that the agency respects and understands the association's position with regard to its status, control of membership and ethics, the profession can with greater clarity understand the agency's plight and lend some help in this regard.

# III. Recruiting for In-Service Training

THE PROPER SELECTION of trainees is the key to the success of an agency's training plan. Educational requirements are among the first of the basic qualifications to be established. As one of the objectives of the training plan is the eventual enrolment of the trainee in a school of social work, the educational standing required or preferred by the agency is that required for admission to a school. The applicant should, therefore, possess a university or college degree.

For the purely internal purposes of in-service training as well graduation from a university is a wholly desirable requisite. A university graduate, it is assumed, has a trained mind. He knows how to learn, to think, to reason, to evaluate facts and impressions. Regardless of the nature of his degree—whether it is in Arts, Science, Commerce— the graduate has, by acquiring it, been "admitted" to the company of people conditioned to the notion that education never ceases, and that, in the appropriate application of knowledge and reason, good will result for themselves and those about them. Education, if it is liberally founded, conditions the mind to make judgments which are free of prejudice; it stocks the mind with ideas and knowledge which, though never exhaustive, can be applied with exactitude or adapted in pursuit of chosen vocations.

The hope that an adequate number of undergraduates will choose social work as their vocation seems, in the minds of many, to have become akin to despair. In the Western world in this decade, the serious manpower shortage has led to keen competition for the brains and energies of the young people in universities, and, on the students' part it seems, to a race for the fields of work which, in the mid-twentieth century, identify him with civilization's progress and stamp him as a success. The choice of vocation requires a measuring of individual attributes and attitudes and an analysis of the fields open to the young in these times. This is a task which educators in high schools and universities have undertaken. Social work—the agencies, the profession, the schools—must, therefore, address itself first to these educators so that they may appreciate the dignity and value of this young profession and may know the qualities it takes to make good in it. The counsellors in high schools and universities are eager to

39

know of all the fields open to the young; it is their professional duty to counsel each student in relation to his innate abilities.

Interpreting social work to the educators is the joint responsibility of agencies, profession and school. One small word of advice which may not be amiss here is that social work needs no apology. That note creeps in most often when comparisons are drawn between the social worker's rewards and those of the older professions such as law and medicine. Besides the fallacy of comparing incomparables, the fact is that this salaried profession of social work permits the practitioner to earn, if he has the ability, a predictably increasing salary over a life-time. Advancement comes fast for the able—within three to five years in this time of shortages—and in the past fifteen years, social agencies have increased salaries by over 300 per cent, inflation not-withstanding. The better the services the easier it will be for the agencies to continue this spiral of increases. Add to the material rewards the system of values on which this profession is based, and the serious-minded young person will not fail to be interested.

This problem of "reaching the unreached" raises the question of when young people should choose their careers. It is debatable whether the young should know what they want to do with their lives before they get to university. Universities exist primarily to prepare young people for life, and to use these years to prepare for specific vocation may result in a life-road which has only one lane. The title of Hilda Neatby's critique on modern education puts this point well: *So Little for the Mind.* Social work could become arid were it deprived of the great ideas of letters, philosophy and history. To start to "train" for social work in the undergraduate years, in this writer's opinion, is to cheat the profession and the practitioner alike.

To begin an "education" for social work in the undergraduate years is another matter. The problem for schools of social work to reflect upon is what courses are appropriate for the students as well as for the profession. The social sciences seem to have an immediate application, but so do history, literature and the classics. Higher mathematics, to inculcate proportioned thought, is not out of place as a prerequisite to social work; neither is the study of commerce and administration. It is a knotty problem and the agencies can be glad that it is not theirs alone to solve. The agency should have a viewpoint, however, and it can only do so if it studies the effect that the various kinds of undergraduate education of its staff have had on agency work. Such a study will also lead to the wide use of the whole knowledge the staff possesses, an advantage to the agency and to the individual concerned.

Now, the thorny question arises of compromising on educational qualifications when not enough university graduates exist to meet the demands of both social work and the older professions. If the number of graduates is small, and in many parts of the world it is, social agencies are lucky when they can recruit a high proportion of them. Accepting persons with less than a university or college degree under these conditions is a necessity. What is not a necessity is accepting such people when there are enough graduates to fill the agencies' needs. Yet, given discernible intelligence, apparent maturity and even hear-say evidence of talent, it is a loss to the agency, and to the profession to turn away people whose only deficiency is lack of educational status. Often, if that person is young enough and not too far away from the completion of his education, he can, while working, finish it extra-murally. Always, however, the agency's objective for his eventual professional training at a school of social work needs to be taken into account. Some schools, facing the facts with the realism of the agency, can and do admit some of these agency-trained and experienced undergraduates. If the agency's initial discernment of intelligence, maturity and talent has been correct—and it will have been well tested long before admission to the school is requested—these in-service trained workers will make very good students indeed, learn deeply, and obtain the maximum benefit from the experience. Once that training has been achieved, although they will have no degree, an agency may, without jeopardizing the chances of the better educated, promote those who merit it to positions of greater trust.

When an agency does employ undergraduates, it is only wise to establish firmly a minimum educational requirement. In the Social Welfare Branch this minimum is successful completion of one year of university study, which offers some proof of intellectual ability. Some applicants who fall short even of this minimum may, if they are serious in their intentions, set about obtaining it, though it is unwise to hold out a guarantee of employment on the understanding that they do so. Instead they are told: "We prefer to take people who have a university degree. When we do not have enough applicants with that status and with the personal qualities this profession demands, we consider next those who have the greatest amount of education short of a degree. Last of all, we turn to those having only this minimum. If you do acquire that minimum in the next year or two, your application will still be reviewed last. Your application will always be in competition with others having more education than you." Nevertheless, when such people return in a year or two having acquired that minimum, their determination cannot be ignored. Given maturity and talent they may be good steady people to have on the job; they will grow on that job; they will be content in it.

Many administrators know the desperation that comes when vacancies pile up and all efforts fail to find persons with the minimum education or better. In this extremity, either the service the agency gives will have to be curtailed, or the work will have to be heaped upon other hard-pressed members of the staff. In public welfare agencies the work cannot be curtailed as a rule. Moreover, higher authorities may ask why a position is needed if it goes unfilled for a long period of time and that position may be eliminated. Here, the minimum educational requirements may have to be dispensed with temporarily, although they should never drop below high school matriculation, which assures university entrance. The in-service training programme will test the people who are selected. The trainee will know that this is a second compromise on the desired qualifications. He will hope to make good and be prepared to admit that his lack of education is an obstacle that cannot be overcome except by further academic study. In all events, he will hold the job open for someone with better qualifications. If his educational lacks turn out to have no correlation with his intellectual ability, then he will probably remain in it, and it will be increasingly well done as time goes on. Although he will know that his chances for advancement will be very slim, he may be content.

Age is another basic qualification. The age-range initially established for the in-service trainee in the Social Welfare Branch was twenty-three to thirty-five. The assumption, based on educational findings, was that learning ability is at a peak in these years, highest at around twenty-five, but continuing, for a great many, until the age of forty-five and often longer. Because of the nature of social work itself, which demands that its practitioners be free of bias, of fixed ideas and prejudices, thirty-five seemed the latest age at which such biases and fixed attitudes, if they existed, could be subject to modification and change. A change in this opinion has slowly come about. Age alone does not account for fixed ideas, which have been found in the very young as well as in older people. Persons over thirty-five, who have a broad liberal philosophy of their own, have blossomed in the breadth and liberality of the philosophy underlying social work. There may be corners of prejudice to chip away, but reason is an effective chipping tool. When there are too many corners, and the tool has grown dull from lack of use, there is more discomfort than comfort in the agency and such a person is usually relieved to go. Therefore, although added care should be exercised in selecting people of thirty-five and over, when they are good they are usually very good. Moreover, they have sought employment for reasons of necessity and they will stay. They will also go to school. Let us find these people and even entice them into the field.

Exceptions to the lower age limit have been made with less success than exceptions to the upper age limit. On the positive side, there is usually boundless enthusiasm on the part of the nineteen, twenty, twenty-one and twenty-two year olds. They enter social work with the fervour, idealism and appealing sophistication of late adolescence. Nothing should ever be done to quench their enthusiasm or to stifle their fervour, or to make them appear ridiculous. Idealism is precious in a materialistic age. But some curb will be needed, for the possibility is that learning will be fast but irregular. There is some danger too. The problems the social worker deals with will always arouse some subjective feeling, but with experience and training that feeling becomes well disciplined. New social workers have not learned this discipline fully even if they are graduates of a school of social work. Young non-graduates—that is, the in-service trained people—can suffer harm or, at the very least, fail to react at all, when faced with even the simplest of problems. Later, when life has caught up with them, when they have rubbed shoulders with many people, some of whom will have obvious problems, the shocks of the agency's cases will not be as great. Real sympathy which can be talked about and appropriately exercised and controlled will develop.

Health is another essential. Social work is a fatiguing occupation which requires physical and mental stamina in abundance. The applicant should provide a recent medical report. It is not easy to measure mental health by direct questions and the interviewer's observations may have to suffice. Being a social worker, the interviewer is especially sensitive to signs of emotional instability or immaturity and when they show up, the application is more exhaustively processed and will probably not be accepted. Questions about general health and major illnesses may, however, reveal a medical history of mental illness or of neurotic conditions, the "nervous breakdown" for example. Experience has proved quite conclusively that it is not wise for the agency to employ people who have apparently recovered from a major or even a minor mental illness. The work carries an emotional impact even for the most robust. Perhaps the schools of social work can see the less robust over some of these harder roads, but an agency cannot do this. If this be discrimination, it is exercised more for the sake of the person concerned than for the agency.

Previous employment is included in this review of basic qualifications because it is of importance when the desired age-range is set at twenty-three to thirty-five. Even the employment of new college graduates of less than twenty-three can well include a consideration of their work experiences between terms. Those who have had none may need help in grasping the necessity of a steady application of themselves to the work, to the rules of employment, and to the new experience of being held accountable for time, effort and thought expended. Older people who have worked somewhere before have these routines of paid employment among their habits of life. The concern now, with them, is not for that, but for the nature of their previous work, their success in it, their reasons for leaving it.

Almost all work brings people in touch with others: employers, supervisors, fellow-workers, or the public. When the importance of relationship in the field of social work is explained with care, the applicant will talk freely or diffidently about his relationships with those he has previously worked for and with.

The agency cannot afford to employ someone who has failed in relationships, even when they promise to try hard to do better. The best way of terminating an interview with such a person is to refer him to a vocational counsellor. However, when the applicant can say it was because his relationships were good that he began to think of social work as a career, then the interview moves on to another kind of conclusion.

A comment may be interpolated here on the young adults of twenty-five or thirty who, on leaving college or university, joined the race for "progress and success" in the business world, and who found it after all not for them, or they for it. After five to ten years of trying to be a success, they are totally dissatisfied. They will not, as many who have not had this disillusionment, be likely to want to try for material success again if they find their niche in a satisfying profession. They often say: "I know now that there is something about the way I was brought up that makes me unhappy in the chase for self-gain." There may be a little rationalizing behind their words: "I am sick of making money. I want to do a job that will be of some real value to the world." They may actually not possess the fibre to make good in competitive fields, but there is no fault in this, and their altruism is, more often than not, genuine. In any profession self must be subjugated to a larger good, and the profession should assist this person to a full realization of his better self. These matters are talked about freely and frankly in the application interview.

The choppers and changers of professions are people to be handled with care. A school teacher who is "tired of teaching" probably means she is tired of little children who were restless because she was not a good teacher. She will scarcely become a good social worker. One who says—"I have been a good teacher, and I like teaching, but I have grown concerned about my children and their problems; I think I can be of greater help to them in social work"—such a teacher will need to be helped to think this through. Social work needs her; but so does teaching. People from other professions—the nurse, the clergyman, the lawyer, as well as the teacher—must, besides learning new theories, reassemble the components of their previous knowledge, philosophy and experience. Some of these components, in their arrangement rather than their values, may prove to have sharp points which will prick if there is unwillingness to rearrange them in the order of social work knowledge, philosophy and experience. Such matters need to be talked about in the application interview. Professions are not changed for light reasons. In spite of doubt, which does not always arise, it may be that the risk of employing such a person is taken. The doubt and the risk should be in this person's mind as well as the employer's.

Family responsibilities may seem strangely placed as a "basic qualification." The question is one of realism versus idealism or pseudo-idealism. A man who is happily married and has a young family may have a genuine, well-founded drive to enter social work. For him the "back-door" of agency training is the only way he can do it. Before anything else is discussed with him, the implications of salary, the time involved to qualify for advancement, the effects upon his wife and children, should be thoroughly discussed with him. If he has been in his present work for some years, he will have gained some seniority, and will have had some promotions, no doubt. This will have to be recovered in a new field. If he has the qualifications and qualities the agency wants, he must be asked to go away, think and talk it over, and then make the decision. It should be a decision his wife helps him to make, and one made with two pair of eyes seeing the difficulties clearly. He must know that the agency will not be able to give him preferred treatment. This is not to gainsay what was said earlier about social work salaries. Those same things are said to the applicant now in question. It is his age, his present circumstances, his chances to overtake the loss he assumes in shifting which he must face squarely.

The pseudo-idealism referred to is sometimes found in young women who are married, who have a home and may have little children. They wish to retain these responsibilities and pleasures and to be a social worker too. On the sane grounds that to employ them would be to threaten the well-being of their own families, a threat social work exists to remove, the answer must be a firm "no." Then there is the childless man or woman whose marriages have failed. They may have accepted their situations with ease. Whether so or not, the implications to them of maintaining equilibrium when helping others through problems which are similar to their own need to be reviewed. On their responses and the kind of thought given to this possible obstacle will depend the outcome of the interview. If they are employed, they and the agency will accept and together try to overcome the risks involved.

*Personal Qualities*

Many "personal qualities" have already been obliquely discussed in the preceding section of this chapter. Much was said about education. Now the emphasis is on intelligence as a "personal quality." Some may have undertaken a university education so light-heartedly that it made little impression. For others it may have been hard bought. Lack of education, where opportunities for extra-curricular study exist, may suggest a lack of interest, ability, or effort. To judge a person's intelligence rather than his educational standing means determining the effects of education or lack of it on this person; deciding if his education is commensurate with his intellectual abilities. Some people are educated beyond their intelligence; others may not have the wit to see the value of education. A mental or psychometric measurement is not required, but if it is obtained from experts along with other psychological findings, it might be helpful in confirming doubts. Brilliant scholarship is not evidence; neither is that overworked quality "common sense." Upon what evidence then is a judgment to be formed?

Tentatively, it will be detected first in speech. The intelligent person is lucid. He thinks before and as he speaks. He listens to what is said to him, questions to be sure he understands correctly, makes appropriate comments. He can express his thoughts about why he thinks he will be a successful social worker. He has thought of questions to ask about the work. He is not afraid of silences. In these he thinks. He does not talk compulsively. He may not express himself fluently, but his words are chosen well. The interviewer can see this person in the interviewer's chair. "He inspires my respect; he will inspire others in the same way, his clients most of all."

The intelligent person has poise, which is revealed at once in his manner. He is at ease, serious, yet responsive to the play of humour the interviewer is wise to inject into this conversation. He displays few mannerisms; he is not frightened. His manners are considerate. He can meet the interviewer's gaze without embarrassment, neither staring nor glancing away. He is natural, neither shy nor overbearing, not too naïve nor too sophisticated, and he can express his feelings, sympathy, kindness, indignation, tenderness and determination, in his face.

Perhaps there are few who entirely measure up to such exhaustive criteria. Where the deviations are insignificant, they are noted but do not usually influence final judgment unduly. Where they are significant they must be discussed with the applicant either to justify turning down his application, or to see whether, with effort on his part and help from the agency, they can be improved. For example, inarticulation may be the most significant of the deficiencies noted. Language is the medium of social work practice. If what little is said is lucid, then this may not be a major obstacle. Verbosity would be just as undesirable. The effect of these characteristics on the interviewer is a fair clue to their importance. If he is irritated or distracted by the applicant's manner, or words, or appearance, the chances are that this would be the effect this person would have on some of his clients. To sum up, intelligence is required to learn in any setting. To learn while working makes heavier demands than usual upon the intellect. There must be a fair assurance in this first interview of mental acuity.

The applicant should also give evidence of having character or moral strength. This attribute can be deduced from the account he gives of his life to date. For example, he offers reasons rather than excuses for his failure to find vocational satisfactions in his previous work, he will not leave his present employer without giving due notice, he defends his family and his friends, he is straightforward in answering direct questions. There are many ways in which character is revealed.

The agency needs to know what the applicant's relationships with his family are. If he has the qualities discussed above and appears emotionally stable, questions can safely be asked about these. A younger person still living at home will reveal his degree of emancipation from his parents and his feelings for them when answering the question, "What do your parents think of you becoming a social worker?" Older people will often talk of their family relationships without direct questioning. At the point in the interview when the social worker's concern with family relationships is being explained, the interviewer can suggest that this is why it is so necessary for all social workers to recognize and resolve any conflicts they may have with their own families. A response is waited for, and whatever it is, it will have its meaning to the interviewer.

Probably all imperfections in personality are due to some problem in childhood, some faulty relationship with family. Without probing for the possible causes of probable defects, the interviewer can safely ask the apparently stable applicant, after admitting that no one is perfect, what faults he sees in himself which might stand in his way in becoming a social worker. This question could follow the more positive question, "Why do you think you would make a good social worker?" The replies to these questions, and the effect they have upon the applicant, are significant. When such questions are easily and naturally put to him, when they are timed to relate to the description the interviewer gives of the work, they will be appreciated rather than resented. Later, if this applicant is accepted, he and his fellow trainees will learn more of the importance to social work of the self-awareness of the practitioner.

What becomes a matter of concern to the interviewer is evidence of relationships which are apparently threatening an applicant's effectiveness in living. Should any emotional imbalance be shown during the interviews—weeping, anger, unrestrained laughter, gross mannerisms— it should be met with restrained sympathy and the interview terminated, or postponed so that it can be concluded at a later time in a quieter mood. It is not by any means unknown to have persons who are under a psychiatrist's care apply for a position as a social worker. Permission to talk to the doctor can often be obtained and he will be able to explain to his patient why the agency cannot give him a job. The less obvious symptoms of emotional strain or imbalance invariably leave doubt in the mind of the interviewer. The interviewer cannot attempt a diagnosis of the applicant's problem, which is unknown to him. He must, however, respect his own uneasiness about this person and make his recommendation against employing him accordingly.

The applicant's interests in life apart from work and family provide evidence of suitable personal qualities. When there are deep interests— hobbies, sports, the out-doors, music, art, amateur theatricals and so on—they are seldom left out of the interview. People like to talk about their interests. Welcome these always, for social workers as a group tend too easily to make their profession their whole interest in life. Of all people, social workers should lead well-rounded lives. Church affiliation is another indication of rounded living. If there is none, or if the word "agnostic" appears on an application form, or any religious denomination around which public controversy exists, it is well to discuss this frankly with the applicant. This discussion is merely to ensure that his adherence to his own faith will not cause him to judge harshly his clients' faith or lack of it, or give him feelings of persecution which could stand in his way. An agnostic, for instance, must acknowledge that little children have a right to and a need for religious teaching and religious observances. Politics? In a free country, the political beliefs of people are their own business. Should they be revealed at all in an application interview—and the interviewer has no right to question the applicant on this—what is important is the degree of feeling with which opinions are expressed, the sanity and moderation of the applicant's attitude to the views held. Rabidly held views of any kind suggest intolerance of the views of others. On the other hand, a person with no clear-cut political convictions may be failing in his duties as a citizen.

The applicant's motives for wanting to become a social worker need careful examination. The new graduate from a university or college may have a clear vocational direction. He wants to be a social worker. He also wants and probably needs a job. He quite frankly says he is tired of classrooms and study and this is probably true. He is not, however, being fair to himself, his chosen profession or the agency when he fails to prepare himself properly for his future career. Before having further interviews with him, it is in everyone's interests that he be interviewed by the school. If there is good reason for his inability to enrol, the school can refer him back to the agency for in-service training. This interest in him on the part of the agency and school will further impress upon his mind the importance of obtaining proper qualifications for a task which he apparently does not realize calls for broad knowledge and many fine skills which must be learned.

Those who have worked since graduation from college, or since leaving college or school, seldom apply for a job in a social agency suddenly. Usually, they have thought about this kind of work for a long time, both consciously and unconsciously. They have found themselves listening intently when social workers they know or meet are speaking. They have read thoroughly, in the newspapers, the items of news and the editorials which deal with human and social problems, as well as books on human behaviour. There has been a gradual building up of conviction that to work with people, to help in time of distress, is a worthwhile occupation, and worthy of them. Some of these people will have convictions about so serving which are beyond their obvious capacities to fulfil. These, and indeed all applicants, in the first interview, should be brought face to face with the realities of the job. The interviewer will ask if this person has thought about himself in the role of a social worker. Then after reviewing, briefly but graphically, two or three case histories, real or hypothetical, he will ask: "Can you see yourself meeting these people, listening to them, observing them, thinking about them and saying and doing the things which will be helpful? Do you see the importance of your being the strong, steady, reliable person on whom these clients can rely and have confidence?" The purpose is to present a vivid picture into which the applicant fits himself. To applicants who are obviously weak, the interviewer may say firmly: "You appear to me to be a gentle, sensitive person. I do not think you could stand the strain. For there is not one case, or two, or three like this, but hundreds." To the stronger people, the interviewer may say: "Come back tomorrow, or next week, and meanwhile think of what you, as a person, have in yourself to inspire the confidence of others, to give them strength, to convey support. Be honest with yourself. You are the only person who can judge yourself in these ways." That test taken, motive is no longer nebulous, but crystallized. Their objective from then on will be to develop their "self" to greater and greater capacity.

Intelligence, character, relationships, interests, attitudes, motives— these are among the more important personal qualities assessed in the application interviews in order to determine maturity. There are other qualities to be added to this evidence: the general appearance of the person, his grooming, dress, and obvious attention to personal hygiene. There are physical attributes which may be serious handicaps, depending on how the applicant feels about them. There are racial, cultural and national differences which are of no moment unless, as a newcomer to the community, the applicant is totally unfamiliar with its culture, mores, and way of life. When any of these less important personal attributes obtrude, they must be taken into account in judging the applicant's suitability for social work. Whether they are discussed then or later with those who are recommended for employment will depend upon their seriousness. There will be an appropriate time to do this, which should not be shirked, if there is really any need to do so.

## Skills of the Interviewer

Assessing these many impressions, observations, facts, overtones, and undertones makes the task of interviewing applicants for agency training and employment a most responsible one. Certain skills are required, which, though they are not used for treatment, resemble closely those implicit in the casework method. The ability to establish the right relationship with the applicant is important. In general terms, the applicant, whether he is accepted or not, should leave the interview with the feeling that the interviewer was human, understanding and genuinely interested in him. He may even be able to say that he got help from the interview.

The help is, of course, vocational help. This implies that the work has been lucidly and graphically described so that its nature can be clearly sensed if not wholly grasped. The interviewer has listened to the applicant's words, made sure of their meaning, and then remarked on their value. He has invited the applicant to speak, and by his ease of manner and friendliness encouraged frank speaking. He accorded the applicant his respect and did not raise—only to leave—questions which have the effect of delving into, or forcing a betrayal of minor flaws in personality. There was respect for the dignity of the applicant's "self." There was, besides these decencies, an effort to think with the applicant about his future. Advice was not withheld when it was asked for. The decision was left to the applicant when he was judged acceptable. Obstacles to success in this field were frankly examined and positive attributes were recognized. There was a realistic look at the future, and no shrinking from stating the difficulties and demands of social work.

Here is how an actual interview should go. It takes at least an hour. This is the first to be conducted, and others, based on the findings of this one, will follow, at least one of which will be with the agency's administrator or personnel director. It is arranged by telephone for a certain hour. It takes place in a room that is tidy, where there are no interruptions, and the interviewer is not pressed for time. The atmosphere is relaxed and welcoming.

A few vital statistics can be obtained easily and pleasantly: the proper spelling of the applicant's name, his address, place of birth, age, marital status, educational standing and present work. His name and address at least are jotted down. The other details will be discussed further and easily remembered as a result. This information need not be obtained by a rapid-fire question and answer routine. A name, a place, a date, a school, a child—any or all of these will make possible a pleasant conversational association of ideas. The interviewer's interest in him and in what has happened to him is being established now, and also the impression is being conveyed that there is something about him that is liked. The interviewer is revealed as being quite human.

The next step is to invite the applicant to say why he wants a job in the agency. It can be put in various ways. One way that leads easily into other matters which will have to be discussed is: "Why do you want to be a social worker?" Here is where the applicant is under some strain. He wants to say the right thing, but he may fumble it badly. The interviewer moves in to help here, guarding against a patronizing tone of voice or choice of words. He uses the applicant's vocabulary when restating his remarks; he uses his own vocabulary when he frames his questions on comments upon the work. (Need it be added that this vocabulary is shorn of the jargon of social work?)

Next the applicant is asked what he knows about the work a social worker does. Here there may well be confession of ignorance. It will help to reduce any feeling he has about this, if the interviewer says that the profession has failed badly in interpreting itself to the community at large. The interviewer may then trace back into history and review the problems of mankind the world over: destitution and poverty, illness and incapacity, ignorance and vice, discrimination and exploitation. He may relate these to the present day, when new knowledge, new methods and a new regard for the dignity of man make social work one of the positive, building, enabling professions. He will speak of the objectives of social work: "to help people to help themselves"; or "to help people to develop the capacity and to find and use the opportunities to lead lives that are personally satisfying and socially useful"; or "to help dependent people to achieve at least a measure of independence, if not full independence." There are many ways of saying it, and it should be said so as not to sound pat, or rhetorical, or bombastic; the sincerity of the interviewer's own beliefs should show in his manner. The response from the applicant will be significant. Cynicism if it appears can be argued against, but it is better left for the record as a piece of evidence from which to draw inferences. Responses which confirm the value of what was said, even though they are a little naïvely expressed are to be registered and approved. He will then discuss the major principles of the profession and briefly describe the method and meaning of casework. At this time he inserts the questions discussed earlier in this chapter, that have to do with his own family relationships and traits of personality.

Without damage to these loftier thoughts the interviewer may now, briskly and in a business-like way (a change in theme and tempo is a relief), begin to describe the agency's work. He reviews its functions, its structure, its scope and limitations. He illustrates the kind of services given, revealing both success and failure. He presents all the difficulties, but along with these, the hopes and ultimate objectives the agency has for the service and those served. He clearly explains that the agency will expect the applicant to obtain professional qualifications if he succeeds. He pauses for questions and comments. He makes a mental note of their quality and appropriateness. When he is finished —and he should discipline himself to see that he does finish— he says, in effect: "That is it. What do you think now about wanting to be a social worker?" Again the reply is significant. It may lead to termination of the interview or into the next area to be explored.

At this point the applicant should again talk about himself. He is asked about his present and past work, and how it may have influenced his decision to change to social work. He is asked about his education, his courses and standing and his general attitude to education. To make it easy for him to talk about his interests, his friends, his church and group affiliations, the interviewer asks if he has thought that this new work in a rural area might change some of these. He is asked if he thinks he has the physical stamina it takes to do this work.

The personnel practices of the agency will probably have been talked about in relation to his present job and the difference in salary, setting, advantages and status. Applicants have been known, however, after leaving the office to knock timidly on the door again and say: "I forgot to ask about the salary." (This should never happen. People have to live, and though social work offers many satisfactions, it does not yet offer commensurate pay.) With these matters covered, the conditions surrounding the agency's training plan are reviewed with care. The importance of the applicant's attaining professional training is repeated. The possibility and desirability of his doing so first rather than last is discussed in detail. An appointment for an interview at the school may be made or his assurances obtained that he will do this himself. The trial nature of the in-service training plan is explained fully, the usual response being that this is only fair to everyone concerned.

If there are vacancies at the time this interview takes place, these may be discussed with him then, or deferred for the second interview. At least twenty-four hours should elapse between these interviews to give him time for last thoughts and family discussion. A longer period for this is preferable. The first interview terminates on the note that further thought on the applicant's part and the agency's part needs to be given to his employment. If it has not been obtained before, an application form is given him to fill out. If he does not submit it within a week, the agency will know he has decided against it. If he does, and there are no vacancies, he will be told that his application and a brief record of the interview will be held on an active, confidential file, and that he may be summoned for a second interview at a later time. It will help if he keeps in touch with the interviewer from time to time. These actions alone suggest that he has made a good impression, that his chances of employment are therefore good. If an application form is not given, the reverse is suggested. When an applicant is rejected, however, he should be told definitely that he does not qualify. He can appeal to a higher authority if he desires to do so. If he does this it will only confirm unsuitability, provided the interviewer has been objective, sensitive and reasonable in his appraisal.

## Application Forms and Letters of Reference

Every agency has an application form suited to its personnel requirements. These documents are valuable in augmenting the findings of the application interviews and may be used in the second interview especially as a base from which to go further, in a practical way, into matters which are in doubt. Besides this use they reveal much by the way they are completed. If they are filled in by hand, the writing itself is often indicative of personal characteristics—precision or carelessness, for example (not "character"). Spelling, however, is so frequently in error in these days of permissive education that it may have to be ignored. Gaps left on the form are to be noted, and filled in later either by mailing the form back, or when the applicant is next seen in the office. Discrepancies in dates, misunderstanding of the questions, "cute" comments and the like create doubt of the seriousness of the applicant's attention to detail and the seriousness of his intentions. The application form gives the first look at the applicant's administrative possibilities, and it would be rather helpful if he knew this.

A device employed by many agencies, and it is a good one, is to leave space, or request an attachment, in which the applicant composes a short essay stating why he is applying for a position in the agency. If it is written after the first interview, no one should be surprised to find phrases used by the interviewer. This is good, rather than otherwise. People remember words which reflect their own ideas, and a good memory for words that are heard is needed in social work. If written before this interview, tritely expressed ideas may appear, which should not be disparaged. Learners of all trades go through this and many more stages before they become sophisticated. (Seasoned social workers sometimes find this tiresome in their younger colleagues. All progress seems to have to wait until these fresh new minds have gone through all the steps of original thinking, talking, planning, abandoning plans and so on. There is no short-cut to achieving professional maturity, alas!) The ideas expressed in the composition on the application form are to be regarded in that light—the first attempt to give form to thought, feelings and aspirations. The gauge to use in judging it is the sincerity it conveys.

The agency should write to the people named on the form as references. These will doubtless be former employers, teachers, clergymen, family friends and often other social workers. The letter will state the reasons for writing of course, but should ask rather specific questions and give general leads to the kind of reply wanted. For example:

. . . Mr. X has recently applied for a position as a social worker with this agency and has given us your name as a reference. He will, if accepted, be given some initial training with us, and later will have opportunity to qualify himself by obtaining professional training at a school of social work.

Social work is an exacting profession. It calls for broad sympathies, patience and tact, for good health, and for intelligence and character. It will be of help to us if you would tell us quite frankly whether you think Mr. X would make a good social worker. Your letter will be kept confidential unless you say that you have no objection to our discussing parts or all of it with Mr. X.

With our thanks for your help in this matter. . . .

The replies are often useful. They frequently tell stories of the applicant's successes and achievements in working with people. They throw further light on the quality of his relationships with his friends and family, with the people he has met in his work and in the community. Invariably the people who write give their frank opinion of the applicant's suitability for social work, which is one way of gauging public opinion about this new profession. Sometimes a letter will draw attention to qualities which may stand in the way of the applicant's success. These are always noted and, if serious, the applicant is asked to talk further about them. In the training period the teacher may deliberately, though not pointedly, raise questions which permit the group to help this person to think through the way in which these qualities apply to the work. His need to change in this respect will be of his own discovering. The letters of reference most often confirm the agency's judgment of an applicant. The fact that they are asked for without fail gives to the whole operation of selection a further dignity and seriousness of intention and purpose.

## WHERE TO FIND PEOPLE

Application interviews are conducted every week of the year in the Social Welfare Branch—never less than fifteen each month. People write, telephone, or drop in to make appointments, and sometimes are seen without one. They usually come first to the Personnel Office of the Branch (in which the Training Supervisor frequently acts as the first interviewer). This practice is agreed upon by the Civil Service Commission; the Commission similarly refers to the Branch applicants who go first to them to apply. Invariably the Commission accepts the recommendations made, for they know they are made only after careful study of the many matters discussed in this chapter.

Many of those without professional training who telephone to inquire say that "they have heard" about the training plan from someone who knows someone who in turn had heard about it. Their information is therefore sometimes inaccurate. Direct questions are asked about education, age, and marital status and little time is wasted discussing the plan when basic qualifications are totally lacking. The door is shut firmly, but tactfully. The few who insist on an audience will get it, but pleading is ignored, especially pleading which is based on "being a personal friend" of an elected or influential person.

This "word-of-mouth" spreading of the news is not all hopeless, by any means. In fact, depending upon who spreads the tidings, it is one of the best ways of finding people. Other social workers are the best recruiters. There are only a few social workers who hold in-service training in contempt because of a mistaken desire to protect the group in which they have found prestige. The majority of social workers adhere to the true ethic of social work: the serving of people suffering social distress. They share in the effort to enlist the best possible people in the total effort. Among their friends and acquaintances, many of whom are interested in their work, they talk about it objectively and, as they do, watch for reactions. They may start someone thinking about himself in this vocation by saying, when they truthfully can, "You have many of the qualities a social worker has to have. Have you ever thought about preparing yourself for this profession?" This is where the agency's interpretation to the professional association of the plan and objectives of in-service training can pay dividends. If the members know and approve, they can direct suitable people to the agency. The agency can place great reliance on their judgment, although the same care in selection must, of course, be exercised. Those who have themselves gone through the agency's plan of training are useful in recruiting. Some reservations must be made when the referral of a friend comes during the early stages of training, when enthusiasm is high. There may be a little danger that the agency will begin to look like a band-wagon. Later, when enthusiasm has been tempered by the realism of hard work and when the nature of that work is more fully comprehended, referrals from this source are more trustworthy.

Clerical staff employed in the agency may have decided possibilities.

Certainly those who expend extra effort to understand more than the mere routine of the work which they handle are displaying attributes of responsibility and concern for the agency's work. Their personal qualities can be observed in action daily. They may be assigned duties which will test their ability to meet people and deal with problems. The agency can be sure of loyalty. Whether the agency or the clerical worker first broaches the subject of transferring to the social worker ranks is of little significance. In-service training will determine to the agency's and the stenographer's satisfaction whether the transfer was wise. If not, this person is all the more valuable to the agency when he reverts back to a clerical position. A placement can no doubt be found which will make the best use of the deeper perceptions gained. Perhaps here the educational qualifications of a university or college degree should be adhered to firmly, especially for the younger stenographers.

Employment services in the community should work with and for the agency constantly. Government employment agencies may come to mind first. In registering staff needs with them, a few safeguards need to be set up. First, not once, but many times during the year, the agency should get in touch with the proper employment officer, preferably for face-to-face talks rather than by letter or telephone. He will have lots of other employers pressing him, and the agency should not wait for him to take action on its behalf. Second, at least once a year, the agency should review with the employment office the qualifications it requires of applicants. Personnel may change in that office; some of its staff do not have files of job descriptions immediately at hand. This often accounts for referrals from them of people who may be totally unsuited to the work. The agency must assume responsibility of clearly defining the job and the qualifications, as it also takes the initiative in using this service.

Other types of employment services may also be fruitful. All universities have employment offices, usually for between-term jobs, but often used by those who graduate, or by those who for some personal reason (not always lack of scholarship) have to drop out. Again it is necessary for the agency to take the initiative, and before the end of each university year, to review qualifications required—personal as well as basic—and to define the job clearly. Many other employers are looking for these university people. The job description will have to be good. A printed brochure or a poster, provided it is both attractive and truthful, may be helpful. The counsellor in charge may or may not know enough about social work to advise people properly, and the agency should tell him to refer those who inquire to it for interpretation. An agency's doors should always be open for this purpose, whether employment is in view or not.

Many communities are blessed with vocational counselling services, some operated as social agencies, others for profit. All should be approached. Counsellors in these services have a professional interest in making referrals. (Conversely, the agency may sometimes use their services to clarify their opinion of applicants.) The person referred will usually give permission for the agency to discuss the counsellor's findings and opinions. Caution rather than over-assurance of suitability can be expected but that is to be expected of all scientific people. This is a good resource in recruiting.

Advertising has its pitfalls, and if it is done, the agency must clear its desks and be prepared for a deluge. Even when qualifications are clearly defined in the advertisement (its wording is important) there will be scores of people who will come to try their chances without them. Of the total number who will have to be interviewed (although for a government agency the Civil Service may do the initial screening) only a few will be able to meet the full test. It may be worth the effort, however, to get these few. The weekly newspapers in the more rural areas should not be overlooked, especially by public agencies which give a rural service. The rural offices will have to take on the first interviewing, which means that the persons who do it will have to be informed and coached in the way it should be done.

Besides these specific efforts to obtain recruits, the agency should undertake to interpret its work to the community. This interpretation is for larger purposes than merely recruiting, of course, for community understanding and support are needed by all agencies. The problems surrounding interpretation stem chiefly from the confidential nature of the work that is done. The use of fiction to present a picture of that work is seldom tried, probably because the writing of fiction is not one of the ordinary social worker's gifts. In these days of high-powered publicity and advertising, an agency may think that nothing short of an expensive reproduction of a masterpiece will get the story across. It should not be necessary to behave like a literary guild or like big business in telling the agency's story. The simpler it is, the more human: the more human, the more appealing. The media of telling it are with us in plenty: newspapers, radio, television, exhibitions, speaker's lists, schools, clubs and the like. They do not all cost money, but the publicity is worth any money spent.

The slant such publicity manages to effect, however, is sometimes dismal, depressing and distressing. Efforts to talk only about successes, on the other hand, may get a cynical brush-off. These are two of the reasons often advanced for social work's failure to attract young people to it. Recruiting publicity is further complicated because it is difficult to show how the social worker does his job. The chief way in which social workers can suggest that their work is not depressing is by their deportment as they move about the community. They are thoroughly nice people to know; they are competent and reliable; they express their feelings as ordinary people do and admit mistakes; and they have a sense of humour, an alertness and vitality which are positive. All these qualities suggest that their work may not be so depressing after all.

Recruiting in high schools and colleges by reaching the students is a continuing responsibility of agencies, the profession and the schools of social work. If high schools do not ask for it, the agency should itself offer to send someone to talk to the students about social work at a time planned for this. Most agencies are plagued by letters from high school students busy doing assigned or elected job studies. A good, clearly mimeographed reply, simply worded, is a time-saver, and will be a better advertisement if a leaflet with a picture of two good-looking, well-dressed social workers, one male, one female, can be tucked in. These are impressionable people, at an age when idealism plus rather amazing good sense are present in liberal quantity.

It may be that in the colleges and universities social work is failing to make an impression. There may be cynicism to deal with, so the story needs to be told crisply and factually and truthfully and without apology. The importance of this group lies in the fact that these people are committed to a university education. Many applicants for jobs in the Social Welfare Branch have majored in psychology, sociology, anthropology, or philosophy. They seem to have done so without a very clear notion of the vocational use to which this knowledge could be put. Perhaps they thought vaguely of getting jobs in industry, government, or teaching, but they have failed to find such niches, for experience as well as scholarship is usually demanded. These are the people to reach, surely, for they have elected to study the social sciences, but whose job it is to reach them is a question. The agency should be willing, but perhaps the schools of social work should take on this task. Recruiting for social work among the youth of our communities is everybody's business. It is not only foolish, but it may be fatal, not to make unusual efforts in the present and in coming years to capture the minds of our young people in this human calling, or, if you prefer, this behavioural science.

# IV. The Agency Teacher Prepares for the Task

LONG BEFORE the agency teacher meets his first group of trainees, he is occupied in preparing to do so. He has many things to establish clearly in his own mind and to get down on paper. Teaching of the kind he will do can never be done without careful preparation and it imposes the further obligation of accountability. Every hour of agency time spent in teaching has to see some progress made.

The teacher must make a frank examination of his attitudes to the unique job he will do, for teaching of any kind must be done with sincerity and conviction. He must establish a frame of reference for his teaching, and foresee and estimate the educational objectives for those who are taught. A broad "intent" and total plan of operation must be established in order to see the teaching as a whole. The whole must be broken down into parts which can be fitted, in logical sequence, into a time-schedule. Study materials, teaching notes and teaching devices must be developed. There must be a regard for the administrative controls which permit the plan to move forward when the time comes with a minimum of frustration and fumbling. The skills needed to make these preparations are obviously among those required in the organization of programmes, which, for people who have a demonstrated or latent talent in this kind of activity, will be developed and refined as time goes on. Skill in teaching embraces this talent among others.

Teachers, they say, "are born, not made." This is true to the extent that a person who teaches must like to teach. To "like to teach" means: to have an intellectual delight in the relationship the teacher has with those he teaches. In-service training, as a form of intensive adult education, provides scope for developing a relationship which could go beyond desirable lengths. The agency teacher cannot help but be exhilarated by the group's responses to him and what he teaches, but he must control his feelings and let them show only for a purpose; for example, to quicken the group's sober application to learning, should it flag, or to reinforce any trainee's own self-esteem should the task of learning become overwhelming. The trainees' feelings, in turn, are energies to be directed so as to enable them to learn comfortably. The agency teacher, through this controlled relationship can provide for those who are taught, the inspiration, determination, and direction in regard to learning for all time to come. It is a grave responsibility.

Achieving the desired relationship depends largely upon the teacher grasping and then employing one essential principle of adult education: these adults should be considered as adults—that is, as mature people —and accepted by their teachers on a plane of intellectual equality. The teachers' only advantage over them is their wider knowledge and longer experience, a broad advantage, to be sure, but one which all good teachers are dedicated to making less. Both the advantage and the dedication to narrowing it will win the respect of those taught, and inspire their desire and stiffen their determination to learn. There can be no patronage, no talking down from a superior height, no ostentation on the part of the teacher in teaching adults.

## The Teacher's Attitudes

The professional social worker who becomes the agency's teacher must believe in the work he is to do. He must not feel, strongly or vaguely, that he is betraying his profession in undertaking to give this initial training for practice in a social agency, nor may he be overconscious of the sacrifices and efforts he made to prepare himself properly for practice. No doubts as to the wisdom of the agency's plan of training should make him, in spite of himself, half-hearted about his role in the effort. He should not fear the criticism of his colleagues in other agencies, or of the school of social work. On the other hand, he should not take on the task with an alacrity which ignores the profession's interests in this form of education for he must keep the trainees alive to the values of the profession and help them to want to belong to it. The agency teacher is the mind, heart and soul of the agency's specific training and general staff development activities, and his feelings about his responsibilities will affect the training plans.

Professional ethics are not being violated in the concept which underlies in-service training. Social work as a profession is dedicated to promoting human well-being by remedying social distress. There is no question that much knowledge and many skills as well as a formal education are required of the social worker in furthering this cause. Precisely because of this, it is beyond conceiving that people should be employed to minister to the socially distressed with no knowledge and no understanding of the skills involved. The crucial point becomes how much knowledge, how much skill can be taught by the agency when it is forced by incontrovertible circumstances—the shortage of professionally prepared social workers—to employ people who, though not unintelligent, lack the specific knowledge and skills required. Not to teach them, not to start the processes of learning, is surely unethical. To teach and to start the process of learning support rather than harm the profession's system of values.

Criticism of in-service training is to be expected, but it will not persist if the agency confides its purpose and plan to those whose active or passive antagonism would be harmful. There can be no criticism of a staff development programme, and the training plan is part of that programme. If any still object to the plan after they understand why the agency must adopt it, they are probably, according to the definition of Edward Lindeman, perfectionists: "those who prefer evil rather than to be thwarted." Constructive criticism of the plan is to be desired, even sought. The agency teacher should welcome the help such criticism will be to him, and must not be blind to other ways of breaking the deadlock of shortages of personnel. He must, indeed, be among those who seek, by study and experiment, to solve the problem.

These comments are addressed primarily to the person the agency employs to carry out its training programme, but the cap may also fit others involved in its planning and operation. Whoever wears it, or, contrarily finds fault with its style, may be reassured in knowing that it is made from the cloth of experience. Though it be a revelation to protest it, it has been said not in defence, but to bring out the largely unconscious feelings of doubt which criticism can give rise to and which can chill rather than warm the mind as that mind addresses itself to the problem. Conviction and sincerity are essential in this responsible work, and may have to be consciously cultivated, preferably before rather than after the work begins.

## THE FOCUS OF THE TEACHING

"In-service training is a form of education for social work." The word "form" needs to be examined with care. Contrasts can be sharply drawn between this form and the form that education for social work takes in a school of social work. The difference lies in the immediacy of the effects to be achieved by agency training and the scope of preparation that this limitation makes necessary. A professional education prepares people for professional practice in any agency. In-service training prepares people for practice in one agency. The scope of in-service training includes only those things which the agency conceives to be its practices.

The term "agency practices" was defined in chapter I, in relation to the content of that chapter. It now requires further definition. "Practice," according to Webster, means, in the sense of practising a profession: "active performance or application of knowledge." The tense is always present indicative; like the law, practice is always speaking. The question remaining is: What knowledge? Essentially, it is knowledge appropriate to the functions of a social agency. Specifically it includes knowledge of human behaviour and of all the many things inside and outside the individual that condition his behaviour. It is knowledge of the agency and the way it performs its service. It also includes the knowledge which conditions the practitioner to certain ways of thinking about and responding to the problems that arise while he is performing his duties. It is knowledge of values. It is knowledge of self.

Such a focus within which to plan the content of teaching may be regarded with dismay. It appears to have no outside rim whatever. This, however, is the "whole" of agency practice. This knowledge cannot be seen in layers, some of which can be conveniently peeled off and laid aside until later. Nor can it be seen as a series of compartments. It is a whole and its parts are indivisible. In what form, therefore, can this knowledge be taught in an agency?

In the agency only the primaries of this knowledge can be taught. It must be stripped of the inevitable and complex variables which arise in actual practice. It must be simply taught, without affronting the intelligence of those to be taught. To use the analogy of the schoolhouse, this is the "primary grade."

This analogy of primary grades suggests what the focus of the teaching will be. Primary grade teachers begin "where the child is" in his maturation and life experience. The trainee is an adult. His maturity is assumed until proved lacking. The focus of teaching can be sharp and much can be expected of his powers of concentration and assimilation. The trainee's life experience will have brought him in contact with evidence of social dislocation or with ideas about human problems. He probably will have had personal experience in this regard. Teaching moves from what the trainees know to what they do not know, as they place what is known in an orderly frame and integrate it with new facts and ideas.

Facts and ideas in social work come from a variety of sources. The facts are scientific; the ideas are philosophical. The social sciences from which facts derive are themselves in a state of growth, and research continues on individual, family and group behaviour. The agency teacher cannot claim to know these sciences thoroughly or to be completely up to date on all the latest discoveries. However, he should be alive to the significance of social research and social findings, and by his attitude to the scientific method, inculcate in the minds of those he teaches a respect for accuracy and system in applying or using facts. He can, by his own attitude, foster a "sense of wonder" towards future discoveries. In other words, he encourages a sense of inquiry, of intellectual curiosity, of sharpened interest in those areas which touch upon the social worker's field. These new people must realize that the open-mindedness of the scientist and his unending search for truth are essential to their new work. In the application of evolving theories and emerging principles, the social worker gives them further test. He learns that there are few if any laws or canons to be committed to memory and applied invariably to every case he will carry.

The philosophical content of social work derives principally from ethics. For example, moral laws are absolute in all religions, and in the conscious and unconscious minds of the people whom religion reaches. The effect upon human conduct of breaking these laws, the consequences of a disregard of these moral proscriptions can be deduced by this group of trainees in respect of society's moral dilemmas. Here are but a few examples. Can whole nations have feelings of guilt concerning the stockpiling and threatened use of nuclear weapons? How do men of reason and goodwill regard capital punishment? What uneasiness, if any, lies behind the possession of great wealth? Do not all people have acquisitive impulses? Discussions of these issues are for the purpose of extracting the truth that guilt is a natural, even desirable, conditioner of behaviour and that conscience universally directs behaviour. These ideas can be applied to homely incidents within the experience of everyone in the group. The philosophic matter within social work practice is seen as inseparable from the scientific. The contemplative faculties of these embryonic social workers are stimulated in this first contact with their new calling. Their minds can begin to stretch in the consideration of abstract ideas. This produces an enhanced vitality which the work itself will later sustain.

The methods of thought and the exactitude of the language employed by the philosophers also must be considered. The social caseworker engages in deductive reasoning every day as he reasons from known facts and observations through generalizations appropriate to the facts, to reach inferences, or a social assessment of the problem his client faces and of his ability to overcome it. These new social workers need to be helped to see how their brains will work in this job. They must have both a knowledge of generalizations or criteria of behaviour and the acuity to select those which are appropriate to the facts.

It can be interpolated here (and with benefit discussed with these new people who are among the social work ranks of tomorrow) that social agencies have failed badly in not inspiring or apparently even permitting social workers to do more inductive reasoning to formulate assumptions from the mass of data every agency possesses. To test these assumptions and proclaim them for the sake of the light they throw on society's problems are obligations the majority of agencies have failed, so far, to meet.

The facts and ideas on which in-service training focuses are not all scientifically and philosophically derived. Far from it. The facts of administration must claim a major part of the time allowed by the agency for training. However, the teacher will be constantly alert to the chances these sober facts often provide to extract their scientific and philosophic implications. The search for the reason for the fact proclaims the student mind at work. The awakening and cultivation of the "student mind" is the teacher's responsibility.

The most significant point to be made in regard to agency training is that its content is so constructed as to emphasize the external rather than the internal forces which condition behaviour, and to reveal how the social worker applies his knowledge of these realities. This emphasis derives from the fact that the administration feels that the in-service trained person can initially assume responsibility only for work which deals in tangibles or which seeks to change the client's environment for the better. This feeling derives in turn from the administration's knowledge of prevailing community needs, or the kinds of problems the majority of those seeking help bring to the agency. These needs will shape and re-shape the agency's functions. In those agencies set up to meet external needs, and few do not have this as part at least of their function, the social workers must obviously apply their knowledge of the realities of living. In-service training deals primarily with these realities, dealing with them, however, as the social worker deals with them.

The social worker in dealing with the problems that arise from external pressures must work with both cause and effects. Psychological or emotional pressures, inadequacies, or deficiences may well be the root of the problem. Whether so or not, one of the effects of the problem itself will be a shattering or severe shaking of emotional poise. Feelings cannot be ignored in the social worker's search for the understanding he must have in order to give appropriate help. Agency training must make this abundantly clear. It must give equal recognition to internal or subjective causes, but it cannot teach directly the knowledge which bears solely upon these internal forces. It has the time to do no more than acquaint the trainee with the necessity of respecting the client's feelings, of observing their effects, of asking for his supervisor's understanding and direction in respect of his client's psychological make-up, individual case by individual case.

The teaching and learning of this knowledge, which must be gradual but consistent in its rate of progress, marks another major difference between agency and academic training. This is the cultivation of self-awareness. The social worker, it was said before, is himself the chief instrument of his profession. The psychological theories he is taught, if they are to be validly applied in understanding the psychological make-up of his clients, must be accepted as valid for himself. When there is any difficulty in this acceptance, time and frequently some help will be needed in resolving the conflict. The less robust student may in fact be severely shaken in the process or may, for the same reason, become so immersed in the morbid joys of introspection that he is rendered ineffectual as a social worker. Such workers are apt to ignore the knowledge they possess of the external forces which are often indivisible from the internal forces in shaping conduct.

The in-service trained person who becomes a student of social work in a professional school is hungry for psychological knowledge. He has had proof of its importance in shaping and affecting conduct. He has walked delicately in respect of the feelings he has encountered as he had dealt with people who have lost their jobs, who are badly housed, fed, and clothed. He has seen and respected the feelings roused by illness, incapacity, neglect, aging. He has tried to satiate his desire for knowledge—and his supervisor has helped in this—by recording and discussing his observations of these emotional effects. He has read much in the literature; he has listened to his more learned colleagues on these matters. As a student he will pursue these subjects avidly, but with one major difference: he can now relate these psychological theories immediately to the external facts of life with which he has been dealing. He has felt as well as observed their necessity. He has seen that changes in conduct, perhaps in personality, can be effected by changes in the environment. He will not then be disturbed or crushed by the search for self-understanding, but liberated.

## Methods of Teaching

The agency teacher will need to give prior thought to the methods of teaching best suited to this form of education. Reference has been made in earlier pages to the two major ways in which in-service training is carried out in the Social Welfare Branch. These are learning about the work by talking about it in group sessions planned for that purpose, and learning the work by doing it in the setting in which it is normally done and under supervision that is normally provided for the whole staff.

The discussion method of teaching has much virtue, provided it has a predetermined objective, is contained within a prescribed time and is limited to the focus the teacher previously determines this subject, in this time, will have. This immediately suggests that the members of the group do not themselves elect to discuss what they want to talk about when they want to. Their talk, that is, their thought, is channelled and directed in the way the teacher deems best. Within that restriction, however, all the dynamic elements of group activity can be allowed if not encouraged.

The teacher remains the teacher and is not part of the group. In its periods of relaxation the teacher does not join it except at its invitation. It will, perhaps, never name its natural leader but there will be a leader. It will develop freedom to consider the opinions and respect the thoughts of its members. It will tend to seal off any one member who fails to measure up to the norm of the whole group. It will cultivate critical faculties in respect of the opinions of those who are "in" and chastise, discipline and encourage when necessary. It will honour the teacher's prescriptions in respect of what they must learn and will quickly display apathy, displeasure or frustration when the manner of teaching does not measure up to a full recognition of their powers of comprehension.

This group becomes a vital entity possessed of energy, feelings and spirit which provide the soil in which to cultivate what is taught. The supervisor in the operative office also knows about these vital elements. It is to the energy, feelings and spirit of the staff of the district office that the trainee is transplanted when he leaves the first group. The larger staff development programme of the agency which sustains the total staff in their continual growth will ensure that his growth will also continue. In short, though learning by doing the work will call for much independent effort, the conditions—the "soil" or atmosphere—in which he learns when working will have an effect upon his progress.

The agency teacher, acting as the supervisor, does most to create the climate favourable to growth. The skill involved is the simple one of being human. Naturalness, humility, dignity, responsiveness, appreciation, regard, humour and occasionally even confession of error give to the group a feeling of comfort and ease. These qualities can be cultivated by the teacher of social work, who must have an acute self-awareness. They are built into the teacher's personality by his education and experience in this profession of social work and by those things within himself which make him want to be a teacher.

The skills that are more precisely related to teaching are those of speaking, listening, questioning, illustrating, relating, extracting, summarizing, controlling, directing and generally quickening the interest and mental energies of the group. The teacher should try not to talk too much and when he must use the lecture method, he should inform the group of what he is doing. In discussions, usually he should speak only to place a proposition before the group, calling for thought to be expressed on it, and concluding the discussion with a quick and telling summary which applies the consensus of opinion to the agency's work. He gauges the tensions of the group and helps to build them up or reduce them by modulating his voice or his expression or by changing his method. He listens and remembers what each one of the group has said. He shows his respect for the mind of that person by referring back at a later time to what he said. "That was the point you made, Mr. A." By judicious questions he encourages deeper thought. The group itself will soon assume responsibility for pursuing thought to arrive as near truth as may be, which may have to be curbed if the subject does not relate to the agency.

The teacher is an experienced social worker who can occasionally draw from his experience to illustrate the facts and ideas being discussed. As he relates his stories, he is revealing the social worker's attitudes to people. As he presents the lesson the story illustrates, his profession and he seem to be one. To illustrate: at least one trainee will say something like this during the first group sessions: "I think you are the nicest person to have that attitude to people." Without losing a moment the teacher can say: "I am an average social worker having no special distinctions whatsoever. These attitudes you admire are the attitudes of all social workers. Once you have decided they are desirable, thenceforward you proceed to absorb them until the time comes when your profession is an expression of yourself." Affirmation of the teacher's belief in his profession provides encouragement to the trainee to reach such a point of conviction for himself.

The inter-relation of all the many separate items considered by the group should be revealed by the teacher. When the group discusses the skills and knowledge required to place a child in a foster home, the similarity between this process and helping an aged person to adjust in a boarding home can be shown clearly. It is not enough merely to direct thought to this transfer of skills and knowledge. The rule of learning involved can be put into words and the moral of the lesson made plain. It is a way of conditioning these people to see similarities among the various parts of their practice and to transfer appropriate knowledge to new and puzzling situations. The effect is to help them see their knowledge as generic. Extracting and stating the "lesson" to be learned is not to be overlooked.

Control and direction of the group's thought is mandatory. Differences of opinion, argument for argument's sake, verbosity, recital of personal experiences having little point, these and many more like things slow up or prolong the discussion or divert it from the main theme. The teacher must be firm in cutting these off and, if necessary, doing it with a display of authority. The social worker is subject to authority, just as his work often demands that he exercise it. Controls and direction will be accepted when the reason for them is made obvious. The group will itself soon begin to exercise acceptable control over its wayward members in its eagerness to get on with the job in hand.

The responses made by trainees to all these efforts on the teacher's part should be remembered by him. When the evaluation interview is held, as it will be before the group disperses, some of them may have to be talked over with the person concerned. Evaluations should cover the strength as well as the weakness of the person evaluated so that he will be encouraged to make greater efforts to improve; both must be recorded when they are significant. When the responses are seriously negative, the trainee must know that the teacher's recommendation will be that he not continue. If the selection during the application process has been wise the responses of the majority of these people will however have been positive.

The learning that has taken place may be a little more difficult to gauge. Written examinations seldom give a satisfactory estimate of this and the subject of social work does not lend itself to precise question-and-answer tests. The gauge must be the quality of the thought expressed by each individual member of the group. There is little difficulty in assessing this quality and little difficulty in remembering evidence of it. The teacher is immersed in this group during the group sessions. Each trainee's articulation, retention of facts, mechanical skills, and, of great importance, his ability to reason and to relate and apply knowledge already gained are obvious to the teacher. The methods of teaching used further provide the opportunity for these traits to show. He must make these traits equally obvious to the trainee so that he will employ his mental energies fully in the next part of the training period. Without fail, the agency teacher must inform the person who will supervise this trainee of his abilities and disabilities. The administration must be immediately involved when the progress has been doubtful.

*Teaching Devices*

The discussion method of teaching and learning requires a focus or a frame of reference for the thought and talk that take place. To ensure that the proper focus is achieved the teacher can prepare in advance a précis or outline of the topic for group discussion. This outline, which should be in essay form but abbreviated concisely, should help the group recall the meanings which they found and which the teacher summarized.

The supervisors who will be in charge of these people in the field offices will study this material and, knowing what has been taught in the first group session, can develop more fully the trainees' understanding of the concepts discussed. The trainee will also use these précis quite frequently for review and reference when he is away from the group. A more immediate value of the outlines is that the members of the group do not divide their attention by attempting to take notes on all that is said. The précis used in the Social Welfare Branch are found in Appendixes II–V.

The discussion method needs to be varied. The principal variation, and one that cannot be introduced too soon, is that of handling, examining and analysing the "tools" the agency provides—especially the manuals of policy and procedure—and also actual case records, or case files. The agency teacher can usually obtain a sufficient number of these files from the "Closed" filing cabinets of the operative offices. The names of the people involved are not disguised, for the trainees are now agency employees, and should, at this early time, be taught to respect the confidential nature of agency and casework practices.

These records should be introduced not later than the second day of the first group sessions, that is the second day of employment. Before they are distributed there should be a review of the casework method as outlined in the précis on social casework. The trainees thus have first in mind that the bones and sinews of this method consist of gathering and recording factual information and observations; of assessing these facts and observations by means of criteria or generalizations concerning society's rules and human behaviour; of arriving at a tentative conclusion or partial understanding of what the problem is and how able the client seems at this point to overcome it; of planning, most often after consultation with the supervisor and always with the participation of the client, the way in which the agency can help to restore this client to a way of life which is normal for him. This discussion should touch upon the skills of relationship and the meaning of relationship; the actual learning of this all-important aspect of the casework process is deferred until later.

Because of this preliminary discussion of casework method but also because all trainees are frankly curious to know what "sort of people" the clients are, it is almost a necessity to satisfy their curiosity at once. The records are selected for their aptness for this first examination. Each trainee has a record in front of him and after discussion of the confidential nature of all case records but before they are opened, the appearance and detail of the cover are commented upon. The cover shows signs of having been well used; it has a name tab; it may have filing hieroglyphics scribbled on the outside. These are explained, and later each trainee will make his pencilled note on the cover and on the charge-out slip, watch the stenographer put the records away in their proper order and next day, when they will be used again, will watch how the stenographer uses the brought-forward system. In other words, one of the first lessons in casework is on filing; the professional principle of orderliness is being taught.

The first part of the record to be examined is the face sheet. Its purpose is reviewed and the term "identifying information" learned. The significance of this information to the social worker is then demonstrated as each trainee reads aloud what is recorded on the face sheet in front of him. The teacher picks up the significant matters; what is the make-up of this family, are there a mother and father and are there children, grandparents? How old are they? Where do they live? What is the father's occupation? What is their religion? From each of these questions and others the trainee begins to learn that the social worker works with the family as a whole and that the face sheet can give him his first picture of its total make-up. The "normality" of this family is reviewed and significant items, such as wide discrepancies in age, marital status, foreign names and so on, raise questions if not "red flags" of danger about possible conflicts and problems stemming from these. The social worker, the trainee learns, begins at once to search for possible causes of difficulty. The trainee will be alerted to see if, in the record when he reads it, these danger signals are real or false.

This exercise has involved all the trainees and satified some of their curiosity. The next day in that period, they will be left alone for half an hour to read the total record. Before they do, the teacher will define the technical terms used, describe the separate parts of the record, and show the group how to read it. He will talk about recording, its purpose, form and terminology. The group will be warned not to expect literary merit in the narrative sections; recording employs chiefly the speaking vocabulary. The teacher will give the group an outline from which to make notes on what they read. From these notes each will be asked to summarize the make-up of the family, the "story" of their problem, the social worker's assessment of the problem and of the client's abilities, the plan of service or treatment, the result of that treatment. (A few of the brighter members of the group will use the record's closing summary as their notes and thereby get full marks for saving time.) This is the way, it will be pointed out, the social worker prepares for supervision when he is on the job.

Three periods can be devoted to the exercise, though these same cases will be used frequently in other sessions to illustrate legal and administrative procedures. Then the discussion, using the précis on casework as a springboard, can resume, moving in each period into further application of the principles through case analysis. This analysis is done best when several of the case records are mimeographed and distributed to the group. Because such records may be taken outside the office identities are disguised in all respects.

The indispensable manuals in which policies and procedures are recorded are of general use to the teacher. If manuals do not exist, the administrator must make good this omission, and in this effort the agency teacher can help. When existing manuals are so detailed that they bewilder rather than elucidate, then the teacher may have to put them into teachable form himself. Perish the thought that they should be taught page by complicated page! An index is indispensable to the proper teaching use of these manuals. Answering questions relating to policies found in the study of cases gives the group a chance to learn how to find their way around in the policy manual. To take a section of the law under study and find in the policy manual how it is carried out in practice further reveals where to look for these operative directions. To follow the cross-references from one manual to another rounds out the exercise. These are frankly "drills," and they go on all the time. "Here is a new policy we have not seen before. Let's find it." Everything stops until this is done. The physical activity involved in reaching for and searching through the pages of the copy each has before him is a refreshing change. These drills inculcate a desire, as well as show the way, to learn as much as possible independently.

The proper use of the forms no agency is completely without can best be taught by filling them out as a group exercise, each trainee having the same form. Data can be supplied by the cases discussed in the casework sessions or the teacher can become the client interjecting extraneous as well as relevant data to help the group focus on the latter and deal with the former with firm courtesy. Such a session resembles a socio-drama and is good fun. All the forms used by the agency cannot be handled this way, but all should be examined, held in hand and their purposes explained. The idea can well be inculcated that, far from being nuisances, forms facilitate the social worker's task, giving him more time to devote to interviewing his clients and thinking through their problems. Forms may also be legal instruments, and their purpose is therefore to be respected and not despised by the social worker.

Assignment of certain passages in the one or two professional texts[1] to be read during one of the periods or at home needs to have some preparation. The books have first to be chosen for their appropriateness, and then the teacher must refresh his memory of what they contain to decide what purpose they will serve, and the conclusions which will reinforce what he learns about the agency's work. Both purpose and conclusions relate to the focus of one or more sequences of study. The group is prepared for the exercise by a discussion of the question: "Can you learn by reading?" Those who say they can, share their methods with those who do not possess good reading habits. A quick poll of the whole group may be inserted here on the question of what their reading includes. The answers will give further clues to evaluating the potential learning abilities of each trainee. The assignment when it comes consists of reading a prescribed passage, noting its central point, the authorities quoted or cited by the author to support the point, the way in which the thought is developed and illustrated. The group is asked to consider the thought and to test its validity or wisdom so that they can say that it is or is not an idea they can now accept. The teacher leaves the group and, at the end of the half-hour of silent reading, note-taking and perhaps some discussion among themselves, returns to hear and talk about the results. A variation on this method may be later introduced by having each trainee write a brief précis of a longer passage read at home. An estimate of reading ability and of the help one or two may need in developing this ability is thereby possible.

Writing letters, memoranda, telegrams and other communications can be a helpful exercise. After discussing some of the correspondence found in the records studied and after a lesson on the techniques in-

[1]The two studied in the Social Welfare Branch's Training period are: *Common Human Needs* by Charlotte Towle, National Association of Social Workers, New York, 1952; *Interviewing: Its Principles and Methods* by Annette Garrett, Family Service Association of America, New York, 1942.

volved, the group may be left to compose a letter to another agency or to a client, and an inter-office memorandum. These will then be read aloud and criticized by the group as well as by the teacher. This group criticism, and few escape it, helps everyone to learn to take it, and to realize it is a part of the learning process.

Films are both diversional and instructive. The teachers should have previewed all those selected for screening and thus be able to direct the group's attention to the purpose of the film and to the points, both obvious and hidden, it makes. After each film is shown, the group should discuss what they have seen. It is well to tell them beforehand that this will be done. The films should, quite naturally, focus upon or blend into the work of the agency.

Observational visits to other agencies also need to be prepared for and discussed after the event. A word to the group about good manners and good public relations will not be amiss, for it may not be apparent to them that agencies receiving these groups go to much trouble to prepare for them. The questions the trip will answer are reviewed beforehand and these will be asked during the tour, the teacher moving in to do so when the group does not. In the discussion following the visit, which will take place in the group's usual setting, the teacher calls for comments and further questions in order to relate what has been seen and heard to the work of this agency, to the total community and to the profession.

These many devices provide variation in plenty to relieve restlessness. They have proven their value in inducing maximum learning, moreover, for aural, visual, verbal, and manual faculties are all employed. Those reviewed above are best suited to group sessions, and some of them can be employed by the supervisor in planning staff meetings.

### ADMINISTRATIVE PREPARATIONS

Everything the agency teacher does, as well as everything he says, will be noted by the trainees. It behooves the teacher then to so move and execute the plan of training that the effects and wisdom of cultivating good administrative habits are clearly seen. Discussions will be planned on the subject of administration—of the agency, the office, the case-load, the social worker's thoughts and actions—but they will be the more effective if the group or the individual trainee feels the effects in the orderliness of the training plan itself.

This order shows up best in the planned sequences of study, that is, in their focus and progression, but the smaller wheels also ensure progression. These include: the care of the materials and the room; filing the papers which constitute a large part of the teaching material; stacking reference books such as manuals, bound volumes of statutes, reports and the like as these accumulate on the table in front of each trainee; rewinding films and returning them to their owners; filling in the out-cards in each library book used; emptying ash trays during the day. These are habits of tidiness that can be learned—and tidiness is first cousin to order.

Having materials ready in sufficient quantity when they are needed is a small wheel but an important one. The secretary to the Training Division will take pride in setting up, typing, mimeographing and bringing forward, at the appointed time, the agency's teaching material and in having a supply on hand of all the forms, cards, graphs and so on, which are used in teaching. Library books needed are summoned back if they are on loan. Films are ordered well in advance from lending libraries if the agency library does not possess all those needed.

When observation visits to other agencies are planned, these appointments are made weeks before. The first time a visit is arranged, it is well for the agency teacher to write to or call upon the agency director concerned to explain the purpose of the visit and to give this official some idea of the in-service training plan itself. Some mutual good usually comes out of these visits and therefore the agencies concerned will make an effort to plan the event to the best advantage. A letter of thanks to the agency directors after the visit is just good manners, and the group can, if there is time, draft this as an exercise in writing letters and a "lesson" in public relations.

The readiness of the teacher for the task is an obvious requirement. The question of his scholarship has not arisen before. From his basic training for the profession, achieved in a school of social work, this person should have used every experience to add to his knowledge and to deepen his understanding of the field of social work practice his agency represents. He has assessed his experience, knows what he knows and is beginning moreover to understand it. He will have taken time to attend academic courses, but selected for their value to his work and to his understanding of the problems his agency treats. He has brought the elements of administration into planning his own development and growth. His knowledge has been put to effective use.

In conclusion, it must be said that the agency teacher's preparation goes on all the time. He is alert to all that is happening about him. He knows the agency inside out and the people who staff it and what they are like. He knows the community the agency serves and the people in it who serve it well in respect of its social and cultural growth. He knows his country, its history, its problems and its blessings. He is aware of what is happening in other nations of the world in the cause of human well-being. He has the social worker's "fair, large and liberal" philosophy that reason can prevail over might and good over evil. He reads as much outside as inside the literature of social work. In preparing for his responsible job as an agency teacher he increases his own stature as a social worker and as a person. His knowledge and his attitudes "rub off" on those who will one day be social workers of whom the agency and the teacher can be proud.

# V. The Extent of the Teaching

THE IN-SERVICE TRAINING PLAN evolved by the Social Welfare Branch is an extension and refinement of earlier forms of training. This earlier training, rather simpler in design, served the agency well enough when the bulk of the staff was university trained, but as the supply of professionally prepared social workers grew less, the administration concluded that the standards of service this staff had achieved were in danger of falling off badly. Hence it decided to give more time to the training of people on the job and, within that time, to make the training as comprehensive as possible.

This plan should be regarded as suggestive only. Each agency, and each agency teacher, will have to prepare teaching material which will suit the structure, function and established practices of that agency. The more complicated the structure, the more extensive the functions and the more professionally derived an agency's practices are, the broader must be the base of this teaching material. The Social Welfare Branch has a fairly complicated structure and, since it gives a generalized casework service, its functions and practices are both extensive and professionally derived. At the same time the teacher has the problem of limiting and condensing the subject-matter to proportions which fit the time allowed for training.

In the ensuing pages, the plan of training is first presented as a whole and significant aspects of this whole are examined. Each major part is then discussed for the purpose of illustrating the effects of the methods used. Appendix I contains detailed teaching notes with comments on the teacher's objectives, the focus of the study and the methods used. The subject-matter, in addition to laws, policies and cases, will be found in Appendixes II-V, some parts of which are repeated in the text to illustrate methods of using this material. These précis are, in essence, "little texts" compiled from the literature or specially prepared as definitions of agency practices which the trainee will use—augmented by other prescribed reading—until he is ready to launch himself into the deeper waters of learning at a school of social work.

## THE PLAN AS A WHOLE

The in-service training plan of the Social Welfare Branch consists of three parts, or three time intervals. The six-month period allowed by the administration for this training is divided as follows:

*Part I*

Four weeks, beginning the day employment commences, are spent in learning about the work by talking about it in group sessions in a central location within the agency. (By asking the staff to declare their intention to leave the agency at least two, and better, three months in advance, the Personnel Office is enabled to arrange in advance that a sufficient number of people to form a group will start on the same day. Some overlapping of tenure can often be provided for. Five in a group is a minimum, twelve a maximum to obtain the best results from the methods used.)

*Part II*

Four months are spent in learning the work by doing it, the group dispersed in the natural settings of the agency's operative offices, which are decentralized.

*Part III*

Four weeks are spent in consolidating, amplifying and deepening the learning that has taken place by further talk in the same group in the initial setting.

An evaluation of each trainee's progress is made at the conclusion of each of these parts, in which he participates fully. Lack of progress in any one part may mean that the trainee leaves the agency.

The most significant point to be made is that each part of this total plan grows out of the last and none is isolated from another. The "content" is the same throughout, the variation being in the teaching methods employed in each part and in the differences which are inevitable, and not undesirable, when a number of people are involved in the teaching.

The Training Supervisor (whom it is simpler now to call the "agency teacher") is responsible for the teaching in group sessions. It has been found wholly desirable and, though fatiguing, worth the effort, for this agency teacher to do all the teaching in the first part of the plan. The greatest integration of all the material which has to be taught can be achieved in this way. In fact, it is this immediate integration and application of what is taught to agency practice which mark in-service training as different from training obtained in a school of social work. The agency embarks on such a training plan in order to get its work done as expeditiously and thoroughly as is humanly possible. Also, if only one teacher does this early teaching, it establishes in the minds of these potential social workers that social work knowledge, method and skill are indivisible and that practice is the application of basic knowledge, method and skill to situations which are never twice the same.

Some of this heavy load can be lifted from the teacher's shoulders if he is given an assistant. The assistant can be present as part of the group and can be assigned some of the technical teaching of mechanical operations. This is not to imply that the dross of the teaching content is left to the "servant." It merely means that the exercises and drills which form part of the method of teaching involve a conditioning of reflex responses while the engaging of minds in thought and reasoning requires a continuing relationship with the mind which prompts that thought and adjudicates upon the reasoning. This suggests that the presence of the assistant as part of the group imposes certain disciplines on him at the same time that it calls for the teacher's wise use of his knowledge and talent, for example, reinforcing points being made by the apt use of his experience. When he is not called upon to help in this orientation period, he has plenty to occupy his time in the larger programme of staff development otherwise held in abeyance during the in-service training period.

If an assistant is not available, these technical sessions can be assigned to the technical people the agency employs to manage and refine its procedures. The statistician or research director can teach the group how to compile monthly statistics; the office consultant or chief clerk can teach filing and mechanical aspects involved in file handling. The teacher will have to be present, no doubt, to make sure that this teaching is not esoteric; the trainees are not being taught to be statisticians or researchers. He can also help these technicians to prepare their lessons, which will take not longer than two periods, and help devise simple drills to make the lessons come to life, using live statistics and handling actual files.

Although the trainees will come into contact with these technical teachers and will meet other agency personnel when passing down the hallways, or when visiting other agencies, the agency teacher is, of course, their focal point in this important period. It is a heavy responsibility but one which is lightened by the stimulation provided by the relationships which develop. They are of a kind however which lead to an easy transfer to other teachers when the group disperses.

In Part II of the training period the supervisor in the operative office becomes the trainee's teacher. This, for the supervisor, means one trainee or at the most two at a time. The method of teaching is tutorial and not constant: that is, not all day every day, but rather on a scheduled basis. Other social workers, at different stages of development, some having a professional education and some not, claim the supervisor's time and attention. The trainee will not be able to reach his supervisor every time he needs to know what to do and thus he learns to use alternative sources to obtain information. Sometimes, in moments of stress, these may be other social workers in the office; sometimes, on mechanical matters, he may call upon the clerical staff, but most often it is to the written manuals of policy and procedures he turns for guidance. Part of the tutoring he receives, when he does have sessions with his supervisor, is in ways of increasing independently his knowledge of the facts of the agency's operation. It becomes, therefore, doubly important that these manuals be clearly written, well indexed and well illustrated.

Assigning the trainee a case-load in this second part of his agency training is not only a necessity, but provides a frame or focus for the teaching the supervisor does in this practice period. In one sense, this case-load is a teacher. It imposes immediately the discipline of the limitations of the agency's services and the limits of the service it is possible for one social worker to give. It exerts controls upon the trainee to which he is highly responsive, sometimes to the extent of being frustrated by this curbing of his crusading spirit. The case-load is a sober teacher whose name is reality.

There are other intangible teachers in this office setting. The tone or atmosphere of the office has its certain influence, the total staff creating this atmosphere in making the clients' needs the whole object of their thought and activity. The orderliness of the office activity is another influence, as are the inevitable pressures which arise when emergencies make special claims on everyone's time and feelings. The community which the office serves is a teacher in that it often places restraints on the conduct of the agency's work and on the conduct of the workers.

This indirect teaching is absorbed almost unconsciously. The absorption is the more complete because the trainee feels that he belongs to this agency, that it is "his" place in the world. He will want to talk about all these things and, if he cannot do so immediately because his supervisor and he must address their conscious minds to the matters which concern his clients, he will have opportunity to talk about them when he returns with the group for Part III of the training plan.

Since the literature of social work is another teacher, it has been found wise and productive to have the trainees undertake a written project during this practice period. This project is based on prescribed reading concerning parts of the agency's work and its purpose is threefold. First, it is an exercise in reading which reveals to the trainee that the literature can teach if it is read for the purpose of precise learning. Second, it provides a deeper understanding of the one segment of the work on which he elects to read and write. Third, what he produces will be used as subject-matter, that is, form some of the teaching content, in the third and final part of the training plan. This project also impresses upon the trainee the fact that he is still learning (it could be forgotten in his immersion in the work itself) and that the agency insists that he learn how to utilize all the media it provides to ensure his development. When he talks about his reading, moreover, as he will surely do, he sets the more experienced social workers around him a good example; reading habits too often deteriorate rather badly as time and fatigue take their toll on energies.

In Part III of the training plan the trainee is taught by a number of people. Those who occupy administrative, consultative and specialist positions within the agency are drawn upon, not at random, but in a way that ensures a logical progression in this total review of the agency. Their skills in teaching will vary, but this is of minor significance. The group itself can be depended upon to extract from each of these teachers the facts and the viewpoint they wish to have amplified and confirmed. The agency teacher, or his assistant, is always present during these sessions. The part they play is that of effecting a continuity and integration: what has gone before is related to what is being said and to what is to come. Other teachers drawn upon in this period are the people whom the group may meet in other agencies or who may come from the other agencies to meet the trainees. The group has its questions prepared in advance of these meetings and the agency teacher is present to ensure that the information given focuses upon the purposes of this session.

The educational values implicit in all these learning experiences, and the effects of the varying but ordered methods of teaching employed, can be summed up as achieving, for the majority of those trained in this way and to this extent, quite phenomenal results. This method of teaching with its definite beginning and ending has further value. Although learning never ends, in this six months the ways of learning have been established, especially how to extract from every kind of experience the new, or confirmed, or developing consciousness of growth towards understanding. Part of that understanding is the trainee's awareness that he does not know enough to help his clients adequately. He will come to anticipate eagerly the longer period of time the agency will give him in two years in which he can devote all his energies to the thrilling task of study.

PART I: ORIENTATION PERIOD

The general plan of this period is as follows, each member of the group receiving a copy of this outline on the first morning.

GOVERNMENT OF THE PROVINCE OF BRITISH COLUMBIA
DEPARTMENT OF HEALTH AND WELFARE
SOCIAL WELFARE BRANCH

OUTLINE OF PART I: ORIENTATION PERIOD
IN-SERVICE TRAINING PLAN

*Monday to Friday—First Week*

| | |
|---|---|
| Sequence A. 8:30–10:00 A.M. | Definition and derivation of "social problems" |
| Sequence B. 10:15–12:00 | The philosophy, purpose and organization of social welfare and social security programmes in Canada |
| Sequence C-1. 1:30–3:00 P.M. | A study of "normal" behaviour |
| Sequence D-1. 3:15–4:45 | Social casework: An introduction, and case studies |

*Monday to Friday—Second Week*

| | |
|---|---|
| Sequence E-1. 8:30–10:00 A.M. | Study of the social legislation administered by the Social Welfare Branch (public assistance categories) |
| Sequence F-1. 10:15–12:00 | Policies and procedures observed in the administration of legislation |
| Sequence C-2. 1:30–3:00 P.M. | A study of the normal development of character and personality |
| Sequence D-2. 3:15–4:45 | The techniques of casework commonly applied in relation to the administration of legislation; case studies |

*Monday to Friday—Third Week*

| | |
|---|---|
| Sequence E-2. 8:30–10:00 A.M. | Study of social legislation (child welfare categories) including policies and procedures |
| Sequence F-2. 10:15–12:00 | Structure of the Social Welfare Branch; statistics; office management |
| Sequence C-3. 1:30–3:00 P.M. | Deviations from the normal; resources for treatment |
| Sequence D-3. 3:15–4:45 | Casework: techniques and skills in interviewing, recording |

Evaluation interviews will be conducted during this week.

*Monday to Friday—Fourth Week*

| | |
|---|---|
| Sequence G. 8:30–10:00 A.M. | Provincial and local resources utilized by provincial social workers. Local government and voluntary agencies |
| Sequence F-3. 10:15–12:00 | Administrative communications, evaluation and conclusion |
| Sequence C-4. 1:30–3:00 P.M. | The literature of social work; assignment of essay subjects |
| Sequence H. 3:15–4:45 | What happens next? |

The teacher discusses the above outline with the group to bring out the significance of each item. One of the relatively minor, but none the less important objectives of this orientation period, is to make sure that correct agency nomenclature is mastered. Therefore, even the title of the agency in the top margin has significance. There is nothing more conducive to poor inter-agency and internal agency relationships than to use wrong titles and nothing more embarrassing than to be corrected in their wrong use. On the other hand, one feels "in" when these are mastered. It takes only a minute and every trainee will be called for making a mistake at least once and sometimes the teacher will be too. When they leave for Part II of the training, they can speak the language of the agency.

The divisions of time have been called "sequences" to keep the idea of progression, or moving forward, in the minds of both the teacher and the group. One of the hazards the teacher is always conscious of is that of rushing ahead beyond his pupils' grasp, forgetting that they are totally uninitiated. The most rudimentary terms have to be explained when they are first used; concepts which are second nature to the teacher must be discussed first from an elementary basis. As meanings become clear, they can then be deepened through conscious observation of them in practice.

The time-schedule divides the working day into four periods of one and one-half hours, the study sequences continuing for a week in a horizontal line through those hours. The sequences have a vertical relationship as well, which will be illustrated, and, even more obviously to the teacher, an interlocking relationship that produces not a chain but a fabric. In this the outline may be misleading here and there. "Interviewing and recording" are shown, for example, as occupying a set time in the third week, but this does not mean that they are not discussed until the third week. Every time a case record is studied, the recording itself is studied and records are selected which will teach, among other things, various kinds of recording. Each time a recorded interview is read, the teacher calls upon the group to reconstruct it to determine what the social worker said to evoke the responses recorded, but particularly to estimate the quality of the relationship the social worker had with this client. When the time comes to look at interviewing and recording and nothing else, these case studies offer the examples the group can use to bring this study to life.

The hour and a half interval has been found neither too short nor too long for covering a sizable amount of the subject-matter and for maintaining a high threshold of assimilation and attention. The morning and afternoon breaks for refreshment are welcome punctuation points in the subject and in the day. Physical fatigue does have to be reckoned with for if work is being done, which means if thinking is being done, energies are being expended. Fifteen minutes is scant enough time in which to be refreshed and to freshen the air in a room which is probably filled with cigarette smoke. A quick walk outdoors, even in inclement weather, is advocated. A coffee shop could be the destination. The fifteen-minute limit should be enforced at least "threshold to threshold"—coffee shop to office—as the unionists put it. It is the employer's time which is being used and time on the job is a factor in management's budget. Enforcement of the rules not only teaches trainees to obey orders but also cultivates good working habits.

The lunch hour is the employees' own time and in it they can do what they please. The room used in the group sessions is their "home" and should be the place in which they may have some privacy. The hour and a half allowed for lunch is a bit longer than the agency normally allows. It permits a leisurely foregathering and gives the group a chance to talk of things which may, or may not, pertain to their studies. The teacher can suggest things they can do as they munch sandwiches or lounge. The morning paper, a popular magazine, a report, in which there are items bearing upon social work can be left in the room with the comment that they would bear reading. The teacher can return a little early and take part in some of the "natter" and, if wise, take a little time out of the scheduled hour for discussion of what has been read. The moral to adorn the tale told in the casual reading the group does is that the social worker draws his knowledge from all conceivable sources and current opinion, current events, reveal to him where people stand in relation to the social well-being of the community, the nation or the world.

Further examination of the sequences will reveal that the subjects to be studied have been placed in the day in order of their interest value. The mornings are devoted to teaching factual matter on the assumption that the brain is readier to assimilate and retain such matter after a good night's sleep. Even so, the teacher may have to inject a certain liveliness into these sessions. When early morning dragging of intellectual feet is found to be chronic with some, this is to be added to the list of observations the teacher builds up on each trainee (not necessarily a written list) to be discussed with him in the evaluation session. If it is very pronounced, it may have to be dealt with sooner in a private talk as the teacher gets tired too and tiredness can lead to irritation. If more than one person is involved, a fifteen-minute lecture on the "Mental Health of the Social Worker" may have some effect. Usually nothing needs to be done except perhaps a little gentle teasing now and then.

Afternoon sequences are on subjects which invariably claim close attention and hold interest. Nothing in the world is more interesting to talk about than people's behaviour, unless it is to talk about oneself. For a future social worker this talk is neither gossip nor self-indulgence, but an objective and sympathetic analysis of behaviour which society at large, as it is now, deems desirable and acceptable. It is the society of which this budding social worker is a part. He will "try on" some of these ideas and find himself deviating from the standard set before him. He will conclude that the normal human being, by this standard, is a pretty dull fellow and that society is the better when it is not mediocre. He will, nevertheless, have ideas about the component parts of the average person's life and of the effect caused by a breakdown in any one part. He will not be dealing with pathological behaviour except to obtain definitions of some of the terms used to denote forms of grossly abnormal conduct. In fact, he will be told that treatment of pathological behaviour is not within the competence of the social worker employed in the agency serving the community any more than is the diagnosis of its symptoms. Therefore, he should not become immersed in introspective thoughts and muddled feelings about his own emotional maturation. Should this happen in spite of all precautions to prevent it, it must be dealt with individually and privately, and it may lead to that individual's withdrawal. The skill in teaching this aspect of behaviour in this setting is that of presenting it objectively, or academically.

The sequence on casework is admittedly the most difficult to make comprehensive enough and, conversely, limit and condense in the time. Yet a synthesis of this subject with all other sequences is possible and, certainly, the broad principles held by the social worker can be introduced. For example, the first time a case record is examined, besides a lesson on filing, the principle of confidentiality is pointedly taught. This record has not been disguised or edited for teaching purposes. The people appearing in the record are real people, they live at that address, they had these problems. The regard for the confidential nature of this information is implanted at once; the respect for the dignity and worth of these people is revealed in the tone of voice and in the words used in speaking of the problems and of the people concerned which are quickly imitated. The need for confidentiality will arise again and again: in the study of legislation, of local government and of inter-professional relationships. It will show up as methods of recording are studied and again in relation to clerical procedures. Similarly, other basic principles are introduced both directly in the casework sequence and in conjunction with other subjects. In the months and years which follow, these principles will be learned, that is, will become part of the trainee's self, through putting them to the test in practice.

The elements of casework which understandably must remain a mystery in this orientation period are those which pertain to the nature of the relationship between caseworker and client. This relationship can be talked about in such a way, however, as to create a special sensitivity to its discovery in practice. It does not hurt if part of this sensitivity is diffidence, as that quality is far better than over-assurance. This relationship is the heart of the casework process. On it depends whether or not the *social* worker has the ability to inspire confidence and transmit the elements of his character which have a healing effect. The trainees will eagerly await opportunities to see if they have such talent.

Some flexibility in the time-schedule can be allowed. Some sequences will be interrupted by the necessity of arranging visits to other agencies at times convenient to those agencies. This disruption can be kept to a minimum, however, when the appointment is made far enough in advance. Other sessions may be interrupted purposely to permit a distinguished visitor to talk with the group, or to inject something humorous as a diversion from too intense absorption. The weekly schedule cannot always be adhered to strictly. For example, the consideration of the nature of social problems, which takes place the first week in the first period, starts on the second day, the first being given over to introductory matters. This subject may not last even four days. It may, if the group is comprised of well-informed people, take only two periods to note the areas of living in which people can become dislocated. The next week's first sequence can then profitably begin earlier. Then, the Social Welfare Branch has been experimenting with having the orientation period last only three weeks, largely because of the trainee's growing impatience, beginning in that third week, to meet his first clients. These matters show up in practice and ensure that planning and execution of planning is never static or stereotyped.

The evaluation interviews announced in the outline will not take place until the teacher has reviewed with the whole group all the implications for him of the process. They will have heard first about evaluations when they were applying for a job. When the outline is distributed there is further reference to it and, before the interviews begin, there is a full review of their purposes and their methods. At the appropriate time, copies of the evaluation outline used by the supervisors in preparing their written confidential statements are distributed to the group and read together, for they need to know of what this measuring rod consists, and any questions about it are then answered frankly and directly. A period of time is set for the interviews and each member of the group is asked to think through the effect of what has happened to him to date and, when he meets the teacher, to talk about it frankly. The evaluation interview in this orientation period lasts not longer than fifteen minutes unless there is reason to question that any trainee should remain on the job.

Much of what is said here about the outline is said to the group when it is distributed on the first day. That first day is of considerable importance and the highlights of it are now reviewed.

### The First Day

The teacher's objective for this first day, an auspicious one for each member of the group, is to create a pleasureable anticipation of what is to come. Specific goals are outlined in the teaching notes found in Appendix I. One of them, which is not easy to define, is to make it possible for the individual members of the group to begin to think, feel and act like a group. The way in which this is achieved is interwoven with the discussion which takes place that first day.

Introductions are important. The teacher is there to welcome each trainee as he arrives and to introduce him to the others. Pleasant small talk will help to reduce any strains there may be and a gracious manner will set the tone of that day and those that follow. The manners of each trainee will be noted and, if necessary, at a later point a place will be made to discuss the importance of social graces in the deportment of professional people. By the time the first session is to begin, and it should begin promptly, the names of all are known and there is a feeling abroad of pleasure and expectancy. (Late comers should be noted and excuses received by the teacher and the group; if unpunctuality persists, it will need to be dealt with forthrightly, though in private.)

A brief ceremony to open proceedings is helpful in creating additional feelings of being welcome. This will be carried out by the administrator or his delegate. It can consist merely of an introduction to each of the group followed by a brief speech of welcome. In this the administrator conveys that the agency expects much of them and that they, in turn, can derive much satisfaction in the work of the agency which is that of helping people to be self-directing and happy members of society. The teacher may have to suggest beforehand that this be all the administrator say at this time. It should take just a few minutes.

Alone with the group, the teacher may carry this theme on briefly, but it is wise to involve the group as soon as possible in discussion. It can be done by framing a proposition and asking a question such as: "It is my contention that no one ever decides suddenly that he wants to be a social worker. There is always a gradual shaping of this desire, perhaps from a starting point which is vivid, until it gets to the point in time, like this one, where you start to do something about it. Has this been your experience?" There may be a short silence, which can be broken by the teacher, who selects someone by name and says: "How has it been for you, Mr. A?" Mr. A. will describe how he decided to enter social work; Miss B. will volunteer to recount her experience. Most of the others will follow, leaving one or two to be asked directly to speak. All should say something and, however halting or brief, what they say should be commented upon with obvious respect by the teacher.

Several things are happening. First, ideas are being shared about the meaning of social work as each member of the group at present conceives it; this has significance for the teacher, and he should remember what they say. Second, invariably a commonly held viewpoint is revealed which at once establishes similarities of motive and conviction among the members of the group. Third, the teacher can study each individual's facility in speaking, his self-consciousness in expressing his ideas, and therefore the probable place he will hold in this group—a leader or a follower. There is, fourth, an exercise in thinking: thought has been addressed to a proposition and then put into words. Finally a principal law of learning is being observed: each individual learns from the basis of his own past experience—as the group listens to the thoughts of its members on the same proposition, a consensus emerges which can be accepted as valid by each.

This first experience in group thinking and speaking on this first morning is in the realm of idealism, which, at this time, has a strong appeal. The discussion could go on endlessly, and it is wise to inject a note of realism without too much delay. A question about the attitudes and opinions of the trainees' families and friends toward social work will provoke a lively discussion. Someone will probably mention the well-known caricature of the "do-gooder." Someone else will report that a friend of his objected to social work because it was "such depressing" work. The teacher, if members of the group do not, can at once provide answers to these objections. Thus, some of the misconceptions about social work are examined, and ways of properly interpreting the profession's place in society are rehearsed. From the diversity of ideas expressed the group has arrived at a unanimity of thought.

The outline can then be distributed, permitting a welcome pause as positions are shifted and some murmuring takes place. After each trainee has scanned the page silently, the teacher claims attention, directs it to the words in the top margin, and introduces the rule, mentioned earlier, that all mistakes made in improperly naming titles of people, agencies or programmes will be corrected on the spot. Some may not know the full title of the agency in which they are now working. They will probably not know that they themselves have a title which they place after their signatures when writing letters and which they can use when speaking of their work. They are called "Provincial Social Workers." They will be warned that people in the community and many of their clients will probably refer to them as the "Welfare lady" or the "Welfare man," or as merely "the Welfare." An amusing anecdote might be used here to show that these terms are not to be wholly despised—they are "of the people" and naturalness is always to be respected. Among themselves, however, and always officially, precision in nomenclature is a requirement.

The immediate response may be this question: "Can we presume to call ourselves social workers if we do not have a degree in social work?" The reply must be forthright. First, it is the agency which decrees that its staff shall be called social workers. Second, it is the in-service trained person who, more than anyone else, knows that he is at a disadvantage in not having professional qualifications. Until he can get them, this person is earning the right to call himself a social worker. "You may, and should, explain to everyone who asks that you are in training for this work. You can say, without embarrassment, when you don't know what to say or do about matters your clients bring to you: 'I need a little time to think about this and to talk it over with my supervisor.' You can frankly say, 'I don't know but I will find out and let you know.' So far as your professionally trained colleagues are concerned, the ethics of the profession demand that they share their knowledge in order to advance the objectives of the profession. You will find no snobbery among those you will be working with. Nor must you be inversely snobbish by failing to realize how little you know. Social work itself makes all its practitioners humble. Your humility is vital rather than abject, for you will find, if you are like those who have gone before you, that obtaining professional qualifications will become increasingly compelling."

The sequences of study and the time-schedule to be followed come up next for examination. The purpose of studying these subjects, the inter-relatedness of each separate sequence is explained carefully. The scope of the first sequence—nature and derivation of social problems—seems limitless. To be sure, many of the trainees will have studied in this field at university, and they will want and should have an opportunity to talk about what they know. The teacher however brings this discussion to focus upon the problems this agency is set up to serve, suggesting that all the other problems enumerated are matters on which education for social work provide understanding. The introductory nature of their present examination of these subjects is designed to quicken their appreciation of the gaps in their education and to give them a guide as to future studies ahead of them. All the other sequences of study are introduced in this same way, with their inter-relatedness carefully stressed. (A careful study of the teaching notes in Appendix I will further elucidate these points.)

Any questions which are asked should be answered directly and simply by the teacher addressing the whole group rather than merely the questioner. The questions are cut off sharply at ten o'clock and the group leaves to spend a little time together in a relaxed way. The teacher is wise not to go with them.

When they return, usually a few moments are spent settling down in which the teacher can make a few quiet observations. There will be a decided lessening of strain but still rather polite interchanges between the members of the group. Any further questions might be answered at this time so that minds will be cleared of any personal queries and ready to launch into the business of the day.

Then the précis on the purpose, philosophy and organization of the agency is distributed (see Appendix II). The ensuing discussion should ensure that on the first day these people obtain an appreciative feeling for, as well as facts about, the agency, and learn words to use in discussing their new work. As they talk about it, and they are encouraged to do so that evening, their own convictions will become firmer and they will also begin to see that when the purpose of the agency is interpreted to their families and friends, approval of its value is a likely

THE EXTENT OF THE TEACHING 91

result. This appreciation will help to strengthen the trainee's own sense of worth and determination to give his best to the task of learning.

The first words of the précis are read aloud by the teacher, the trainees reading silently from the paper in front of them. (They should have pencils in their hands in case they need them.) Here are the first words:

"Provincial public welfare services are organized for the purpose of administering a Province's social legislation. That legislation may be regarded as an expression of the citizens' concern for those persons who suffer from social disabilities which not only affect them adversely but which, unless treated, could have equally detrimental effects upon their families and ultimately the community."

It is not enough just to say: "Can you agree?" Each of the thoughts expressed must be talked over, that is, thought about. A quick review of the meaning of the term "public welfare" is followed by a call for someone to define "administration" and "social legislation." The teacher can move the replies about to obtain a final definition of administration to be "the means to an end" and emphasize that the end is to bring the benefits of legislation to the people who need them. Defining the term "social legislation" gives an opportunity briefly to review the processes of democratic government. Two further points may be made. One is that, as this agency is a public welfare agency, its social workers are working for the people, at their behest. The term "public servant" is seen in a new favourable light (for, like the social worker, the civil servant has also been subject to ridicule). The second point is that in coupling "administration" with "social legislation" the two are seen as inseparable. "Social legislation is only as good as the way in which it is administered."

Moving on into the next sentence, the phrase "an expression of the citizens' concern" is considered next. "Is this thought too sanguine altogether?" Here the inspiration behind all good works may be reviewed in an historical way, better if illustrated from local examples. "In British Columbia, child welfare legislation was prompted in 1901 by a small group of citizens, who in turn were prompted by one or two of their number, who had observed and pitied the plight of one twelve-year-old child whose parents were, in their terms, 'drunken and dissolute.' Thanks to their active efforts, the Infants Act was passed that same year. When, in 1943, a new Act was passed, more appropriately called the 'Protection of Children Act,' it was drafted by social workers who had, in using the old Act, found certain gaps in it. Their experience in working with children who needed the protection of the state, and new evolving knowledge about meeting the needs and protecting the rights of children, had revealed more clearly what form the state's protection should take. Onto the original Act, the best parts of which were retained, 'expert' thought was grafted. Was the origin of this legislation an expression of citizen concern?"

The ensuing discussion may devolve into an argument on whether law makers are "politicians" with an eye to catching votes. (Such cynicism can be noted, as it may arise again at a place where it could be more significant than this.) Whereupon the question may arise: "Does it matter so long as the desired results are achieved?" Some will say that even for that much-maligned figure, the politician, our concept of justice requires that the accused be deemed innocent until proved otherwise. There need be no conclusion, merely the comment that if democratic processes are respected by electors and elected alike, the statement as it stands can be accepted. The thought could be left that actions to express good-will toward men leave behind them a feeling of right-doing which adds to the stature of a citizenry and brings closer a realization of precepts of behaviour taught over the centuries by all religions.

"Persons who suffer from social disabilities which affect them adversely" is discussed next. "Suffer" is defined as being in a state of pain or sickness which temporarily or permanently causes one to be dependent on others or to become ineffectual in action, or to have acute discomfort which may have an affect upon temper and temperament and, if prolonged, upon personality and character. "Social disabilities" are situations which arise to cause suffering. These will be looked at more exhaustively later, so the term is left without definition although several synonyms are offered—"social distress," "social dislocation," "social problems." That all people at some time suffer some distress or dislocation can be agreed upon by the group. One or two examples will be forthcoming from them: a tragedy such as a fire; the sudden death of the father of a family; loss of a job—a few will suffice. "The adverse effects" are seen then as common enough but why some are able to overcome them, while others are not, is left for future study. Those who are rendered helpless by these problems, it will be said, may need outside help at the time and be quickly restored to their normal patterns. What about people who have never been well "located" in life, whose "abilities" are such that they find it difficult to meet the pressures of living? Here the group will grow thoughtful. One member may say that this, too, is where social work can help. Another will say, "Yes, but how?" The answer must again be deferred. This question can only be answered by training and experience. Part of the answer will come before the end of four weeks; more by the end of six months; still more when education proceeds in a school of social work. Toward the end of a career, the practitioner may have the full answer.

The concluding thoughts in the paragraph being read need as thorough discussion. That adverse effects upon the individual will affect those about him introduces the significance of relationships among humankind. Adverse effects spread in ever widening circles, as indeed do good effects. Why bother about correcting adversity or promoting good? The next paragraph in the précis on the philosophy and functions of the agency will give some clues and these can be related to professional philosophy and functions as follows:

The social worker is employed in social agencies which are created by communities for humanitarian purposes. Essentially, these purposes are to relieve suffering. Social work, in turn, can extend a community's concept of humanitarianism. It can reveal that relief of suffering is not enough. By further effort, people may be restored to independent states of being in which they obtain satisfactions, render their duties as citizens and realize their own destinies. Still further effort may prevent problems and in this a total community is involved.

By the end of this period, the group will have lost much of their initial restraint. They have been talking about things which are, to them, fairly obvious but in a way which focuses upon their new work. They have caught glimpses of things about their work they did not know. They have been absorbed in the subject because they have both heard and read words which have deeper than obvious meaning and they have, themselves, thought and talked about these meanings. They have heard others express their thoughts and ideas. At this point the group has become, intellectually at least, a dynamic entity with a positive direction. In not denying the difficulties which lie ahead for them, they have begun to see the power for good their efforts can eventually have. The noon-hour break is needed as a relaxation from the fatiguing pitch of interest they have achieved.

The next period begins on a different footing. In assembling, there has been more ice-breaking conversation; some have gone to lunch together. There will be pleasantry and some laughter. Their interest in each other will be as great as or greater than their interest in the teacher. By the end of the first day, the teacher should be able to say: "They are now a group, or so near to being one, I need not worry that it will not happen."

Upon these diverse people soon becoming a "group" depends much of the success of this form of adult teaching. Though diverse in background, age, education, work experience, appearance and manner, these people have a common and compelling interest in the subjects to which they are addressing their minds. They have common aspirations to do well in this vocation. They are all at the same stage in their development. They find in all this both inspiration and protection. They will get inspiration as much from themselves (from the reactions of the total group to what is taught) as from the teacher. They will grow apprehensive later when the protection of the group is to be withdrawn. The teacher has to be aware of all these feelings. He is quite correct in calling the sum of these feelings "the spirit" of the group. Its quality will inspire him, but he must guard against an over-identification with it and permit emancipation to take place when the time comes. Meanwhile, he watches for the emerging of group spirit in these early days, which is best detected after short absences from the group.

Before the précis on "normal behaviour" is distributed, the teacher talks about this subject in this way: "It would be an affront to education for social work if we thought that we could, in the time we have ahead of us, teach you all you eventually must know about human conduct or behaviour. Even when you have obtained a formal education, it is doubtful that you will feel you know enough. More than that, the knowledge that now exists in transmittable form is imperfect. Study of behaviour is far from finished and among those who have, and are, engaged in this research, there is often disagreement. One precept, however, can be established from that inconclusive viewpoint: every human being is different, not only in respect of his endowment and his nurture, but also in the way he or she reacts to situations which confront him. Such reactions can seldom be accurately predicted. Is this a concept you can be in agreement with? It is one of the basic 'ways of thinking' of the social worker." Discussion will ensue, and should, on the ease with which people are typed and on the way such typing affects the development of prejudice, punitive attitudes and so on. Some will draw upon courses they have had in psychology to illustrate their ideas. This should be asked for if it is not forthcoming voluntarily. All that anyone ever learned is useful in social work. Old wives' tales, the comments which begin, "they say," platitudes and pontifications are, however, exposed for what they are.

The teacher resumes:

All we can do to teach you what theories of human behaviour are known and applicable to social work practice is to lead you up to doors and perhaps give you some keys to open them. The pathways you will see ahead of you disappear into the horizon, but the exertion of exploring them will be health-giving and captivating at the same time. More precisely, what we will do in this hour each day is to try to get a clear view of what "normal" behaviour consists of and how it develops. We will probably conclude that "normal behaviour" is a myth, but if we try to capture the "normal" or "a norm" of conduct, in an orderly framework, it will help you to determine in what segments of life a particular client of yours is so lacking that he is far from even a relative "normal." From a standard definition of normality you will be able, tentatively but appropriately, to see not only the inner and outer deficiencies which cause his problem, but also his inner and outer strengths. The inferences and conclusions you draw from these findings will help you decide how you and the agency can make up the deficiencies, and use the strengths the client has to help him help himself. You may often, in the first year you are practising, have to conclude that you do not know enough to be of help.

The discussion that will ensue in this hour follows the pattern revealed in the review of the first session, and the précis on which it is based is found in Appendix IV. The objectives, timing and methods of presentation are in Appendix I. These and the matter itself are only suggestive but are offered as a point of departure from which other agencies could build their own definitions of behaviour which form the diagnostic criteria used in casework. The great service Dr. LeRoy M. A. Maeder rendered social workers, in preparing the paper on which the bulk of this material is based, deserves every agency teacher's grateful acknowledgment.

The final hour of the day begins after another break for refreshment. The mood of the group by this time is one of eagerness bordering upon excitement. There is virtue in deliberately delaying the introduction of the next sequence of study for a few minutes, perhaps by bringing out a paper punch, stapler and fasteners, and having some one in the group who knows show the others how to use them. There can be pleasant chatter while this filing is going on and, when it is finished, the teacher can comment on the fact that tidiness is a utility as well as a virtue. One of the papers fastened to the file-back in the manilla folder provided them is the précis on social casework (see Appendix V).

These principles will be discussed in the same painstaking way. The material contains terms which are a part of the terminology of social work, and need definition as they appear. It may be well to pause here to discuss the "jargon" of social work with the group. "Every calling, vocation, profession, craft, or trade has a vocabulary which instantly communicates what the speaker has in mind. Sometimes they overlap. One writer points out, for instance, that a "joint" means a piece of pipe to a plumber, a part of a bone to a physician and, perhaps, a "low dive" to a social worker. Social work indeed has borrowed many of its terms from other professions. "Client" is taken from law, "diagnosis" from medicine. The obligation we have is to use these terms precisely and accurately; the objective is that these terms will have definite meaning and come to mean the same thing to all social workers. "The right use of words is as much a matter of obligation as any activity whatever," is an admonition from the writings of the learned philosopher, Bishop Butler, we would all as social workers do better if we heeded. One final word: the right time and place to use the words of social work is when with other social workers. In all other places, the simplicity of the words we use will reveal us to be "of the people" and therefore worthy to serve them.

The précis on social casework is not recondite, but it does require close attention. The initial part on the concepts, functions, methods and philosophy of the profession of social work is read in order to extract from it the deepest meaning that can be apprehended at this time. Before the end of the four weeks of training, some of the passages in this précis will be read again, and will reveal a deeper meaning. They will be read and discussed again during the four months' practice period and again when the trainees return to the group. At that time, in essays and from the consultants who will teach them, further basic principles will be added to give breadth as well as depth to their comprehension of these underlying truths.

This first statement as it is read on this first day repeats much of what was said when the purposes, philosophy and organization of the agency was discussed that morning. The teacher refers back to the earlier discussion, explaining the inter-relatedness not only of these sequences of study but also of the basic concepts on which agency and profession are alike founded. This will be done as often as may be necessary in the next four weeks, but in time the trainees will themselves be able to see and refer to the "wholeness" of their study. Moreover, their memory will be the more reliable because they will be remembering their own responses to the ideas; they will recall the responses of the others in the group; and they will have participated with the group in reaching an agreement.

A close study of the teaching notes found in Appendix I will augment the foregoing comments on the methods employed in the orientation period, and their results. This method of group teaching and learning in which all that is heard and much of what is read are discussed under the leadership of one teacher is an educational process uniquely suited to adult education. The teacher recognizes and utilizes the degree of maturity each member of the group possesses, and in sharing the thought, reasoning and feelings aroused by the subjects presented, each achieves knowledge and is stimulated to grow towards a greater maturity. Further study and experimentation is needed in the methodology of education for social work. Meanwhile, this method is commended as having proven value in in-service training.

# VI. Learning by Doing

ONE OF THE CHIEF ADVANTAGES of the orientation period is that the important second stage of "learning by doing" can commence on the day the trainee reaches the office in which he will do this learning. Without such an introduction, each supervisor would have to spend precious time in teaching the trainee the most elementary things, and in organizing these things for teaching. Unless they had some help with this, each supervisor would do it differently, probably inadvertently under-doing some parts and over-doing others. When the trainee is already familiar with the work the agency does, then the supervisor is free to carry out his part of the whole plan with relative ease. There is also no danger that the trainee will feel frustrated by being given desultory "busy work" or plunging into his duties blindly to make mistakes which would be harmful to the client, the agency and himself.

In this chapter, the methods the supervisor employs in teaching are examined in some detail. This examination may, for many readers, seem to labour the obvious, but it is often the obvious that escapes notice in this kind of teaching. The supervision of the trainee demands full thought and planning. While all of the usual skills are employed by the supervisor, many of them have to be sharpened to a finer point and all have to be applied, at first anyway, in slow motion. He must make haste slowly and spend much time with the new person in the first few weeks even when pressures are mounting because work is undone. The first days are the time when good habits will be started and the positive attitude of the trainee to supervision and to the supervisor will be formed.

Another important matter examined here is the effect of supervision upon the trainee. The nature of the efforts he makes to grasp the implications of his work are either discussed directly or strongly implied. His development proceeds from "where he is" in that development when he arrives in the office to begin his learning by doing. He has graduated from the first to the second primary grade.

### WHERE THE TRAINEE IS NOW

When the trainee leaves the group, the teacher, and the place in which the group has had its being, he is aware that he is respected for what he is and for the value he will eventually be to the agency.

But, above all else, he knows how little he knows. Rather than being overly anxious, he is reasonably comfortable about that because he realizes that the agency also knows it. Moreover, he and the agency together are pledged to do something about it. Coupled with these feelings of comfortable apprehensions there is, on the day he leaves, a keen anticipation for all that is now to unfold.

He has already heard about the office in which he will work and about the community of which it is a part. At many points along the way, he has talked about and heard about supervision and what it means in casework practice, agency administration and teaching and learning. Not only has the trainee thought and talked about the agency's clients, but he has also visualized them realistically from the case records and the agency teacher's illustrative stories. He has attempted to find the cause of their problems and to assess their strengths and weaknesses, that is, their maturity. He has found his judgment changing as he has read further into each record. He has used these cases to discover how to help them, using the legislation he has studied and the casework method he has talked about and read about. He has done no interviewing himself, but he has learned something about the techniques. The nature of the casework relationship is something he wants to experience. Since he has an appreciation of the dignity and worth of people, he is willing to accord them his respect. He knows that there are some kinds of problems which he is, as yet, inadequately prepared to comprehend, let alone treat. With all this in his mind, he quite literally cannot wait to meet his first client.

Besides his growing understanding of the direct work he will do with his clients individually, he has been helped to think through the volume of the work for which he will be responsible. Since in some agencies the size of the average case-load might worry the trainee somewhat as he thinks of what is to come, the problems have been discussed. The trainee has heard that careful management of his time, and organization of his work, will be among the first things he will learn in the office to which he goes. He has been led to see that the social assessment he and his supervisor will make on each case will determine priorities of need for his service. He has thought about time as an indispensable element in the healing of society's wounds, and as an enemy which no one ever completely defeats, but which responds to a firm controlling hand. He has seen, in his drills and exercises on statistics, how much work other social workers, better prepared than he, can accomplish in a day and in a month. He has weighed in his mind and accepted the grave responsibility that rests on his shoulders to give a service to those who seek the agency's help.

The trainee's supervisor has prepared for his coming. The administration organizes training groups for the purpose of filling vacancies as they occur. A beginning staff member is seldom called upon to move into a position which is totally new and unformed. The social worker whom he will replace has worked with the supervisor to arrange the transfer of the case-load when the trainee arrives, and has also prepared as many of his clients as possible for the change. However, these clients may not, in fact, be among those the trainee will have in his case-load, since the arrival of a new staff member sometimes provides a good opportunity to shift geographic boundaries that have grown unwieldy. However, although all the clients may not be told who their new social worker will be, they can be told of the dislocation in services which a change of staff always brings about and that the supervisor will make sure there will be a minimum of interruption in the services that are being given. Those clients who would not be seriously affected by the knowledge that the next social worker will be in a learning position may be told of the shortage of professionally trained social workers and of this agency's way of trying to maintain its services in spite of this shortage. The clients can be assured that the greatest care is exercised in selecting people for the work and that the agency itself goes to much trouble to give them some preparation. Many clients may not ask the questions which will prompt such an explanation by the previous social worker. The trainee himself will then be the one to make his learning position clear as this becomes necessary.

The social worker who is leaving will have much work to do in readying his records for transfer. Summaries will facilitate the trainee's work, especially if the record is a long one and the case at that time requires priority attention. It will further the trainee's grasp of the nature of the services he will continue to give and of the casework method if the transferring summary can state the social diagnosis or social assessment, outline the plan of treatment being followed, estimate the progress or movement of the plan, and intimate the goal the agency considers it should reach before terminating the service. The previous social worker, with the help of the stenographer, makes sure that the face sheet, work-box cards and other administrative records are up-to-date. Added point is given to these operations when it is known that the trainee has been instructed in the proper use of these mechanical instruments of casework. The trainee's advent, in short, can mean a general effort to put the house he will enter in order.

This review of the case-load the trainee will carry involves the supervisor heavily. The social worker who is leaving brings to the supervisor all those cases in which complication or change or progress in the client's situation or attitudes, or no change or progress, is obvious. After study of them, the supervisor will decide what is to be done. Some cases may be transferred to more experienced, more adequately trained staff members, provided adjustments can be made in their case-loads to enable them to give the time and thought these more complicated cases require. Some may be selected as being at a place where transfer to the trainee will not cause the client difficulty. Others may be held in the open files with the definite understanding that they will remain quiescent, but will be studied by the trainee. Others may be closed.

If none of these things can be done with any of these more difficult cases, the supervisor prepares himself to take over responsibility, the trainee to devote extra time to their study and to work with him in carrying out the needed service. The supervisor does not "carry the case" in the sense that he does the interviewing and establishes a casework relationship with the client. Often the administration has to take a firm stand on whether the supervisor should or should not "keep his hand in" himself by giving casework service to one or two clients. In controlled settings, such as hospitals or clinics, this may be wise and possible, but in the majority of public welfare offices, the supervisor's administrative and teaching duties are usually too heavy to permit it. The supervisor may have to interview clients some of the time, for example, when intake schedules are disrupted by the absence of a social worker. Whenever he intrudes in the work of his staff, the client must be told that what is said will be communicated to his own caseworker. Dual relationship, when one of them carries superior agency authority, can confuse the client and defeat the efforts being made.

The supervisor is concerned about the size of the case-load to be assumed by the trainee. He may be able to change boundaries to trim the numbers, but this means loading other staff people with the excess. Whether he can make changes or not, he looks critically at the case-load as a whole. Using work-box cards which provide the same identifying data as the face sheet in the record, he notes the movement of these cases, the time they were last active, or worked upon, and when the next activity is planned. If the agency employs a system of bringing foward its records through a filing system, he may have those which are to be worked on the week the trainee arrives, drawn from the filing cabinet for his own review. He will have them put back again, however, if time permits, so that they will be brought to the trainee in the accustomed way on the day he arrives. He knows the trainee is by now familiar with the filing system the agency employs. These preparations will take time and the supervisor is a busy person, but their value will be apparent.

## THE TRAINEE ARRIVES

The supervisor has kept the first half-hour of the arrival day free to devote to the trainee and has planned the first supervisory conference for a precise time, say eleven o'clock. The first half-hour is most informal. There is a relaxed chat, about living accommodation or other personal matters the trainee wishes to discuss. This is the beginning of a relationship between this new worker and his supervisor and first impressions on both sides are important. Though he is relaxed and the talk is informal, the trainee should, nevertheless, get an impression of the dignity of the supervisor's position in the agency. Manner, speech, posture, assurance, interest in the trainee indicate what enjoyment and profit are to come from this relationship. The supervisor who has been a good caseworker will have no difficulty in creating a feeling of confidence in his office and in himself.

The trainee at the same time is making his impression on the supervisor. He may be a little self-conscious for he knows that the agency teacher has sent the supervisor a written evaluation of his progress during the first part of the training plan. The supervisor is wise to ask him about his feelings about the training plan as a whole and to tell him that his experience in the next four months will prove his conviction about and his aptitude for the work.

After having been introduced to the rest of the staff, the trainee is shown to his desk and left by himself until the time for his first working conference with his supervisor. He needs an hour or two for the work he will do and to gather composure. He knows how to use this time because this was talked about before he left the group. First, he will check his desk for the equipment he knows he will need: policy, office, accounting and legislative manuals; writing tools, forms, calendar pad, telephone book, brief case and other such indispensable items. He then turns to the real work of the morning, a study of the work-box or card index which reveals the size and make-up of the case-load for which he will be responsible.

First, he checks the size of the case-load by counting the cards unless the previous worker has left a copy of last month's statistical report, in the desk which will give him this count at a glance. The cards may be arranged geographically if the office is a rural one, which will reveal the extent of the district he will cover. There may be a map under the blotter to study. The categories into which the cases fall, if this be a multi-service agency, will claim his attention. He may already have formed some opinion as to the parts of the work he thinks he will do best and these cards will, perhaps, be closely examined. Those cards which have "signals" on them he will study more carefully.

In this solitary exercise the trainee is beginning to feel the weight of responsibility any case-load exerts on any social worker. His eagerness to get on with the job will sustain that weight, even add to his determination to do a consistent job in all parts of the work ahead of him. He knows, as the group talked of this, that the administration expects even standards of work and that agency standards are judged on total coverage rather than on isolated spectacular successes. By eleven o'clock he is ready to go, work-box or card index in his hand, for his conference with his supervisor.

General information comes first. The supervisor tells the trainee something of the history of this office and of what it has grown to mean to the community. He reviews quickly the total case-load of the office, the kinds of problems which predominate and mentions the load of work carried by the other social workers. This leads directly into a definite presentation, preferably prepared also in writing or in graph form to be taken back to the trainee's desk, of the time-schedule he will observe in the course of any week. He will have the use of one of the agency's cars on, say, Tuesdays, Wednesday mornings and Fridays. His interviews in the homes of his clients must, therefore, be arranged for those days. On Mondays and Thursdays, he will have a two-hour period for dictation. The dictaphone is used by informal arrangement among the staff. He will not be given intake duty for a month or two, but he will make appointments for office interviews in the time he is in the office, but not in dictation hours unless it is unavoidable. A portion of his time each week will be spent in case study and case planning alone and with the supervisor.

Here begins the first experience in the organization of time. Soon enough the trainee will find that some disruption is inevitable. Emergencies will arise among his cases, or another social worker's, to make a shifting of scheduled activity essential. The give and take is generous, but the supervisor must be kept informed of any changes which are made. The supervisor, the trainee learns, has among his many functions the co-ordination of activity to ensure that the work gets done.

The next matter to be discussed in the conference is the area the trainee will cover in his work away from the office. This is introduced by a description of the total area the office covers and its general and particular characteristics: its population, industry, communications, its educational, cultural and recreational facilities, its government, its unique problems such as slum areas, juvenile gangs, seasonal unemployment and the like. The chief causes of the social problems the clients bring to the agency are mentioned in general terms. Then the particular area to be covered by the trainee is described. Its boundaries and chief roads can be shown on a map and the problems of travel in various seasons of the year mentioned. The other professional services provided in the district may also be reviewed and a tentative time set for the trainee to be introduced to the people in charge of these. The help forthcoming from the community itself, as well as its sensitive spots where the social worker must be unusually tactful, will be discussed. Employers, business firms, churches, service clubs, women's organizations, leading citizens and others may be mentioned in this review. The trainee will have many questions to ask; the answers to some will be deferred until they are encountered in practice. He will not remember all the details he is told, but he will find them out soon enough as his work proceeds.

The logical next step is to review the case-load. The supervisor and the trainee together sift through the work-box or card index and the supervisor describes again what is meant by "total coverage." The supervisor tells the trainee:

One of your principal objectives in this four months is to analyse this case-load and in this I will help you. There are, of course, too many cases to make it possible for you to devote an equal amount of time and effort to each; you will probably not meet all the people involved in the next four months. We will decide which of these many cases need most attention and which are at a stage where we know that all we can do is be here when we're needed. We will decide how best to B. F. (bring forward) all these cases so that they are spaced over a period of not more than a year to permit you, and the client too, to know when to do the things that both of you have agreed need to be done. Some cases you may see once a week, others once or twice a month, others at intervals of several months. Most of this organization has been done for you by the previous social worker and by me. There are ten cases which are at a place where a lot of time and thought is needed. The cards for these are flagged for us. You and I will carry these cases together. As far as I can foresee what may arise, I will help you to get ready for these interviews. When you have had them, we will talk about them in detail. They have all been B. F.'d for next month and you will have time to study the records with me. One or two may require attention before that. We may both have to do a little overtime work to get ready for them. These cases will, at that, not take all your time; the others must be served too. By the time you return for the last part of the training, you will, yourself, have planned for your absence for a month. When you get back, you will find you can move right into high gear and move forward with greater ease on this case-load you know so well.

The conference adjourns for lunch, to be resumed next morning when the office opens for business.

Back at his desk, the trainee finds five to ten case records which have been brought to him by the filing clerk or by his stenographer. These are the records which normally would have turned up in the B.F. system for the social worker who covers this district. One or two of them may be there because of in-coming mail. These case records represent the afternoon's work; in them are the clients the trainee is so eager to meet. He studies them, pencil and notebook ready as he has learned to do in the group sessions. At the appointed hour next morning he is ready to discuss them with his supervisor.

## Second and Third Supervisory Conference

The second conference proceeds immediately to an analysis of the cases needing attention. The trainee has already been taught how to present the facts of the case. Although the supervisor may know these cases well, he lets the trainee tell him what they are all about, except for a little coaching as it is needed. This exercise can be abbreviated as time goes on, for the trainee learns in time to select the cases and the facts about them on which he needs help from his supervisor.

The trainee has made his notes against this general outline: the names and make-up of the family with special reference to any marked deviations from the average or normal family make-up; the source of referral of the case; the problem as the client has stated it; the data required to satisfy the eligibility requirements (which should be the same as the data every social worker gathers in any agency setting) which have been checked against the policy manual to see if they are or are not complete; the previous worker's assessment of the problem (if it is recorded, this is simple; if not, the trainee will speculate upon what the previous social worker's understanding seemed to be); the trainee's assessment of the areas of "normality" or strength possessed by the client and of the areas of deviation or weakness; the plan of the services or treatment the previous worker had worked out and followed, with the client's co-operation or lack of it; and, finally, questions about the purpose of the next interview, where it will take place and when.

Each of the five or more cases will be reviewed in this way. On each the trainee will have questions to ask as he goes along and, if he does not, the supervisor must ask them for him. Confusion is bound to arise on points of procedure: "How do I go about getting these glasses for this client?" The supervisor will explain the process involved and cite the section of the manual in which the instruction can be found if the trainee forgets, as he will. The answers to all questions on procedure should be in that manual; knowing how to find them is a skill to be learned.

If this review has been done well, the supervisor should say so, though economically. Social workers need commendation occasionally and the trainee may especially need it in the early days. Moving from the known into the unknown, the supervisor now asks: "Have you thought about how you will introduce yourself when you go to the homes of these clients?" There has been some rehearsal of this in the group sessions but not much, on the premise that it is best for the trainee to do it in the way which is most natural to him; anything "stagey" is anathema to casework. The supervisor wants to know what feelings the trainee has about doing it for the first time. From his knowledge of the cases the supervisor can say that this client will probably be glad to see the trainee; this one may be a little hostile at first; this one will make excuses for not seeing him now, and so on. The problem of being at ease and at the same time business-like may be discussed for a few minutes. This is not a "visit" but an interview. It has a purpose of which the social worker and the client are not in doubt. The trainee may say he fears he will forget what is said to him in the interview. Sharpening his faculties and giving his whole attention to the client, he can be assured, will result in his remembering more than what was said. He will have impressions and observations to add to the total memory he will have of these interviews. Part of that memory should be of himself, what he said, and how, during that visit.

When this case-conference ends, the time is set for the next one, marked on the supervisor's calendar pad and entered on the trainee's. Between now and then, the trainee will interview all or some of the five or ten clients he has been discussing and, besides, will have studied the records B.F.'d daily in the next few days. Before he leaves the supervisor, he will get a quick briefing on the procedures involved in using the agency's car; how and where it is garaged; what to do if repairs are needed; what statistics on mileage have to be kept and how this is done; the necessity of obeying all traffic laws for the sake of his own safety and the agency's place in the community. When all these many things are absorbed, the trainee can literally feel himself growing. The supervisor must watch that this growth is not too fast in the first few weeks. Emotional and physical fatigue could cause this young plant to languish.

One of the things that helps to level off and keep steady his rate of growth is the rest of the staff in the office. By the second day, the trainee has begun to feel at home among them; if he is the sort of person people like (and he will both unconsciously and consciously try to be), the others will soon make a niche for him. His contacts with them, at lunch time and in other free parts of the day, will contribute to a feeling that this place is "just like home."

From this human base, the trainee begins to find the qualities he has in common with them. He patterns his manner and his speech after theirs. A feeling of identification with them develops easily and the more intimate identification he had during the first weeks with the group and the agency teacher soon slips away. He finds these new associations more agreeable because they make real and not vicarious impressions as they did in the group sessions. He belongs here as of right, the right of his evaluation and of his wages. The result is not a straining to prove himself but rather an attempt to be like those around him and to reach for the knowledge and assurance they possess which he does not. Sensing his desire to emulate them, the rest of the staff will respond, as it is flattering to be accorded virtue.

This teaching is of a subtle sort and when the administration can do so, placement of the trainee in an office which is known to have the felicitous attributes mentioned above is consciously made. The administration has, indeed, a duty to make conditions such that all its offices have these attributes. When a supervisor fails to help the staff member who cannot accept the shortcomings of others, particularly when his air of superiority affects the relationships he has with his clients and with others he works with in the community, then the administration must be drawn in to deal with the problem. If the offender is a professionally trained social worker, the conclusion must be drawn that his education has failed to take. There are few such people who cannot be helped to see the folly of their manner when they are faced with the results of it, but these few can have a disproportionately disruptive effect upon the atmosphere of an office. The in-service trainee may not be the whole object of his scorn. Whether so or not, it is a state of affairs which must be corrected, if not by the supervisor, then by the administration.

The trainee's duties on the second day will consist of interviewing his clients. Among other things, he may have to confirm previously made appointments by telephone and here is the first test he gives himself of the naturalness of his manner of speaking; telephones can often give rise to affectation. He may have to write a letter to make an appointment for next week. He will struggle to frame his words simply and directly, yet with some warmth. Finally, he will leave the office, with the policy manual and the forms he may require in his brief case, to take his first step into the unpredictable and uncertain. He gives himself a head-start in gaining self-assurance by making sure he knows, before he leaves, what roads and streets to travel to get to his destination. At the end of two days of interviewing, both in the clients' homes and in the office, he is more than ready to have his third conference with his supervisor.

This interval of two days between the second and third conference has given the trainee time to do the hard work that interviewing is and to do it as if it were his kind of work and no one else's. That is, he has been allowed time in which to feel a sense of possessiveness: these are "my" clients; "I am responsible for helping them; they will look to "me" for that help". This is a necessary beginning in cultivating his devotion to people. Hitherto the "people" was an abstract idea which, though he was devoted to it, had neither urgency nor complete reality. Now, in these two days, the idea has become real and has taken a definite shape. There is a conscious reaction to this and a little time is needed to have this reaction settle down and become familiar before attempts are made to analyse his responses. The possessiveness will disappear when he is helped by his supervisor to analyse what he has done as an agency worker.

The supervisor does this quickly when the third conference begins. There are a few comments to allow general reactions to be expressed: "I feel very much at home; everyone in the office is friendly and helpful; I seem to have been around here for months." Then, a discussion follows of the interviewing he has done, the people he has met.

"What sort of reception did you have from Mrs. A?, welcoming, co-operative, anxious, indifferent, hostile? Why was this do you suppose? Did you meet Mr. A or any of the A children? What was their response to you?" Here some fundamental comments are made to reduce the trainee's anxiety about his own failure or to reduce his over-estimation of his apparent success. For example:

You, as a new worker, provided this client with a new ear into which to pour her troubles. Does this slow up or hasten her insight into what is wrong? Can we expect any change in the situation until she is ready to see her own complicity in creating it? You were made welcome but was it a helpful interview? Probably not altogether. This was inevitable, no doubt, and we shall have to mark time until your relationship is established firmly enough to help her to take some definite step to correct what she thinks is now wrong. The action of taking such a step—for instance, this idea you have of helping Bobby get a paper route—may, in itself, begin to change her feelings towards and about Bobby. The environmental work you will do in this case is the only way we in this agency can help. If you get nowhere in six months, let us face the fact that it is beyond our resources to be of any help at all. Meanwhile, think through ways in which you can help her to take even a small step to make a change. Write these ideas down: better, put them in the record. Be encouraging in what you observe to be her capabilities. Let her feel that you think she has some value and some good points. This is psychological support. Watch for opportunities and seize them when they come to introduce positive suggestions. Timing of these things is probably intuitive, although your direction of the interview may create the moments you are looking for. What was the result of this interview? What is to happen next? When did you arrange to see her again, and why? Record this briefly for your own guidance.

The supervisor is teaching directly. He is putting this case in the frame of the agency's functions. He is discussing overt behaviour rather than probing psychological depths. He is dealing with some essentials of interviewing skill. He is revealing the agency's insistence that all interviews have a purpose and a reason. Much of what the supervisor says will fairly clearly repeat what the trainee heard in the group sessions. What was said there, the trainee discovers, is a part of the reality of his work here.

One of the interviews, perhaps one or two of them for contrast's sake, should then be totally recalled by the trainee at the supervisor's request. (At this point the supervisor may further the integration between Part I and Part II of the training plan by drawing from his desk the précis on social casework which the trainee has studied in group sessions and turn to the pages devoted to interviewing skills and techniques.) The emphasis in this total recall will be on what the trainee said, the words he used, the expression he gave to his words, the feelings he had in respect of asking definite questions, steering the discussion, replying to questions asked of him, responding to feelings the client revealed, and so on. Whether the story is told with restraint or off-handedly, the supervisor is measuring the trainee's apparent ease in dealing with his feelings about himself. If there is heightened anxiety in recalling all this, the story is not pursued but a note is made, probably by both supervisor and trainee, that discomfort exists and is to be watched for in its effect upon the client and in its obstruction to the trainee's growth.

The notes made by the trainee for his recording are next reviewed. It is sometimes well to have the first interviews recorded in longhand for the supervisor to go over before or during this interview, though economy in the use of time demands that this practice be abandoned before it becomes a comfortable habit. It will help the trainee if his first recording is fairly detailed and it will further help him if the supervisor blocks out general headings under which he may organize his data for dictation. The policy manual should, if it is well illustrated, outline such headings as well as the general form of the record. Imitation of preceding parts of the record may or may not be wise, depending upon the quality of the recording that has been done.

Throughout this conference the supervisor makes use of any question, response or reply, from the trainee to extract the appropriate principle any of these points of discussion may suggest. "Here we are operating on the principle of weighing the outer pressures on this woman against her inner capacities as we have so far determined them to be." "Here the principle of self-determination is at war with its effects upon others in the family." "Here we are exercising the authority of the legislation; the legislation is 'for the public good,' it is not your own authority you are exercising but the community's." "Here is an example of physical abnormality which is seriously affecting behaviour." The précis on normality and maturity can be brought out for reference.

Further questions on procedure will be answered with dispatch. There will then be a quick review of the additional cases to be worked on within the next few days. Relationships outside the agency will have to be dealt with if any of these new cases involve community resources. This conference is the one in which the trainee gathers confidence in his supervisor and in the agency, and confidence in himself. It is the most important of his whole future career. When he leaves it, he is ready to move forward with greater confidence because all that was said was related to his learning to date and to his immediate experience. He will not have another two-hour conference with his supervisor for a week, although he will see him for quick directions no doubt.

To recapitulate the timing and purposes of these conferences, they are:

(1) A brief half-hour at the beginning of the first day in which the necessary courtesies are extended to the trainee to make him feel wanted and at home.

(2) A full hour, or hour and a half, on the first morning to review "totals"—total community, total agency, total case-load.

(3) A full two hours on the morning of the second day to review the results of self-study of five or six records on which cases the trainee will give his first services.

(4) A full two hours on the morning of the fourth day to review all that the trainee did, said, observed and put in motion.

## SUPERVISION CONTINUES

In the first week the supervisor has given the trainee six hours of his time. In the second week he can reduce this to four. Depending upon the rate of progress, and it may fluctuate, he will probably budget the same four hours for the third, fourth and fifth weeks. After that, the trainee should be given the same amount of time the rest of the staff are allowed in any week for supervision. There will, of course, be visits to the supervisor's office throughout these first weeks for quick help in respect to procedure. If frustration or serious confusion arises, talk after-hours may be necessary, or time made available to help relieve mounting anxieties or deal with crises.

The scheduled conferences in the weeks that follow, although all will follow the same general pattern of analysis of cases and of the work to be done on them, will ensure that new duties are carefully taught. For example, the first time an outside agency, doctor, public health nurse, teacher, clergyman, community organization, is approached for assistance, the supervisor will teach the trainee how the social worker does this. He learns that it is never done without the client's knowledge if not his consent; he finds it requires self-imposed disciplines in order not to betray the confidential information the agency has about this client; he discovers that it is not enough to suggest a service be given but that appointments should be made and some assurance obtained that the service requested will be carried out; he discovers that the results of the service will have to be ascertained from the agency giving it and from the client; he is aware that good agency relationships are sustained by the manner in which a service is requested. These matters have been discussed in the group sessions of Part I, but the supervisor repeats them when they are first implemented.

Similarly, the techniques of intake, case-conferences, psychiatric consultation, court procedures, case summaries and the like are taught as they occur in these four months. Very literally, this trainee is learning by doing, but he is also being taught directly how to do what he does and helped to reason through why he is doing it. He is thereby performing as he learns. He is filling the vacancy the agency had with a growing competence. His diligence never falters even though occasionally his footsteps may.

The agency teacher does not intrude anywhere in this teaching except that the materials he prepared for use in Part I, the various précis or "little texts," are used by the supervisor in deepening the trainee's consciousness of what he is doing. The trainee and his teacher are in the same agency. The supervisor is also an agency teacher and such contacts as are necessary to mark progress or lack of it will be between these two teachers. Channels should exist to make this communication possible, and will exist if the training division is placed close to the agency's general administration.

The chief connection between the agency teacher and the supervisor is the evaluation the latter prepares at the end of the third month of this practice period. Its details are reviewed in a later chapter. The timing of its preparation is of considerable importance to the agency teacher. By the end of that third month he is preparing for the trainee's return for the last part of his training. He has a course of study on which to schedule the sequences for discussion, to be sure, but knowledge of the points of confusion, of the areas of the work which present special difficulty, of the lack of conviction in regard to employing basic principles, of problems in retention and reasoning, all help the agency teacher to plan the detail of the second group discussion in order to try to overcome these deficiencies. It may not always be possible to do so by design, but with the supervisor's findings in mind, the teacher can, at appropriate times, lead the discussion to these points. It will not be done with direct reference to any one trainee. What his colleagues, and the consultant who will be present, have to say about this point will make an impression upon the halting member, perhaps a more effective one than admonishment from the teacher or supervisor.

The trainee, too, has been getting ready for his return to the group. He has had the interview with his supervisor for the express purpose of being evaluated. He has participated fully in it by first getting ready for it and second, because he is ready, by expressing what he thinks has been his own progress in understanding and performance. He has readied his case-load for his absence, making sure that agency commitments will be carried out without fail; telling some of the clients he is working with most actively that he will be away; signalling certain records to remain inactive until he returns; covering eventualities by knowing who will take on emergencies as they arise.

Before he does any of these things, however, he has been working on the assignment he was given before he left the group. The agency teacher waits six or seven weeks before sending him the outline of the essay he will write and the literature he will read in preparing to write it. When it goes to him, the supervisor receives a copy of the covering letter and of the outline and list of reading. In the covering letter, the dead-line the essay must meet is firmly given. The suggestion is also made that the supervisor give his work constructive criticism, help to find or select case examples to illustrate the points made and give the trainee an opportunity, at a staff meeting, to practise presenting this kind of material. The whole office will know he is writing an essay and the criticism of his labour by this staff group, all more advanced than he, and their sympathies will be eagerly sought. The chances are that his colleagues will also do the reading he has done; his supervisor will have to. The trainee, himself, will seldom fail to say that the effort he put into it was worthwhile.

In these ways the trainee is made aware that there is some educational form and order to this six-month period of training. The form, although not the order, will stay with him when the six months is over. As he goes about his work, as he learns from supervision, as he learns independently, as he participates in staff meetings and other means the agency uses for staff development, he will rejoice in the increase in his own stature. The work itself will have its effect upon his spirits. Frequently, as his sensibilities increase, he will know that he could have done better if he had known more. He will develop an impelling desire to take time in which to do nothing but learn.

Meanwhile he has learned these things in the four months:

(1) He has grasped the meaning of his responsibilities to his clients and to the agency. He has, perhaps, experienced the satisfaction of seeing some good results from the work he has done.

(2) He has analysed his case-load through keeping abreast of current work and through study of quiescent records on which he plans the work that he will do, and when.

(3) He has learned by practice how to analyse existing records succinctly and inclusively and how to set up a record so that it is succinct and inclusive.

(4) He has learned the feeling as well as the purpose of interviewing, and made a beginning in learning how to use the casework relationship constructively.

(5) He has searched for causes of the problems his clients present; he has observed the feelings the problems created and has had his curiosity stimulated to know the causes and the effects of these feelings with greater accuracy.

(6) He has learned to organize his activities within agency schedules, in relation to time, priority of need, geography and travel.

(7) He has learned to use references such as agency manuals of many kinds in order to get things done. He has learned to use many, although probably not all, the resources available for specific services the agency itself does not give, and to realize the position of the social worker in initiating and synthesizing their use.

(8) He has had the stimulating experience of being evaluated by his supervisor; he is proud of his progress; he has a humility about all that he still needs to learn.

(9) He is a totally different person to the one who left the safety of the group four months before.

# VII. Consolidation

FROM THE MOMENT the trainees begin to arrive, the agency teacher marks the change which has taken place in them. They belong; and they are glad to be back. Probably one of them will say: "This comes at exactly the right time. Another week and I would have collapsed from the pace of what has been happening to me." This kind of learning, which may not always be visible in the four months of learning by doing, gathers momentum as it proceeds. Mental muscles which are used almost every hour of the day need an atmosphere of calm and a setting away from everyday pressures for a change. Although they will work just as hard, this "return engagement" provides that atmosphere and freedom. (Indeed, some such sheltered harbour is needed for short periods for all the staff from time to time. The buffeting they get produces a spiritual, if not a physiological, state of stress. This may be a reason why professional people leave the profession, as they sometimes do even when they are successful.)

If this three-part training plan is followed, the order or sequence of the study in the third part will differ from agency to agency. The outline of the order followed in the Social Welfare Branch is included in this book merely as a pattern (see Appendix VI). In this final part of the training plan, a professional emphasis is placed on discharging agency functions—that is, on the integration of professional practice and administration—and many people within and outside the agency have a part in teaching. As the majority of those who teach are highly skilled social workers, even though each teaches differently, all present the same basic ideas, the same viewpoint. This does not make for tiresome repetition but for impressive confirmation of professional principles.

The plan for Part III utilizes four methods of teaching: essay-discussions, administrative "clinics," visits to other agencies (in some of which lectures may be given) and two or three quizzes on procedural matters. The essay-discussion sessions make full use of the study and writing assignment each trainee undertook during the learning-by-doing period. They also make use of the specialist supervisor or consultant, or of the administrator whose function in the agency is to supervise or administer and develop the particular service on which the separate essays are based. That is, if the essay is written on the casework skills implicit in administering public assistance, the director or consultant of that division or department of the agency is present to direct the discussion the essay provokes. The essay was received by the agency teacher in time to be mimeographed and a copy forwarded to this consultant a week or two before the date of its presentation. Its content gives the agency teacher and the consultant a clear indication of "where the trainee is" in his present understanding; he is still in the "primary grades" but his maturation is obvious.

Besides reading what the trainee read, the consultant studies the essay with care. He marks passages to be queried, sentences to be developed, ideas he wants to expand, principles he sees to extract, details he thinks need emphasizing and so on. In case the group will not readily produce illustrations of the points being made, this consultant searches out such case material and may have it mimeographed for distribution to the group. He takes a vow, administered by his friend the agency teacher, that he will "lead a discussion" and not "give a lecture." He further agrees that he will never leave a point dangling to give rise to doubt as to where he and the agency stand in regard to any matter discussed.

The members of the group also do their home-work to prepare for these discussions. They literally do this study at home as the time-schedule does not permit much individual work during the day. They do it faithfully, partly because they have a vicarious sympathy for the efforts this writer expended in preparing his essay, partly because they want their own essay to be studied as diligently when the time comes, but principally because they are intensely interested in the subject. They, too, mark passages to query, points to emphasize, sentences they wish to have developed. They will also, almost automatically if they have had experience in giving this service, relate the points made to the cases they know.

When the day arrives, the consultant is introduced to the group and he to each member of the group. The consultant has a vital place in the agency and this session will make it known and appreciated in a lively way. On the agency teacher's suggestion the consultant makes a plan of the seating arrangement so that he can call each trainee by name as discussion proceeds. The geographical location of each trainee in the agency is noted too as sometimes he may wish to point out special characteristics of a trainee's community.

The method of presenting the essay can be left to the consultant's preference. The procedure that seems to get the best results is to have the writer read it aloud, the rest following the written word. The consultant, any member of the group, or the reader himself can interrupt the reading to comment upon, question, dispute or illustrate the points made. If no one interrupts, the agency teacher must.

His part in this discussion is unique. The attention of the group is held by the trainee who reads his essay and by the consultant who sits alone at the top of the room or table. The agency teacher sits nearby but only interrupts to suggest that a question is perhaps irrelevant at that moment and should be saved for the next session. Or he may suggest that a certain trainee has had an experience which would illustrate a point most appropriately. Or he may come to the rescue of a consultant who may be unskilled in arousing responses from a group, by asking "loaded" questions or by summarizing adroitly. At times, the group benefits from hearing two such practised people discuss a point between them. Mainly, however, the agency teacher serves in the capacity of co-ordinator, connecting the thought of these sessions to that of others which have gone before or will come after. He is also observing the responses of each member of the group for purposes of their evaluation.

The virtue is that it is the result of painstaking reading and thought, rather than being a literary gem. Felicity in writing, however, can be detected in these essays as can its opposite. They provide clues to the ability of a trainee to read and to relate that reading to practice. An essay is deemed good when principles read about are related to a segment of practice by apt case illustrations. It is not wholly a lost cause when an essay merely copies out what has been read, with or without benefit of quotation marks or footnote references. The very act of copying has set some psychological process in motion. This could, however, prove that the trainee does not know how to learn by reading or it may suggest that he does not have the ability to integrate theory and practice. Either lack may in the end remove him from the agency. During the discussion of his essay, on the other hand, as he observes how the others have achieved this integration, it could happen that a key may be turned in the lock and suddenly this lack comprehended. Partial comprehension, at least, may come at this time. Perhaps there are few such moments of insight in the learning that is involved in social work but sometimes they occur.

The "clinical" sessions are interspersed among the essay subjects, and relate to them. That is, the essays focus primarily upon professional principles and methods, relating these to agency practices chiefly by means of the case illustrations contained in the essay, or brought out in discussion. These examples do not deal primarily with legalities and agency policy, or with agency procedures. The "clinics" are designed to consider these points more closely. The separation is not artificial as these administrative bones and sinews are examined immediately following the examination of the professional matter. Moreover, at this point in their learning, the necessity of relating the generic and specific, which determined the method of teaching in the first orientation sessions, is not so immediate. Now, the indivisibility of administrative practice and professional practice is more obvious. The attention paid to professional meanings in the essay-discussion offsets the possibility that some might consider that all the social worker need to know is administrative procedure, while the realities of these clinical sessions obviate that some might consider that professional concepts are all a social worker needs to know. They will be integrated, if not at once, then when the brain is later called upon during practice to remember something from each. The agency teacher, playing the part of co-ordinator, vigilantly watches for evidence that this integration is taking place; if it fails to, everything stops until it does.

These clinical sessions are prepared for before the trainee leaves the office in which he has done his learning by practice. When he and his supervisor are notified of the exact dates of his return for Part III of his training, they are reminded to gather up the things about administration that have been perplexing and confusing to the trainee. On the first day of the trainees' return, the agency teacher calls for their questions and records them. They are then sent to the administrator of the part of the service they are concerned with, who studies them and prepares his answers. At the agency teacher's behest this is done from an historical point of view. How did this policy develop? From what original premise? Through what stages? At whose instigation? With what primary intention? With what extenuations or exceptions? If there are few or no questions from the group, the administrator will present the legal and procedural matters he selects to teach in this general order. He will, doubtless, select the areas where errors or misunderstandings most commonly occur. He, too, takes a vow not to review, painfully, clause by clause, the statutes and policies he administers. When the group has no specific questions to ask this administrator, the teacher puts before them those enumerated above as keys to what they may expect to gain from these sessions. He urges them to ask directly if the answers are not forthcoming. He will investigate the notes taken by the group in these sessions to ensure that they are accurate and adequate.

Field trips, or visits from the personnel of another agency, have much more meaning than they had in the beginning group sessions. There, one of their principal purposes was to confirm what was taught by hearing other social workers use the same language, seeing other social workers at work with people within their agency and carrying out its precise functions. Now the field trips and visitors to the group are introduced for the sake of extending exact knowledge of the major resources available to the trainee's agency and to learn how, when, for whom, and why these other agencies can be used.

Great benefit derives from these experiences. There is usually little need to alert the group on what to ask. They will now have cases in their case-loads to relate to all that they observe and are told. They are now able to understand and speak the language they will hear: "referral," "eligibility," "intake," "ceilings," "residence," and the like. They will sense the overtones of professional sensibility sounded by this other agency; when they are alone with their teacher, they will criticize any lack of such sensibility. The teacher will know what to say about the struggles of that agency to give an adequate service; he will leave no room to doubt that non-professional practices can often achieve results that contain much good; he will show by his own respect for these agencies that social work is by no means the only way, or the only discipline to effect public good.

Inter-agency courtesies are learned again through these visits. The teacher will accompany the group on the majority of them, but it is wise to let them go unescorted once in a while. One of the group can be elected by the others to conduct them, that is, to make the introductions and express their thanks. This gives them further proof that they are trusted and trustworthy. They will want to share all that happens with their teacher when the visit is over and time can be found for this. The longer lunch hours provide opportunities for the teacher to meet for fifteen or twenty minutes with them alone so that they can tell him their impressions. In these informal sessions the teacher is a familiar mentor. Thoughts can be expressed freely because they know how well they are known by him. Not being "leader," or yet "father" or "mother" to the group, the teacher is nevertheless "family."

It, too, is a delightful relationship but very different from that established in the first group sessions and different from that which the trainees established with their supervisor in the practice period. This group, in truth, now knows more about some aspects of the work than the teacher does. The teacher is wise to say this and to ask to be put straight on small points of procedure now and then. They are aware that the teacher is devoted to the task of doing all that can be done to help them develop in understanding and skill. They respond with liking and freedom which redounds to the good of the agency. They are non-competitive in their regard for each other and copy the teacher's early manner of commending each other's good ideas. This imitation is a way of learning and it, therefore, imposes upon the teacher the necessity of attempting to be an example to them in thought and deportment. The significant point is that these feelings and relationships are engendered within the agency. In turn, the devotion of the agency personnel to the people they serve creates, in these trainees, a similar spirit of devotion which they never lose.

The "quizzes on procedural matters" are placed near the end of this four-week period to bring before the group the daily routines they will soon be moving back into in their operative offices. It would be wasted effort to reteach all the mechanical devices the agency employs. The accountant, the statistician, the office consultant make brief appearances to throw questions to and catch answers from the group; both questions and answers often lead to further clarification of the reasons for this or that procedure. This is not a game, but it is not a heavy-handed way of handling a part of the work which is often irritating because simple rules are not observed. As a result the trainees have a livelier appreciation of the good that comes out of orderliness and a realization that here is one part of the work which, by the establishment of good habits, may become reflex action.

### THE FIRST DAY

Like the first day of the first group sessions, and the first day in the actual office, the day the "return engagement" begins has considerable significance. It is spent with the agency teacher and his assistant if he has one.[1] The first hour is spent in "reporting back"on the things that have happened to each of the group in the past four months. The teacher asks the same questions of all: tell us about your community, its good and bad features. Tell us about your office, the setting and accommodation, how many colleagues you have, how many clerical people, your supervisor. (The latter is invariably described by each trainee in some such words as: "I expect I have the best supervisor in the whole agency.") Tell us about your total case-load (we will look at it more closely later today) and the predominant problems it represents. Tell us about yourself, how you now feel about the work. Tell us of any highlights or episodes that made a special impression on you.

[1]After this first day, should an assistant teacher be available, he may with added advantage co-ordinate and lead this entire four-week period. It can be assumed that this assistant teacher has been recruited from the ranks of the agency's supervisors. Since he has come more recently from practice, he can make reality doubly real, and knowing the facts of the everyday life of the social worker, especially the rural social worker, can reduce any overly idealistic notions to practical proportions.

This recital helps to bring the group together again as a group. It does not establish the teacher as its leader necessarily as this leadership is not needed now as much as before. There is a spirit of independence abroad but on independence based on similar, not diverse, experience and interest. The teacher merely facilitates the return of the members of the group to each other and makes no effort, beyond revealing the keenest interest in what they say, to do more than that.

After this the schedule they will follow in the ensuing four weeks is distributed (Appendix VI). They are told that it is constructed to cover first the areas of the work which account for the bulk of the services the agency gives. This follows the teaching-learning principle of beginning with what they know best. The sequences then move on to cover the entire service the agency gives. The group is left at this point to read the outline and to discuss it among themselves. Just before the morning refreshment break, they have a chance to ask their questions and to make comments.

In the first part of the next hour they make a list of the questions they want to put to the people they will meet in the "clinic" sessions. The rest of the morning and part of the afternoon are spent reviewing their case-loads. This is a case count rather than an analysis. It is done so that they will see that they have all had a similar experience in assuming heavy responsibilities and so that they will have the cases they have worked on firmly in the front of their minds as session succeeds session. They are told that the teacher will remind everyone at the beginning of every new field of study to think about the cases he has in this category. A quick poll will be taken of each member of the group at that time so that the consultant who is present will also know how much work they have done, or will be doing, in respect of this part of the total service. Some of their own cases will serve to illustrate the points being made in the discussion. All the points made in the essay should be related to these cases to determine whether they apply. In short, these discussions, or these learning sessions, are not carried on in a vacuum. Experience is always present; knowledge transmitted is always immediately and realistically applied to something that is known. There has been virtually no time lag between this group session and the practice done. There will be no time lag between these sessions and their return to practice. They will be able to remember and employ what they learned with relative ease.

There is an obvious pitfall in this procedure and it is often one of the trainee's making. This is their effort to obtain from the consultants they meet an opinion on the conduct of the cases they bring forth as examples. The agency teacher watches for this for the consultant might unwittingly fall into the trap and give an opinion which would be contrary to that of the trainee's supervisor. The teacher says firmly, echoed by the consultant: "No one can advise on or guide the conduct of a case unless all the facts of the situation are known and studied. There is not time here to review your case so explicitly. We can deal only in general principles and review the appropriate body of knowledge against which you, through logical reasoning, make your diagnosis or reach an understanding of the problem and then plan your services." The supervisor is thus protected from the temporary relinquishment of his authority in favour of many others who are senior to him. One or two other obvious lessons are taught at the same time and a clue is also furnished of the obstinacy of this trainee. Such obstinacy is not uncommon. Everyone resists authority to some degree. It has its virtue. This trait may have been mentioned in the supervisor's evaluation. If it is serious enough to provoke a resistance to any learning, the administration is advised and one of two courses followed: the trainee may be placed with another supervisor or he may be asked to leave the agency. If it is not as serious as this, the supervisor may welcome help in learning how to teach the independent mind which is not so much resistant as slower and more deliberate in its learning pattern.

The review of the case-load completed, which is done by reference to the monthly statistical reports the trainees have brought with them, the discussion moves on to the administrative and professional aspects of the management of this case-load. The weekly time-schedules are reviewed and assessed for the efficiency they make possible. The system of filing and of "bringing forward" cases, according to the time interval between interviews agreed upon by client and social worker, receive similar review and assessment. People who say "I haven't got the hang of that system yet" will be asked to bring the points that confuse them to the office consultant during the quiz on office procedures. The techniques of using the policy manual to determine how to put various services in motion will be discussed. Forms are alluded to and their uses criticized or commended. The absence, or presence, of "bottle-necks" in all these procedural matters will be mentioned, but full explanations will come in the "clinic" on agency administration.

This obviously is a quick cataloguing of all the agency's devices for bringing its services quickly and smoothly to the client. It serves the purpose of establishing that these devices have a purpose and have been given much thought, and that there probably is much trial and error behind them. They are seen "whole" as a starting point and will be dissected only as the study progresses.

The management of case-load does not depend wholly upon administrative devices. The method of social casework itself implies management. The précis on "social casework principles" is now reviewed in part, the pages devoted to the method getting particular attention. The workability of this method can now be discussed:

Have you yet been able to find this method at work in the records you have read? Have you used it yourself in the casework you have done? You have recorded the data which the legalities of the services we give demand you collect to prove eligibility. Does that information follow and contain the data a social worker needs to determine how, and how seriously, this client is dislocated in society? Have you specifically recorded the social diagnosis—your understanding of the client and his problem—which you and your supervisor have arrived at? Have you recorded what you and your supervisor and the client agree to be the plan of treatment or service to be followed? Have you worked long enough on any of your new cases to determine what the goal of treatment will be? Have you closed any cases when the goal established by the previous worker has been achieved? Have you, in four months, closed a case because the client has become independent through his own and your efforts?

The purpose of this discussion is to bring before the group the application of the casework method in their agency. It is the professional method the agency's administration demands be followed and which is specifically mentioned in the laws administered.[2] It is economical to a degree, establishes priorities of need and of service, imposes disciplines, gets things done. At the end of this discussion many of the trainees previously puzzled will have gained a new understanding of how casework principles are integrated with casework practice.

This discussion and others in this period do not attempt to do more than mention the relationships the trainee has established with his clients. This inter-personal aspect of social casework, which gives effect to the intention of the method, is a matter for individual cultivation. The appropriate time and place for examining this talent, for these relationships comprise the "art" of professional practice, are when and where the trainee is practising. This examination of talent, moreover, is in effect an effort towards establishing the need for "self-awareness," a process which sometimes causes pain. The agency supervisor is wise to walk delicately as a growing self-awareness is revealed by the growing poise, the seriousness of mind, even by the appearance of these earnest people. This growth in awareness is one of the major effects, as was said before, of education for social work as carried out

[2]Social Assistance Act Regulations, 1945, Statutes of British Columbia; section 2, sub-section 2: "Social worker means a qualified social worker performing casework in the field."

by a school of social work. It is fitting that the introspection which is required be deferred until the trainee reaches the school. The contention that this is then done with a minimum of pain and with its true purpose—to know oneself before presuming to know and judge others—safely accomplished, has been borne out far more often than not in the writer's experience. After another two years of experience and after a year of study at the school, the maturity of these social workers is impressive.

This has been a heavy day for these trainees in many respects. However, it should tie together the two previous parts of the plan with what is to ensue in the next four weeks. It proves again that none of the three parts of this training is in isolation from any other. It further establishes the limits of this training and quickens the trainee's determination to absorb all the agency can offer, then moving on, after further practice, to obtain more thorough professional education in the proper setting.

During this four weeks, the agency teacher notes the responses of each member of the group for evaluation purposes. If the assistant teacher conducts this part of the training plan, he confers at least once a week with the teacher on the difficulties he encounters. At the end of each session taken by a consultant, all three discuss the consultant's opinions of the trainees. All this serves to confirm or change the earlier evaluations of their learning abilities and of their sensibilities to their new vocation.

It is useful to have the trainees evaluate the in-service training plan before they have done with it. At the time interviews are held with each trainee separately for final evaluation, the rest of the group can review, singly or as a group, the effectiveness of the studies they have undertaken. They are asked to review the programme of the last four weeks in some detail, and to write down their frank opinions of the teaching given. A set of questions is sometimes drafted for them to answer in writing. This is not intended as an examination but as a critique of the training plan itself. From the criticisms—and no one need sign this written evaluation—have come many admirable ideas for changing the plan for the better.

The comments made, however, reveal the workability of the plan more often than not. The following samples are chosen for their criticism as well as enthusiasm:

. . . Personally, I feel that my understanding of social work, which began with the cultivation of attitudes in the first four weeks, has been both deepened and broadened by my experience in the field. From the last four weeks of classes, I have gained a confirmation of these practices and a reiteration of the philosophy and policies of the Branch in regard to the following points:

1.  The client-worker relationship is the basis of any or all casework. This relationship, friendly, relaxed and still having an air of business-likeness is the key to success or failure.

2.  The principle of self-determination of the client is worthy of deep thought. There may be times when this principle must be over-ruled (in the case of protection, for instance), but this does not occur too often and, even then, the worker must be sure of his grounds. . . .

. . . The inherent worth of man, whether he be a six-months-old child, a delinquent boy, a mentally deficient man in his thirties, or an old man, appeared to be the common theme, both underlying and on the surface of all we were taught. All the people we met seem to have an awareness of the needs of people and are trying to answer those needs to the best of their ability and the resources available. It is good to find that such people exist and I feel good about being identified with them. I have lots to learn. . . .

. . . This is a field in which one could never stop learning. At the moment, I need most help in the actual casework process, in recording and in organizing my caseload. . . . [This is a common criticism and is welcomed. It proclaims that educational goals are in sight and that the agency is not presuming to go beyond the "primary grades" in teaching professional matter.]

. . . I believe that we are working in a young and growing field. Even if anyone could learn all there is to know at this point, there would be continually more to learn. But our aim in learning should not be to "keep up" with but to help build the profession. . . .

. . . The in-service training plan has definitely given me a start in social work. It has incorporated and developed views that I have previously had. I also think that I have a relatively clear understanding of the specific work of the Social Welfare Branch. My only regret is that I did not know all this two years ago when I might have been able to get to the school of social work. I have plans to do this as soon as I can get leave. . . .

. . . The initial in-service training period gave me the bare bones of the set-up, initiated me into the way of thinking and talking as a social worker and presented me with a general picture of the total set-up. It surprised me that I remembered as much as I did of these things. The practical work floored me for the first four or five weeks and then it began to have meaning. By the time I came back, I was ready to absorb the finer points because "the client" had become a reality. It is certainly only a beginning in my understanding of casework principles, however. . . .

# VIII. Evaluating the Trainee

THE EVALUATION OF TRAINEES in each of the three parts of the training scheme is governed by considerations beyond those usually implied in the term "staff evaluations." In a sense these considerations embody the educational intent of all agency training plans. This suggests at once that evaluation—the objective assessment of the progress each trainee makes in learning—is inherent in the total concept of in-service training. (Later, in the chapter devoted to discussing an agency's staff development programme, evaluations will be mentioned again and the thought conveyed there that evaluations are inherent in the total concept of agency administration.) As far as the social worker is concerned, evaluations are a measure of self-growth, indispensable in perfecting his practice. All evaluations are administrative, educational and professional necessities, but in-service training evaluations have certain special implications in regard to administration and education.

## ADMINISTRATIVE CONSIDERATIONS

First, in-service training is a learning experience, planned and executed at the agency's expense, for the purpose of maintaining its services in spite of shortages of qualified personnel. The administration of the agency must be satisfied that, both during and following this training, its standards of accomplishment are met. The majority of those recruited will succeed and many will exceed the agency's minimum requirements and expectations. The few who do not will have to leave.

For those who sway on the fence, there is always the possibility that the training period has not been long enough to provide the evidence required to justify a negative judgment. There is sometimes a possibility that the agency teacher and supervisor may, in spite of their self-discipline and good intentions, be weighting their judgment by including subjective or personal feelings about this person. If judgment is to be deferred there must, of course, be evidence that this person has made some progress in areas of the work which count. The evaluation interview of such people will begin with the supervisor or agency teacher, but will continue in the office of the administrator or the agency personnel director. This is not a frightening experience, for the administrator has already interviewed this trainee when he first applied. At that point he had enough confidence in him to hire him. In this interview, as then, the trainee talks about himself. What he says, weighed with all the other evidence—which the administrator discusses frankly with him—may result in replacement in the agency. Another supervisor, or a different community, may see improvement. A definite time interval of not longer than three months is set for the next evaluation. Meanwhile, everyone tries, the trainee most of all, to make the next interview a success story. It more often than not is just that, not a spectacular one, but one which tells of steady development.

Of the seventy-six in-service trainees employed in the two-year period 1953–5 by the Social Welfare Branch, four terminated their employment before the end of the six months' training period because they failed to achieve the minimum development expected. Two had B.A. degrees, one two years of university study, and one only high school matriculation. The latter was always in doubt; his employment was a risk taken with everyone's eyes open. He failed because of a language disability. The other three could not co-ordinate their learning faculties to make use of this form of education. They themselves concluded that vocationally they belonged in a setting where intelligent routine or manual activity was demanded. One of them is now a laboratory technician and a good one. Another is heading the dispatch office of a large trucking firm. The third is working in the woods of British Columbia, saving to complete his university education. He may return to social work some day.

There were three other trainees in this period who presented a problem, and of these two have remained. A transfer to another office away from parental influence (which had not been fully known about before the evaluation interview with the personnel director) freed one of them to apply herself to learning. An adjustment in the caseload of another proved helpful and, in the area of work this person now covers, his performance is well above average. As he grows in confidence no doubt the time will come when he will want to stretch his wings in other parts of the work. For him, as for a few others like him, education at a school of social work may have to be deferred for several years. The third doubtful one left of her own volition after a further three months of trial. She had lately come to Canada from the Old World, and though she was frank in saying "in spite of myself I find I like the clients I have known," nevertheless, her own cultural conditioning in another stricter way of life made her uncomfortable in working in the non-authoritative field of social work.

The above examples serve to illustrate both the agency administration's firmness and its flexibility in acting upon the evaluations made on the trainee. Those who fail and those for whom some doubt exists are seldom hurt by the actions taken. They are based on conclusions the trainee arrives at himself, although sometimes he needs patient help to attain this understanding. The agency has to write off the costs that were involved in reaching these conclusions. Few agencies can afford many of such failures, but they are reduced to a minimum when the recruiting is done with the care suggested in chapter III.

A second administrative consideration in regard to evaluations is also embedded in the recruiting process. It is that both agency and trainee are prepared to risk the use of this experience for the ulterior purpose of determining whether or not this trainee has the necessary aptitude for social work. The agency wants people who are convinced that social work is the career they wish to follow. When candidates say they are not certain, but *think* they have the qualities and interest needed to become social workers, the agency is obviously taking a risk in employing them. But it is a risk calculated against the experience that such ability and interest are usually confirmed. Often these trainees, after obtaining professional qualifications, have moved into specialized parts of the work. Their original doubt has turned out to be a form of discrimination as to their abilities, and this in the end has been a gain. Only a very few have concluded that social work is a totally wrong field for them.

Experience also proves that the agency can expect in-service trained people to withdraw for the usual reasons. Some on the outside of the agency are sceptical of in-service training on the grounds that it fills positions which qualified people, turning up later, should have. There is always a strong implication in these words that unqualified people, sensible of their good fortune, stay in their jobs forever. Nothing could be farther from the truth. The turn-over for "natural causes" among the trainees is as great as among the professionally prepared staff. As was stated in chapter I, a third go on to obtain professional training. Those who leave before doing this meanwhile give a service, thanks to in-service training, that has value to the agency and the community.

The criticism levelled at the smaller agencies when they retain the in-service trained person even when a qualified social worker turns up unexpectedly is not wholly justified. The agency has already expended much effort to prepare that person for the job he is doing. He is growing perceptibly; he is performing beyond minimum requirements; he is perhaps slated to have leave of absence the following year to obtain professional training at a school of social work after which he will return to the agency with his value increased beyond price. Most agencies, to be sure, can employ every qualified person who applies at any time of the year. Smaller agencies, on a limited budget, may not be able to employ a qualified social worker immediately, but somewhere in the community he will find a job. In fact, the agency may well ask why he is looking for work at this particular time. Has he a history of job-hopping? A few social workers with good qualifications on paper are not good employment risks, unfortunately.

Added to the in-service trained people who leave for "natural causes" —marriage, child-bearing, more adequate pay, sickness, moves to other parts of the country and so on—are the people who leave after fulfilling the unwritten term of employment to stay for two years following successful completion of the agency's training plan. In this longer period, they find that they are not as happy in the work as they had thought they would be. Their subsequent evaluations prove that although they are not necessarily unsuited to it—they have given a commendable performance at the level the agency expects of them— nevertheless they are, for some reason, not completely satisfied in their work. Some have grown fearful of themselves in the work. Some have found it both physically and spiritually fatiguing. They are not quite willing, or they have not the fibre it takes, to spend themselves fully in fulfilling the demands made upon them. Some have regressed in their powers of learning; others are content to stand still. They come to the conclusion that either social work is too big for them, or they are not big enough for it. They then leave for other fields. The evaluation and separation interviews seldom fail, however, to produce spontaneously this thought: "Whatever I do in the future, this experience has helped me as a person. I shall carry over much of what I learned and practised into my everyday life. I shall always believe in, and, as a somewhat privileged citizen, support the cause of human well-being."

Of the seventy-six people mentioned in an earlier part of this chapter, in two years twenty-one have left for one or other of the above reasons. When the five who left at or before the end of the training period are also subtracted, thirty remain. Some of those who remain may leave before they obtain their professional training. Those who stay will obtain professional qualifications, some receiving training grants from the agency. Those who do—and half of the number do not receive financial help—then return for a period of time sufficient to repay all the efforts invested in their learning and growth. They may make this agency their "field" within social work for the rest of time. Many who preceded them have done so.

A third administrative consideration implicit in evaluations is a positive one. They provide the assurance that learning is taking place which will result in the work getting done. More than this, they present a fairly specific catalogue of the growing strengths of each of these successful people. Every administrator needs to know who possesses what talents in order to place his people in the positions they can do best, and which employ best their individual abilities. It is not possible for the in-service training evaluation to do more than intimate these assets. They may be sufficiently clear intimations, however, to suggest that, as soon as a grounding in general practice and school training are accomplished, the person evaluated can be groomed for a special niche in the agency. The promise of steady dependable growth nevertheless calls for continuing help from the agency, individual by individual, to realize the full and unique potentialities of each. Knowing through the evaluation process that the agency values him in this way, for himself and not in comparison with others, each trainee will be helped to make the efforts required to realize this goal.

## STAFF DEVELOPMENT IMPLICATIONS

Learning on the job can proceed best when certain goals of achievement are in clear view of the learner and the teacher. These are interim not final goals: achieving one merely means that new ones will be set. As these are overtaken, the setting of new goals becomes the responsibility, gladly accepted, of the learner himself. However, the agency must take the responsibility for starting the process. Agency evaluations set the pattern which gives purpose and form to self-evaluation, which, in turn, promotes self-learning and self-induced growth.

Learning on the job should enable the trainee to function so that the work will get done to the best possible advantage of the people for whom it is done. This fact crowds the trainee's mind and consciousness, and leaves little space for the joy of learning just for learning's sake. This does not mean that there is no pleasure associated with it. There is. It is shown in the delight and vitality the trainees bring with them when they sit face to face with their supervisors, or in a group with the agency teacher, to address themselves to the meanings and intentions of the work they do. This enhanced vitality is charged with projected feeling, arising from their concern for the needs of others with whom they have identified themselves. It arises also from a sense of urgency, heightened by their lesser knowledge, to do something about those needs. Thus they commit their minds, readily and eagerly, to discovering the full range of services of the agency, which they can use to meet the needs they know and have felt. This gives them a sense of security which partially compensates for their lack of professional knowledge. They will find later that their knowledge of the agency is a part of professional knowledge.

A social agency is the concrete expression of an abstract concept. Its concrete form is learnable, and this learning is measurable. This side of learning pertains to the order of executing the agency's benefits and services. It is the step-by-step procedure, each step having a known purpose, by which the client is assured that the agency is doing something about his problem. The measurement of this aspect of learning includes more than checking and recording a trainee's mastery of procedure. His understanding of the reason for each step taken, and his appreciation of the significance to the client of the attention to administrative requirements, must also be measured, as well as his accuracy and dispatch in discharging these duties. It is also necessary to make an assessment of the trainee's ability to interpret the agency and its procedures to the client, and to measure the cogency of his arguments when, as the client's advocate, he presents to the administration a problem which calls for an exception to be made to existing rules. Finally his attitude to these activities, which is another clue to mastery, must be considered.

The trainee's attitude is conditioned by the abstract concept out of which the social agency has grown and which permeates the concrete form it takes. The concept may be as old as civilization itself, but whether ancient or modern, it remains the lode-star of all social agency endeavour. This is the spirit of altruism: "regard for others as a principle of action," as the Oxford Dictionary defines the word. The comfort the trainee feels in occupying his place in the agency is a measure of his attitude to the altruistic base of all that the agency does. His response to his duties—his willingness, alertness and well-directed energies—is another indication. His identification with his supervisor and colleagues is another, as is his eagerness to know, to question, to understand. His way of speaking and thinking about his clients and his reaction to their needs betray his "regard for others." His supervisor can say, when his attitude reflects the spirit of altruism, "he likes people." He possesses the simple virtues of kindness of heart, consideration for others, thoughtfulness and good cheer.

This assessment of attitude is the beginning of an assessment of his potential ability to become a social worker. Later, after a year on the job, it will be possible to begin to measure skills and talents in relationship, in reasoning ability, in self-discipline, but these skills are merely suggested during the first six months. They are not ignored in the in-service evaluations, for they are set as the next goal of achievement. The initial goal, meanwhile, is that of ensuring that kindliness prevails. No one is ever hurt by kindness. Even when methods are uncertainly or unskilfully applied, the supervisor and the agency can be sure that the client will not suffer injury from the ministrations of a trainee who is kind. That he also knows his way about in the concrete form the agency takes makes his ministrations effective.

## USE OF AN EVALUATION OUTLINE

Any outline followed during the evaluation interview and in recording it—for this is a "process" thus having form and order—will divide the total learning goal into segments, each of which will become a specific goal to be accomplished. The effect of this on the trainee is something like this: "this is the minimum the agency expects of me now; I can do better than that." He soon finds that the minimum is none too simple, but simple or difficult, the learning he is expected to do is not amorphous or diffuse. It is concrete, yet imbued with the abstract. It is conditioned by his feeling and spirit. To measure evidence of facts learned is to discern the quality of the learning and the learner; to do this is to see total growth and to make the meaning of total growth clear to the trainee.

Contained in these evaluative considerations is another which must not be overlooked. This is the fact that in-service training does not attempt to prepare people to be social workers in the full professional meaning of the term. It can only begin that preparation, hence the yardsticks of measurement applied when evaluating qualified and experienced staff members, or students placed in the agency for field work, cannot be applied to the in-service trainee. A different set of criteria has to be established, and this is not easy. The examples given in this chapter are forever under review and have evolved over many years.

Then, the criteria applicable in measuring the trainee's development are hedged about by another set of unknowns. The training given or the learning undertaken is intensive. Adults are expected to have the ability to learn quickly and with considerable thoroughness. Each will learn differently and according to his life-experience to date. Their experience in coping with their own affairs has given them experience in reasoning in practical matters, and the attitudes and viewpoints they hold when they come into the agency suggest some familiarity with philosophical and abstract reasoning. Together with their emotional poise and relationships among colleagues, friends and family, all this gives some assurance that they measure up adequately to the definition of maturity which they will study during the training period. Nevertheless, in-service training is sufficiently condensed, and its pace sufficiently rapid, to suggest that progress or growth may be forced. The agency must trim the content and slow up the pace when the majority are found to slip back or reach a saturation point during the total training period. For some, such regression can be predicted, tolerated for a time and eventually recovered. When, on the other hand, the training objectives for this period are reached, the learning does not cease. The next evaluation, at the end of a year of supervised practice, will measure further growth. The supervisor can then begin to apply to the trainee the criteria of evaluation used for all staff. By then there is fuller comprehension of the ways to apply total knowledge and one's self to achieve effective results. The trainee is conscious of his development and learns consciously and deliberately.

The criteria used in evaluating the in-service trainee should properly derive from education. Not being educationists, neither supervisors nor agency teacher can apply the scientific forms of testing or measuring used in education. Any attempt to do this would be ludicrous. Rather, an attempt can be made, by using the social worker's skill in observation and deduction, to determine whether a trainee appears to be learning. An examination of the criteria developed thus far in the Social Welfare Branch to set goals of attainment and to guide the evaluation interview may make this somewhat clearer.

Here is the outline followed by the agency teacher—and the trainee himself—at the conclusion of Part I of the plan.

OUTLINE FOR THE EVALUATION OF IN-SERVICE TRAINEES

PART I: ORIENTATION PERIOD

A. *Information about the Trainee*
    1. Age, place of birth, marital status, religion
    2. Education, including vocational courses and elective non-credit courses taken for pleasure and in pursuit of avocational interests

3. Work history
4. Original vocational aspirations
5. Appearance, articulation, mannerisms
6. Attitude to further education, and planning for this
7. Significant life experiences which are either useful in social work practice or which may intrude upon learning

B. *Responses to Teaching during the Orientation Period*
   1. General responsiveness to matters discussed
   2. Particular interests revealed, if any
   3. Areas of apparent indifference, criticism, or cynicism
   4. Quality of questions and comments
   5. Perception
   6. Degree of intellectual curiosity

C. *Learning Abilities*
   1. Application to learning
   2. Powers of concentration and attention
   3. Ease of verbal expression; vocabulary
   4. Retention of facts; transfer of knowledge
   5. Reading and writing skills
   6. Independent learning

D. *Attitudes and Feeling*
   1. With respect to differences among races, creed, colour, political opinion, behaviour
   2. With respect to laws, morals and social custom
   3. With respect to particular social problems
   4. With respect to family responsibilities and privileges
   5. With respect to professional conduct
   6. Sensitiveness and possible vulnerabilities

E. *Manner*
   1. Apparent sense of responsibility
   2. First impressions
   3. Poise
   4. Humor
   5. Acceptance of and by the group
   6. Negative traits

F. *Training Supervisor's Summary and Recommendations*

This outline (together with those used in the next two parts of the training) is distributed to the group at a time planned for this, usually at the end of the third week of the first group sessions. Perhaps it is shock tactics to do this, but the fact that these people are adults and that this evaluation process is a "requirement" of the training plan and will be applied to each alike carries with it teaching and learning value. Should any feel apprehensive, they will, in facing this anxiety, find that they are themselves putting their own maturity to a test. The way in which the agency teacher introduces the subject, the interpretation given to each part of the outline, as well as to the whole intention of evaluations, will include comments upon the agency's assumption of their willingness to be evaluated. They were given to understand in their application interviews that evaluations would be conducted. Now they see of what precisely they consist.

Some strain can be expected in the first few minutes of the interview when it does take place (the evaluator indeed may feel a little strain in anticipation of some of the interviews), but this is allayed by the naturalness of the evaluator's manner, by the attitude he adopts of presuming that the trainee wants to know where he stands in the agency, and by his dealing first with the positive indications of growth which at once suggests to the trainee that he is succeeding. With this encouragement, strain subsides. The evaluator can then move into the phase of the interview in which the trainee is asked to examine the evidence the teacher has gathered of his apparent learning disabilities and of those attitudes and feelings which may stand in his way in learning and performing. Attitudes to education and ways of learning are discussed rather than the emotionally derived problems which may have shown up in what the trainee said, and how he said it. Any personal mannerism is frankly looked at to see if it might hinder efforts to establish good relationships. The restless person will agree that physical composure is necessary when interviewing; those trainees whose voices are low or otherwise weak will agree that modulation of the voice has an effect upon people; animation may need curbing or promoting. This discussion does not probe for causes; it merely offers the trainee help—from one who is liked and respected—to speed his progress. Some have been able to say at the conclusion of this first interview: "I gather that social workers practise what they preach; they try to see themselves as they are so they too can change for the better." This is the professional purpose of these evaluations: to begin the journey into self-awareness. The stress is on the word "begin."

The agency requires this evaluation for administrative purposes. Not only does the evaluation set specific goals for the trainee, but it also reinforces them with the authority of the agency. The agency acts on the assumption that the staff will make efforts to learn, continuously and consistently, in order to give an increasingly effective service. It, therefore, replaces the usual laissez-faire of adult education—the election by mood of what and when to study—by definite requirements.

This kind of discipline needs at first to be imposed from outside. Later it will become self-imposed. All new social workers perhaps could, with benefit, be subject to authority in learning, but for the in-service trainee, it is imperative that this discipline be felt from the outset, so that self-discipline is established as soon as possible and maximum use is made of opportunities to learn and grow. Learning and growth are wholly within the individual's power. The agency's efforts to induce growth would be of no avail without this self-determination. Stimulating determination by sublimating the purpose of education—"it is for the sake of the better help we can give"—and providing media to be used in learning imply authority and impose discipline.

The written evaluation as a record of the evaluation interview follows the rules of good recording: brevity, relevance, confidentiality. The teacher will know much more about this trainee than he records, but these unrecorded items are the positive things which are implied as being possessed merely because they are omitted from the record. The relevant matters are those which the teacher and the trainee have discussed as being less positive attributes of learning, which he requires help in overcoming. The ultimate disposal of the written record—and its possible though scarcely probable misuse at some later time by persons not convinced that social workers can and do grow out of early-found faults—demand that the record not resemble a social history nor yet record evidence which invades the trainee's right to privacy. When necessary, such evidence is verbally conveyed to those who must know it in order to take whatever steps may be required. The confidentiality of this written evaluation, in other words, places major restraints upon the evaluator.

This first evaluation is prepared for the supervisor who will teach the trainee in the next part of the plan. The evaluator must make use, also, of what he knows about this supervisor in preparing the written evaluation. If the supervisor has had much experience, the evaluation can be considerably shortened. If he is new to supervision, the agency teacher may go so far as to make specific suggestions about ways to help the trainee over some of his self-acknowledged difficulties. If he knows that this supervisor tends to hear alarm bells when only precautionary signals are intended, he tempers his written evaluation by highlighting positives before he mentions negatives. In these and other ways the written evaluation attempts to bridge the separate parts of this learning experience and make it a whole.

The samples of written evaluations given below will serve to illustrate some of the points made in the foregoing discussion. They are all fictitious, yet near enough to experience to make them real.

## EVALUATION

### PART I: IN-SERVICE TRAINING PLAN

To: District Supervisor
From: Training Supervisor

#### A. *Information about the Trainee*

Mary Elizabeth Frome is 29 years of age, born in Victoria, is single and an active member of the United Church of Canada. She was educated in Victoria elementary and high schools, and attended Victoria College attaining second year university standing. Her education was interrupted by her necessity to earn her living as her family suffered financial set-back at that time. She took a course in stenography and, thinking to continue her academic education through extra-mural courses, obtained a job in a business firm in Vancouver nine years ago.

She remained with this firm until leaving to join our staff. Her advancement was rapid. She became supervisor of a department within four years and for the past five has carried certain personnel duties as well. It is in her favour to note that she is on excellent terms with the management of the firm, whose letters of reference both recommend her move into social work and express regret at losing her able services.

It had been Miss Frome's intention to become a teacher of high school English, first because she had enjoyed her own 'teen days so thoroughly she wished to work with adolescents who, like some of her friends, had had "difficult problems," and second, because English literature was her favourite subject and one in which she did well in high school and college. Her feeling for literature is reflected in her ease of speaking and good choice of words.

Miss Frome is an attractive young woman, not "pretty," but alert and full of quiet vitality. She dresses becomingly and has a good sense of colour. She is relaxed when she is listening.

She is delighted that she will be able to obtain professional training at a later time. She has saved some money, which she had thought to spend on a trip abroad. Now she will add to it as "an investment in the future rather than the present." She would rather finance her own education than get "something for nothing." A brother whom she helped finance through medical school would probably be able to help her if she needed help.

#### B. *Response to Teaching*

Miss Frome's attentiveness and total response to all that was taught was a delight. In one area she may need help. She has herself a strong feeling of family responsibility. In the discussion of a case involving an absconding husband, she revealed impatience over his conduct and said forthrightly that he "ought to be brought to task." As the discussions progressed, she listened silently but alertly as the others talked about the provocation behind his actions, of the total lack of example in the man's own life of assuming responsibility, of the small but significant display of maturity he showed in sending his wife a money-order. It was she who summed up the discussion. "I've been lucky, I think I've got the point. We behave in these ways because we have never learned anything different. When we run away, as this man did, we need help and understanding help at that." This was an exercise of the mind. Watch for a slightly punishing attitude affecting her work in some cases, as she will, for we discussed this in the evaluation interview.

### C.  Learning Abilities

These have been contained in the foregoing comments. The test of her apparent ease of learning will come in the application of herself to the work.

### D.  Attitudes and Feelings

Miss Frome displayed no feeling in the discussion of cases where social and cultural differences were factors to be considered and was the one in the group to quote (inaccurately but aptly) Voltaire's famous dictum: "I will never believe as you do, but I will die defending your right to believe what you please." Our clients are safe in these respects with Miss Frome.

### E.  Manner

Miss Frome conveys an immediate impression of responsibility and trustworthiness. Enough has already been said of her poise and humour. She was liked, if not loved, by the group, and was a constant delight to the teacher. Her negative traits may be a shade too much sophistication and self-assurance, but this is so natural to her it does not overwhelm or detract from her essential kindness.

### F.  Summary

It should be a pleasure to supervise Miss Frome in the work she will do in the next few months. It may be necessary to cause her to think penetratively rather than superficially. She will want more of her supervisor's time than is possible to give, for she believes she learns best by "thinking out loud." She agreed to discipline herself by using manuals to learn facts. The professional study she does independently should be planned with the supervisor. It should not be at the expense of leaving undone the job to be done.

We have in Miss Frome a mature intelligent young woman, who, in my opinion will progress in spite of her educational shortcomings.

TRAINING SUPERVISOR

### A.  Information about the Trainee

Robert Henry Shane, 32 years of age, born in Ontario where his parents still reside, is a widower. He received his B.A. degree this Spring, majoring in sociology (honours) having returned to university last year after an interval of several years. He feels he has been at a cross-roads since his wife's death sixteen months ago. His former work—business administration in a large motor firm—paid him good wages, but having to make a major adjustment in his family life and affairs, he left it to resume his education. He had no special vocational purpose in majoring in sociology. He is anxious now to "get the feel" of people. He is by no means sure he wants to be a social worker, but from his studies he thinks he may find it "engrossing."

### B.  Response to Teaching

Mr. Shane was an active participant but inclined to be learnedly argumentative; here and there he was cynical in a sophisticated way. We talked of these traits during the evaluation session, and he thought he saw the point of watching for their effects upon his colleagues. The need to have an open mind in learning even the simple operations he acknowledged as necessary. He has an intellectual virtuosity, but whether it can be toned down sufficiently for him to apply what he knows steadily and with purpose and effect, his practice work will reveal. He was told this, and has agreed to hasten slowly and to make a consistent effort to understand all that he will do.

### C.  Learning Abilities

The question is whether Mr. Shane can apply his considerable knowledge and himself as a person to the task of helping people who are in trouble. Specially acute observations should be made of his relationships with clients, and also with colleagues, supervisor and clerical staff.

### D.  Attitudes and Feelings

Mr. Shane has a militant attitude toward those who are prejudiced against people because of race, creed, colour, politics, religion. It probably ensures that he himself is free of such prejudices, but the "militancy" may be a clue to something else: a general intolerance of society's immaturity and a crusading idea about using shock tactics to change the situation. He is a champion of penal reform, and considers that all adult offenders are reformable. In short, he has positive convictions which have not been put to a full test. It was not around these topics that cynicism burst through. This happened in the discussions on casework and in the case studies, where contempt, however mild, can be tolerated least. It was, however, levelled at the caseworker rather than the client.

### E.  Manner

Mr. Shane reflects his good family background and gives one a first impression of dependability. He has a nice sense of humour and can laugh at himself. He was at first an irritation to the group—and they to him—but by the second week he was their natural leader. He has many endearing qualities beneath his superiority. He is superior, and he will not be hurt but helped if we acknowledge this.

### F.  Summary

In my opinion the next four months of practice will confirm our wisdom in employing Mr. Shane. In that time, he will discover either that he can employ his mind in developing skills, or that he cannot. If not he will withdraw, but if he does find the work a challenge to his best thought and effort, he will make considerably higher than average progress. His former work experience will be of value in quickly learning procedure and routines. Once these are mastered his supervision can then be devoted principally to casework. He should be kept busier than most.

TRAINING SUPERVISOR

To: A.L., Personnel Director
Re: Mary Inkler, B.A., aged 20

This will confirm our lengthy discussion in respect of Miss Inkler's lack of progress in the orientation period. Her determination to become a social worker need not, in my opinion, be lessened by our inability to retain her. Her kind attitudes seem sincerely based, and she has a good mind. She is, however, still a schoolgirl who is dramatizing her notion of a mature adult. Her immaturity is a little too obvious to entrust her yet with the serious situations encountered in our practice. In three or four years time, if she does not marry, I would say we might re-engage her if she applies. She has been advised that it would be in her own best interests if she obtained professional training before again seeking employment in a social agency.

TRAINING SUPERVISOR

To: A.L., Personnel Director
Re: William Harver, age 24, Junior matriculant

Mr. Harver will see you at one o'clock on the last day of the orientation period. He has, he informs me, thought seriously of all he and I talked about in the evaluation interview, and concluded himself that it is better for him to withdraw. He attributes his failure to his lack of education, and thinks now that he will try to get his B.A. degree before he is 30. He said he was grateful for the help we had all been to him. He will never cease wanting to be a social worker, he said. I replied that he could use his interests and kindly feelings in many ways, and help many people to be happier just because he was a happy person himself. He may write us for character references, which I shall be pleased to furnish.

TRAINING SUPERVISOR

THE SECOND EVALUATION

The outline followed by the supervisor in evaluating the trainee's progress after three months of learning by doing in the second part of the training plan is as follows:

EVALUATION

PART II: PRACTICE PERIOD, IN-SERVICE TRAINING

A. *The Trainee Himself*
  1. Any additional information pertinent to learning, not contained in first evaluation
  2. Use of leisure
  3. Unusual demands made upon us by the trainee or *vice versa*
  4. General comments re personal adaptation to the community

B. *Response to Supervision*
  1. Relationship with supervisor
  2. Receptivity to teaching

3. Progress in independent learning of procedures
4. General attitude and application to learning

C. *Relationships*

1. With clients as revealed by trainee's own estimate of this as given during case supervision; as implied in recording; as observed by the supervisor
2. With colleagues, professional and clerical
3. With community people met on the job

D. *Progress in Learning*

1. Administrative procedures: attitude, understanding, accuracy, dispatch
2. Casework: ability to obtain accurate relevant data, ability to isolate problems, ability to recognize clients' abilities, ability to detect clients' feelings, ability to interpret agency function to client, ability to plan or quality of thought in planning, degree of identification
3. Interviewing: growing ease or self-confidence, sense of purpose in interviewing, skills in listening, guiding, interpreting, encouraging, planning next interview, special problems in interviewing
4. Recording: organizing material for dictation, facility in dictation, grammar and syntax, letter and memo writing, face-sheet, work cards, forms, etc.
5. Value of orientation period: application of facts learned, discrepancies

E. *Areas of Confusion and Weakness*

F. *Time Table of Week's Activities*
   1. Supervisory conference
   2. Interviewing clients and collaterals
   3. Dictation
   4. Travelling
   5. Case study
   6. Projects

G. *Statistics*

(Kept by trainee and brought back by him to concluding sessions)
   1. Daily work sheets
   2. Monthly statistical report

H. *Supervisor's Comments*

Concluding with recommendation for continuing employment, transfer, or terminating employment.

This outline, like the first one, is intended to give the trainee a guide in preparing for the interview, to give form and order to the interview itself and to the written record which is prepared following it. The record can be brief. It could allude only to those segments of the outline in which difficulties are being experienced by the trainee in learning or by the supervisor in teaching. It usually gathers up the positive signs of growth in a sentence, "the trainee is making satisfactory progress in all other areas," though special mention may be made of the parts of the work in which he seems to have progressed beyond expectation. In the interview itself, all these segments have been discussed, and the supervisor and trainee have come to their own agreement about the way in which learning will proceed and be deepened when he returns from the third part of the training. The recorded evaluation gives the agency teacher an indication of the special needs of each trainee, which helps in planning and conducting the second group sessions. These concluding sessions will add to the trainee's insight and understanding, confirm what he has mastered, add to his fund of facts, and reveal further knowledge that must be sought. It will give him the assurance that comes from knowing what social work and the agency "are all about," and where he, the developing social worker, fits into the whole.

Carrying forward the illustrations of the two written evaluations prepared at the conclusion of Part I of the training, the second written evaluation on these two people reveals much.

To: Training Supervisor
From: District Supervisor

### Re: Mary Elizabeth Frome

A. *Information about the Trainee*

Miss Frome has fulfilled all the predictions of the first evaluation in respect of relationships among her colleagues and in the community. Her poise, charm and good looks in fact have been helpful in reducing the strain our whole office has experienced in our relations with one local government official. This she has achieved without knowing that strain existed and by being completely natural. She is accepted by and accepting of the people in the community and is active in two separate young people's groups, one a church organization.

B. *Response to Supervision*

Miss Frome's naturalness makes supervision a pleasure. She prepares for our conferences and has never twice asked the same question about procedures. She has mastered to her own satisfaction the way to use the policy manual and has more than once brought to my attention situations which it does not precisely cover. Her attitude to learning is not so independent as to suggest that she resists being told, for she checks the steps she will take over with me each time to confirm her grasp of them. She has a thorough appreciation of the need to dispatch procedures in a business-like way. Her previous work assists in this.

C. *Relationships*

It has been possible for Miss Frome to talk easily about her relationships with her clients. She has herself marked the change in herself in this regard. She could say that her first interviews were "meandering," her clients conducted some of them. She agrees they were not therefore lost, but were unplanned and their purpose not too clearly understood. Now she uses "meandering" as a release when tension seems to mount and can bring the interview back to the matter in hand with some ease. She thinks she can "feel" the meaning of the casework relationship, but cannot put it into words. She has a nice sensitivity, but may be a little over-fearful of hurting the feelings of her clients. She thinks this makes for some constraint on her part. She sees the importance of naturalness and as she put it: "letting her kindness show." She is on safe ground in this. Later, she will be readier to apply her reasoning powers to further her understanding of the use of relationship.

### D. *Progress in Learning*

Administrative procedures are carried out accurately and without fumbling or distress. She learns them easily and understands their necessity.

The progress in using the casework method is praiseworthy. Her lack of knowledge is frustrating to her. She has used the outlines on maturity and normality and on casework to good advantage, and has read Overstreet's *The Mature Mind*. Her recording is a little stilted but is improving; a piece of it appears in the essay she wrote to illustrate a point.

Learning is proceeding with results that are visible to her as well as me. She is moving out of the realm of "What do I do now?" to "What lies behind this problem?"

Miss Frome moved right into her work the day she arrived. Her analysis of the first cases studied was almost a model. The orientation period "took."

### E. *Areas of Confusion or Weakness*

Besides some trouble with recording, the principal point of confusion is the management of case-load. The categorical count of cases is mastered but not the qualitative count. The problem is one of seeing the case-load "whole," and of apportioning time adequately. She has some confusion with respect to the use of the Court to prosecute absconding husbands.

### F. *Time-Table of Week's Activities*

After the first three weeks, Miss Frome has had one two-hour period of supervision in each week. Five to six P.M. conferences were necessary around three critical cases on six separate occasions.

Twenty-eight hours a week are available for interviewing, ten in the office and fifteen in the district. Her district is relatively close-in and only three hours is devoted to travel per week.

Five hours are allowed for dictation on three separate days, one hour for case-study and one for projects. Some overtime use of the dictaphone was necessary, but that is normal for this office.

### G. *Statistics*

Miss Frome's case-load is 263: 120 old age categories; 15 Disabled Persons' Allowances; 3 Blind Persons' Allowances; 52 Social Allowances; 3 Mothers' Allowances; 15 family services; 3 protection of children; 8 adoption applications; 6 children in adoption homes; 12 approved adoption homes pending placement; 3 children of unmarried parents; 20 children in foster homes; 3 boarding homes.

She has given services in respect of approximately half of this number, and has studied, made some plans and B.F.'d the remainder.

### H.  Supervisor's Comments

Miss Frome is a "natural" social worker. She has interest in pursuing further undergraduate courses extra-murally, but I would not advise this until she has grown into the job more firmly. She is in good health, but is tired after a day's work. Next year will be soon enough to undertake academic study.

I consider we are fortunate to have Miss Frome in this office and warmly recommend her continuance.

DISTRICT SUPERVISOR

Re: Mr. Robert Shane

### A.  Information about the Trainee

Mr. Shane has made a study of this community in his own time, and at a recent staff meeting, he was given time to tell the rest of us his findings. It was a good job; he intends to write it up for his own future use. Apart from this he has not, he agrees, become a "part of the community." His working relationships with other professional and municipal people have been purposeful, but a certain element of superiority has tended to make his relationships rather "starchy."

### B.  Response to Supervision

There has been a growing, rather than diminishing reliance on supervision in the past three weeks. Our relationship has strengthened. From the beginning I made it clear that I respected his intelligence and except for one unimportant situation, Mr. Shane was able to grasp unaided most of the routines of the work. Lately he has wanted to talk about his relationships with his clients.

He confessed that he felt himself inadequate in this direction. He thinks the reason is that he is scientifically interested in people and may, therefore, not have "the human touch." We talked about sympathy and empathy. He is not sure that he wants to "feel with" his clients; he is not sure that he has true sympathy. He protests it is not a superiority feeling on his part, but this may be it. In our latest talk he thought he was cultivating humility. We related this to the cases he had brought to discuss. He got closer to the people involved in them, he said. I think this is true, but I do not know whether he is willing to give up his first preoccupation: his purely intellectual interest in people and conduct. In all events, he is thinking about his feelings, and about the feelings which prompt the client's confidence in him. He is using supervision to talk this out.

### C.  Relationships

These are sufficiently indicated in the paragraphs above in respect to his clients.

Among his colleagues in the office, he is admired but one or two have shown signs of being put off by him. These people have not reached out to bring him in, however. Those who have find they enjoy him.

### D.  Progress in Learning

Mr. Shane has found administrative procedures easy to master. He has used the casework method intelligently. His facts have been accurate and he has interpreted them simply and appropriately. He has done the things that were obviously needed. He has shown imagination in respect of rehabilitative planning. His recording is succinct and well organized. As stated above he is now trying to discover why he has not had a better response from his clients.

E. *Areas of Confusion or Weakness*

The skills rather than the techniques of interviewing comprise Mr. Shane's greatest question about casework.

F. *Time-Table of Week's Activities*

This is attached.

G. *Statistics*

Mr. Shane has a case-load of 305, fairly evenly distributed among the categories with the exception of children in foster homes. At his own request, made after we had talked over the cases which were originally in his case-load, the five foster homes were transferred to Miss K. and some of her O.A.A. cases transferred to him.

H. *Supervisor's Comments*

There is no question about Mr. Shane's interest in his work. His attitude is in question in his own mind. This is a healthy sign. It seems to me that his scholarship and intellectual curiosity are assets which we must respect. His "human touch" is lacking, not to the injury of his clients, but to the detriment of achieving fuller helping relationships. As he has himself a growing realization of this, I think he should continue on the job. In another year, he may know himself whether casework or some other field within social work is his forte.

DISTRICT SUPERVISOR

Such written assessments of sensitive people may seem a violation of confidentiality. The fact that the trainee knows what is written, and the use to which it is put, makes him a partner in the whole undertaking. These second evaluations are seen by three people, all of whom know the trainee well: his supervisor, the administrator and the training supervisor. The sharing of this knowledge brings about an integration and sharpened focus in teaching which has much value.

This practice of preparing written evaluations has a variant possible when time and the geographic coverage of the agency permits conferences among the three people whose business it is to know each trainee well. The conference is undoubtedly more satisfactory in the sense that discussion may reveal more than the written evaluation can hope to do. Even here, however, the confidential nature of the matter discussed must be carefully respected. Besides this, the evaluators need to keep the educational nature of these two evaluations uppermost in mind. Only when there are quite obvious signs of emotional disturbance, brought about by the trainee's reactions to his clients or to the responsibilities assigned him, can the evaluators feel free to account for this by probing personality deficiencies. They are faults, perhaps, only in relation to social work. Elsewhere they might not obtrude. The "diagnosis" is made in respect of the effect of this person on the work of the agency. Whatever the cause, the "treatment" is counsel in finding a niche in another field than this.

At the conclusion of the training plan a written statement is required to satisfy the administrative purposes of evaluation. In this, the most important item is the recommendation about continuing employment. The next most important is the statement, prepared on the basis of the final interview the trainee has with the agency teacher, about future educational planning. After six months, the trainee's convictions about further education are usually clear. He can often talk about the plan he has tentatively made to save for his education for social work. Putting this down in the final evaluation gives him assurance that the administrators are aware of his intentions, and concerned about his future. As further evaluations proceed at yearly intervals, and in the course of other normal contacts with the personnel director, these plans will again be discussed. This educational light is not permitted to go out, in other words, and the training supervisor has a responsibility as well, to keep the wick trimmed.

An outline for the final evaluation at the conclusion of the total training period follows:

CONCLUDING EVALUATION

A. Summary of two previous evaluations.
B. Statement of progress made during the training period.
C. Estimate of continuing teaching needs.
D. Special problems if any.
E. Plans for further education.
F. Recommendation.

This outline is now followed, in significant part only, for "Miss Frome" and "Mr. Shane."

To: Personnel Director
From: Training Supervisor

*Miss Mary E. Frome*

C. *Estimate of Continuing Teaching Needs*

Miss Frome and I agreed that it would be easy for her to continue as she has started, getting enjoyment from her work and letting it go at that. She admits she needs to "stiffen her backbone" about study. She learns easily, but needs self-discipline to get started and sustain what she undertakes. This showed up in her work on her essay, which was a good one.

She has pleasure retrospectively in such efforts. Encouragement will therefore be needed in respect of pursuing purposeful study. Help in planning courses of reading, and the use of what she reads, perhaps, in staff meetings, would be helpful.

### E. *Plans for Further Education*

Miss Frome has set a definite objective for enrolment in the school of social work. She believes now she will be able to finance this herself and with the help of her family. In view of her own confession of needing to be prompted to carry out good intentions, it will be helpful to keep this one before her from time to time.

### F. *Recommendation*

It is the opinion of all who have shared in training Miss Frome that she should continue in her present placement.

TRAINING SUPERVISOR

### *Mr. Robert Shane*

### F. *Recommendation*

In view of Mr. Shane's progress to date, it seems obvious that his abilities or talents lie more in the area of research or administration. His interest in community life may suggest that community organization is his field. It is my recommendation, which he knows I am making, that he continue where he is for another six months in order to come to a fuller appreciation than he now has of the meaning and purpose of social casework. After that, it is his and my present thought that he resign and either attend the school of social work or go on to obtain his Master's Degree in sociology. His experience with us, which he considers to have been a helpful one to him, and which has been an intensive learning period, will ensure that his future study and work, in whatever field it is, will result in a "cross-fertilization" of ideas between social work and that field. He is needed in those areas of social work for which he has a special talent. He may elect to take courses in social work. The longer view of his future, however, suggests an even greater usefulness in the synthesis of scientific theories of society through research, writing and teaching. It should be possible for us to assist him to obtain scholarships from university sources.

TRAINING SUPERVISOR

This latter evaluation is perhaps the exception to the rule, but it was inserted as a result of experience with more than one "Mr. Shane." The initial temporizing the brilliant student does in seeking employment in a social agency before qualifying professionally is growing to be a fairly common thing. It would be senseless to say that they were "too brilliant" for social work practice. It is their adaptability that is in question. It is the agency's business to help such people detect their true talent, and to channel that talent so as to use it, now or in the future, to the advantage of the cause social work serves.

These written statements are all forwarded to the office of the personnel director. The summary in the concluding evaluation often suffices to satisfy questions about the trainee's progress. They are all filed on the personal and confidential file kept for each employee. One copy of the concluding evaluation is sent to the local administrator, who shares it with the supervisor. It is then kept in the local administrator's staff files, to be drawn at the end of the year when the supervisor will next evaluate the trainee. The trainee knows all this.

The significance of these evaluations lies not in the fact that they are recorded, since this is accepted by the trainee as one of the requirements of his employment. Rather, the true significance of the process is that it is a process. It goes on moreover, almost daily. Each conference with the supervisor makes use of the evaluatory techniques. The periodic interview for this purpose alone is not therefore feared, but welcomed. It answers the question, "where do I stand in relation to my employer's expectation of me in the total job I do?" In recognizing the trainee's value, it at the same time underlines the necessity of continuous assessment of experience. It induces self-effort in regard to learning. For the in-service trained person who succeeds, formally conducted evaluations give him a security he needs and provide opportunity to set his vocational and educational compass for the remainder of his career.

# IX. The Form of Staff Development

THE ETHICAL DERIVATION, and administrative and professional purpose and intention of staff development, as well as its place in the agency structure and its nature and effect as a progressing educational process have probably had enough attention to establish its pervasiveness and in-knitted pattern. The abstract idea of staff development makes compelling good sense. Transposing it into concrete form is guided by the same good sense. The programme devised to carry it out should obey all the dictates of good agency administration, should exist for the sake of the agency and should use the media which are, for the most part, already available. Staff development is necessary to the completeness of the whole intent and meaning of the agency.

Three things should be taken into consideration when a programme of staff development is set up. These considerations may be thought of as "principles." There may be others which other agencies, as they proceed to develop and test such programmes, will extract and proclaim, but these three have survived the test of many years of experiment and are apparent also from a study of the experience of other agencies.

The first consideration, or principle, which has already been alluded to in this book, but which deserves repeating here, is that learning, development, perfecting of knowledge, skills and self-awareness—that is, growth toward a trustworthy professional maturity—must be self-motivated. The old maxim that you can lead a horse to water, but cannot make him drink is most applicable here. Basic education seldom fails to create a thirst to know more and more with increasing certainty and conviction. To pursue the analogy a little further, thirst is slaked, not with one continuous draught, but as and when the organism signals its need. It is thus in relation both to constant and to special needs that a staff development programme can be effectively devised and carried out. Such a programme must be wanted by those for whom it is designed. To ensure its effectiveness, it must be asked for and partly planned by those who want it.

A second consideration is that the specific programme, any study undertaken as study, be both inclusive and conclusive. Inclusively, the objective is so to involve the minds of all those concerned that penetrative, disciplined thinking develops, is voiced, listened to and given recognition. Conclusively, the objective is that this thinking produce

147

some tangible results. Experiments may be undertaken, evaluated and passed on to the appropriate people within the agency for further refinement which leads to agency action. This fulfils the concept mentioned earlier in this book that staff development is agency development; the professional minds are exercised to achieve the objectives of the agency for the good of the community. In this exercise there is positive growth.

A third consideration is simply to ensure that the staff should not become so intent upon their own development that they fail, or are overly hesitant, to give services to the best of their present ability. This attitude is as contrary to the purposes of staff development as is the attitude of considering administration as an end in itself. The middle course, of making learning certain through practice, is achieved when specific programmes are geared to a time budget. Programmes based on common needs are scheduled constantly: one two-hour period each week for conferring with the supervisor; one two-hour period each two weeks or each month for staff meetings; one three-day period each year for staff conferences. Special programmes required to meet special needs are also planned. A time budget further ensures that these programmes are anticipated with eagerness. They will be prepared for as eagerly. They are periods of refreshment necessary to relieve the spiritual and physical stress which, unrelieved, leads to static or dragging performance and sometimes to a resignation from the agency and the profession.

These principles are illustrated in the following discussion of a programme of staff development. It begins with the most significant part of any staff development scheme, supervision.

### SUPERVISION

Few within an agency are not supervised by someone senior to them, whether he or she is called a supervisor or not. In ascending order, the social worker is supervised by his supervisor; the supervisor is supervised by his closest administrator and by specialized consultants if these invaluable people exist; the administrators and consultants are supervised by their immediate seniors in the line of authority; they, in turn, are supervised by the chief administrator. Only the latter seems free of supervision. However, somewhere above the middle of this ladder of authority the nature of supervision changes and becomes a sharing of ideas among equal partners in the agency's hierarchy. These "senior officials" devote their thought to devising methods to meet new needs as they are found in the community and to refining old methods to better the agency's services. The facts they consider are provided by the staff under them. By means of periodic conferences among themselves, they discuss their ideas, which are reinforced or modified by their colleagues' opinions and judgments. The disciplines of their profession and their offices are fully employed in this planning, and the effort results in learning and growth. At the very top, in considering their submissions, the administrator learns from his lieutenants. What he learns he uses to make decisions, and his authority when he exercises it earns the respect of his whole staff.

The leadership or statesmanship of the chief administrator can best teach the staff how to use this authority when it is delegated to them and, of as great importance, how to take authority. This he does by making himself known to his staff, not for the sake of popularity, but so that he may know, respect and like them. When he makes decisions, as he must and as the staff should know he must, the communication announcing them explains the thought behind them. As he exercises his duties, he follows the established line of authority without fail, dealing firmly with bottlenecks when they occur. He has a trust in his staff which inspires their trust in him. He has a belief in the principles on which his agency is founded and is fearless in upholding it. His decisions reflect this belief. In other words, the chief administrator is the principal teacher within an agency, by his example and by his recognition of his staff's value, showing them how to assume responsibility for their own work and that of others. Staff development begins there.

The authority delegated specifically to the supervisor is usually regarded as twofold. He is charged with seeing that the work is done with accuracy and dispatch and in conformity with the rules, or policies, laid down by a higher authority. He also must teach the staff to use the professional methods and knowledge the agency deems to be best suited to the discharge of its functions. As a rule the two sides of the job of the supervisor are labelled "administrative" and "professional," but in reality, the one cannot exist apart from the other.

This concept of the supervisor's function has two immediate implications when staff development programmes are planned for supervisors around the common needs that they have discovered for themselves. The one has to do with business, the other with skill. The teaching of business operations is the supervisor's function. These operations cannot be taught unless the teacher knows both how and why they are carried out. He must have an appreciation of the whole, moreover, which gives perspective to the agency's work: total case-load equals gravity of community need; total costs compare with results in terms of cases closed; total time measures the possibility of meeting needs adequately. The actual adding up of figures, the handling of papers, the checking of other persons' addition, the ordering of supplies for the office may take so much time that they become obstructive to the real function of the supervisor. These duties, which are important because they facilitate smooth operations, most often were assigned to the supervisor because he was nearest to the operation, or simply because the administration developed this way. It becomes apparent when it is examined that this detail belongs in the administrator's job. He can delegate some of it, but not necessarily to the supervisor.

The illustration given above may be valid only in a large public welfare agency. What is valid in any agency, however, is the necessity of defining the supervisor's functions clearly. This definition becomes a staff development operation when, under the leadership of the administration, the supervisors themselves set about analysing their own work and themselves in it. As a result, some of them may find they are administrators at heart, which is something the chief administrator wants to know. Others may see the meaning of administrative motions with a new clarity. If there are far too many forms, for example, such a group of supervisors may be able to suggest how to consolidate and simplify them. If there are too few, they may be able to design some which will speed operations. They will gain a new respect for the principle of accountability. They will realize anew that administrative method and professional method are an integrated whole, a fact which can escape notice when paper-work is felt to be purposeless. It may result, too, in a realignment of duties as suggested in the preceding paragraph.

Clear job definitions are just as essential for the administrators who carry delegated authority. From both job studies will come statements which can have use in orienting newly appointed or newly promoted supervisors and administrators to their work. The chief administrator can use the deeper understanding he obtains in many ways, one of which may be to obtain equitable recompense for the responsibilities his officers assume. Certainly he will know better from such studies what qualifications supervisors and administrators should possess to do their jobs adequately. If he follows the wise course of a Canadian leader of social workers, the late Dr. Laura Holland, he will alert his officers, as he himself is alerted, to look for their successors on the day they assume office, and thereafter make opportunities which help to develop their potential individual talents.

The orientation of new supervisors to the task of supervision is discussed in some detail in the next chapter. After the orientation, continuing help in learning and perfecting the skills of supervision is forthcoming for them as for the more experienced supervisors, from their nearest administrator and from consultants, all older and wiser and more professionally assured than they. This help is a constant element in the staff development programme for supervisors. This function, to support, sustain and develop the supervisors in relation to the everyday problems with which supervisors are faced, will be written into the administrators' and consultants' job descriptions. In his relationship with the people who are senior to him in experience and position, the supervisor will learn as much by example as by precept. Although administrators and consultants have different functions, their professional maturity will ensure that their lines of authority in respect of personnel do not become crossed and that, by collaboration, they will work out how to meet the special needs of any one of their supervisors.

One of the special needs of all supervisors, in these days of shortages of qualified social workers, which quickly becomes apparent when an in-service training programme is launched in the agency, is learning how to teach. Teaching, after all, is the heart of their work. It ranges all the way from "instruction" to "consultation" if wise replacement policies are observed. That is, the administrators see to it that in each office there is a careful blending of available staff: a quota of qualified people to effect a balanced performance from the office as a whole; a mixture of older and younger people, of men and women, of experienced and inexperienced. This arrangement has obvious values, but for the supervisor of this well-mixed crew, it presents problems. Problems, however, exist to be solved and one should enjoy solving them. It helps to sustain that enjoyment (a condition in which teaching is best done) if the agency recognizes the expressed wish of the supervisors for special help in meeting the challenge of teaching.

In this special area, the agency may not be able to meet the need itself. Even if it can, it may be wise to enlist the help of people who can speak authoritatively on the subject of supervising or of teaching social work practice. This is not class-room teaching. It is inextricably bound to the lives of people—the clients—it is bounded by the scope of this agency, and boundless in the knowledge it supposes the teacher to have. Those who comprehend these vital components best are surely the teachers of social work. Though they may be distant from the agency, it is in everybody's interests, none more than the school's, that a member of the school faculty conduct these special programmes for supervisors.

There are ways of doing this which guarantee returns for the time and expense incurred. (Part of the expense is the payment of a professional fee for the services the faculty member has given.) The supervisors should devise the outline of the plan and determine the subject. They should also provide the leader or the faculty member with materials from which to teach—cases and everyday problems on which the leader may fashion the content of his presentation. Being within the context of an agency's practice, the faculty member himself learns much as he prepares for this experience. After it, he has a greater appreciation of the realities of that practice, which he can share with his colleagues and use in his teaching. The supervisors concerned, meanwhile, have the benefit of skilled teaching which is focused upon their everyday work. What they learn can immediately be transposed into action.

The matter of time or timing is significant in setting up these special programmes. Preparation takes time, but besides the prior thought it inspires, it also quickens the supervisor's powers of self-awareness. He will come to the class with his questions and observations ready. The execution of the plan also takes time. Not less than two days (preferably five) are needed in larger agencies to permit all that should be said to be said and all that can be absorbed to be absorbed. With this time for study made as generous as possible, the agency arranges a special programme annually, or semi-annually if a shorter period is all the time that can be spared. It can become, with benefit, a constant programme. Its constancy ensures a carry-over from year to year among those who remain in the agency, and thus a sure development of skills. It ensures a progression of ideas for subject outline and study materials from year to year which, in themselves, mark development, not just of the supervisors, but of the agency. It ensures a harmony of purpose and a deep good-will within the agency: in being recognized in this way, the supervisor's loyalty becomes a commodity of great value. It may be of interest to report that in the Social Welfare Branch in which such an annual programme has taken place for several years, turnover among the supervisory group has been almost non-existent. Nothing is of greater value to a social agency than a constant, and a constantly developing, corps of supervisors.

One last word should be said about programmes to meet the needs of older and newer supervisors. Consultation on everyday problems, the detail of arranging, of timing, of evaluating the special needs expressed, and of preparing findings of the special plans as they are executed should be funnelled through one office. This should be the office of the Staff Development or Training Division if the agency is large enough to have one, otherwise, someone must take on the duty. If no one else can be spared to do it, then the administrator must.

## EVALUATIONS

Evaluations become a part of staff development only when those who are evaluated take part in them. Human fallibility makes any attempt to judge another, or to accept the judgment of another, a process fraught with difficulties. Both the evaluator and those evaluated have to know what evaluations are for, so that they want rather than fear them. As a medium of staff development, the evaluation should be geared to agency practice and effectively timed. Experience with it will make its meaning clear to the social worker, the supervisor and the administration. However, it is probably wiser for the whole staff to have the opportunity to study its purposes and values before the scheme is launched. Staff meetings can be used for this study. Thus, fears will be replaced by enthusiasm when all discern, before evaluation, the values of the process.

A statement on evaluations prepared ten years ago by the staff of the Social Welfare Branch is found in Appendix VIII. The years have proved its validity. Though it is principally focused upon benefits to accrue to the social worker and supervisor, it also applies to the evaluation of supervisors by administrators. At the upper levels the element of self-evaluation is strongest, of course, especially if the incumbents in these offices have had the experience of being evaluated when practising at the operative level of social worker. There are special skills involved in these offices—teaching and leadership, for example—which do not pertain to the social worker to the same extent, but these need only be mentioned to become the object of self-analysis. The statement found in the Appendix is thus deemed applicable to all levels of staff, and as they originally had a part to play in preparing it, it follows that the staff at all levels enjoy and benefit from the evaluation process it describes.

That statement has another implication in respect to the purposes of this book. It is an example of a "clear definition of agency policy" which, in chapter II, was advocated as necessary for in-service training purposes. This particular definition is necessary in acquainting all newly appointed staff, qualified and unqualified, with the agency's policies in respect of evaluations. It is used in both in-service training and the orientation period planned for professionally prepared staff. In reproducing it, one significant paragraph has been taken from the preamble (which is too domestic to deserve complete quotation). This paragraph reveals the application of a recurring theme of this book: the necessity of administrative decision, based on conviction, in the establishment of any part of a staff development programme. It also illustrates the method used in developing a policy which intimately concerns each member of the staff.

Following that statement of purposes and principles, there is a job analysis. This again is too domestic to warrant reproduction. It is, however, a necessary corollary to any study of evaluation if the first principle—that his evaluation be conducted in relation to the job the social worker is to do—is faithfully observed. The further uses to which a job study can be put need no elaboration.

The form the evaluation takes, its focus and content, is suggested in the following outline. This is a modification and an abbreviation of the earlier outline devised at the time the study of evaluation was undertaken. One of the pitfalls of a written evaluation is that it can suffer from verbosity and repetition. This is especially true for the second and third evaluation made on the same person. The outline below attempts to pinpoint the significant and to do away with the possibility of repetition. The evaluator is reminded to be brief and concise when he is asked for an evaluation. He is also cautioned not to use the jargon of social work to obscure his meaning.

GUIDE TO THE EVALUATION INTERVIEW AND RECORD

District Office
Date
Supervisor
Date of Last Evaluation

Social Worker's Name
Date of Placement (in present post)

A. *Administrative Ability*
    (1) Experience and training (particularly in first evaluations).
    (2) Description of case load and local setting.
    (3) Knowledge and handling of legislative aspects.
    (4) Work habits: organization of job; coverage of case load; selectivity and focus; application of office manual; capacity for steady flow of work; adjustment to pressures and emergencies.
    (5) Knowledge of community resources.

B. *Professional Practice*

(1) Knowledge and understanding of human behaviour and social forces: degree of intellectual curiosity; the interest and type of questioning by the worker, and retention and application of learning in beginning social workers.

(2) Method: interviewing skills, such as planning, timing, directing, focusing, and concluding. Understanding the necessity of securing, and the ability to obtain and confirm, necessary factual data, statistical and social, for study and diagnosis, and of the developing of relationship in this area at this early time.

(3) Integration of administrative knowledge and case handling, ability to interpret the scope of the services and the client's responsibilities to the agency.

(4) Understanding of recording as scientific data; preparation, quality and promptness.

(5) Referrals, within agency or without: proper channelling and preparation of client and agency.

C. *Relationships*

*With client.* Courtesy and respect; warmth and understanding; professional assurance, resulting in a relationship that is meaningful, helpful for client's maximum benefit, and which meets his unique needs.

*With supervisor.* Acceptance of supervisory role; ability to share thinking, accept criticism and use this constructively; problems which derive from personal qualities such as resistance to authority, too great dependence, etc.

*With community.* Agencies, schools, public health, other professions and community organizations.

*With department as a whole.* Other staff members; ability to share and contribute, acceptance of agency limits and capacity to work productively therein.

D. *Summary of Professional Development*

(1) Supervisor's opinion of worker's adequacy in terms of job performance, productivity, helpfulness, and professional growth. Assessment of the worker's present development in relation to his training, experience and personal suitability; his potential for further growth and increased responsibility.

(2) Worker's own awareness of where he is.

(3) Special interests or capabilities; areas in which he needs further development.

N.B. Evaluation to be fully discussed with worker before it is written by the supervisor, the worker reading the written evaluation if he so desires, and being free to add his own comments if he wishes to amplify or disagree with comments made.

Comparison between this outline and those used in evaluating the trainee will reveal their differences. The essential difference however lies in the intention of the two. The training evaluation is an assessment of the trainee's learning abilities; the staff evaluation is an assessment of the professional performance of all those employed as social workers.

Neither, incidentally, is required or seen by the Civil Service Commission which has its own methods of rating the performance of all civil servants not excepting the provincial social worker.

There is this final word to be said here on evaluations. Their significance as emphasized in the foregoing paragraphs might suggest that they could obtrude on the consciousness and work of the social worker to an unwarranted extent. They have, rather, or come to have, an imperceptible influence, something that quickens and stiffens determination to grow. The agency, acting upon the findings of these evaluations, provides what is needed to help each member of the staff to achieve that growth. The evaluations are planned for the end of one full year of practice and thereafter biennially. They are, moreover, kindly rather than hurting in their intention, compilation and interpretation. They recognize value and help the administrators to use it wisely.

### STAFF MEETINGS

In no aspect of a staff development programme are the principles stated at the beginning of this chapter more necessary than in staff meetings. These meetings must be wanted and initiated by the staff to ensure the active participation of all. Their content must come within the functions of the agency. They must include everyone's ideas and reach to conclusions which lead to some action being taken. They should be carefully timed and the time strictly observed.

In the staff meeting, the staff is all together, which is in itself significant. It means that individuals and their individual efforts are replaced by the agency and the agency's efforts. This, indeed, may be one reason why some individual staff members may approach a staff meeting with apparent indifference or, worse, apparent antagonism. It is not the agency to which they are indifferent or antagonistic, it is merely that they are reluctant to give up their preoccupation with their own place in the agency. However, the preparation the staff does individually before the staff meeting, and the nature of the matters discussed in it, can bring about the desired sense of "togetherness" or the "sense of agency" which will foster growth. This growth is partly the result of the individual's identifying himself with a larger unit to achieve more good than he could achieve alone, just as the agency, in its turn, can achieve more good by identifying itself with national and international organizations having similar aims to its own. This propensity for growth is also partly the result of the resolution of feelings which free discussion in staff meetings makes possible. These are not grievances since they are not aired for self-gain—there are other channels for such problems—but rather misunderstandings, or under-understandings, arising from incomplete knowledge. Growth cannot take place amidst doubt or confusion. The understanding of the whole staff dispels doubt; if the doubt is justified, the whole staff endeavours to make their feelings known in appropriate ways to the proper authority.

What is discussed in staff meetings concerns the agency itself. It is expected of the staff of any agency that they, more than anyone else, know what they do, and that they, therefore, "know what they know." It is in the staff meeting that the latter knowledge is attained. Concepts are crystallized and perceptions deepened; curiosity is sharpened and thought quickened; in the interchange of ideas, opinions, experiences and feelings, convictions and principles are reinforced. Seldom is any staff made up completely of people with identical training and experience. The seasoned speak with the authority of their experience. They are listened to and challenged by the young; as long as they are respected by the young, they will give of their experience and be willing to listen to, and even learn from, those who bring forth new thought to bear upon old familiar matter.

It takes wise leadership to bring all that about. Perhaps one reason that staff meetings are sometimes dull and boring is that the leader, knowing it is up to him to make them successful, gets himself into a panic. He may make this state of mind worse by studying hard to correct his feelings. The key to leadership among people with like minds is naturalness—a natural liking for the people led, a natural interest in how they think and what they say, a natural manner that permits a show of good humour. Buttressed by the observance of a few good rules, staff meetings cannot then fail to have good results and to be enjoyable.

They will be worthwhile and enjoyable if they are prepared for and if they result in tangible action. The preparation may amount to no more than knowing what is on the agenda long enough ahead to think of what to say about any part of it. Contributing to that agenda makes it more appealing. Now one and now another member of staff can prepare a statement on a faulty policy for discussion, review a learned paper which throws light on the agency's work, write a report on a staff committee's findings, summarize a case record which has special teaching and learning properties. The administrator may request the staff to study this or that aspect of the everyday work and submit recommendations for changing it for the better. When a community group has asked for enlightenment on the agency's work, a member of the staff may compose an interpretive piece which the staff as a whole can tear to pieces and put together again. The opportunities for preparation, for productive, that is, educational, results, and for subsequent action are legion.

Subsequent action is surer to be taken when staff meetings within an agency of some size are authorized for all levels of staff. Assurance of action is doubly sure when there is an interlocking leadership among these levels. The supervisor is the leader of the district or unit office's staff meeting. The administrator is the leader of the meeting of district or unit supervisors. The chief administrator is the leader of the administrators' meetings. The findings of each are thereby modified and made more precise in the order of the authority and understanding of these higher levels, which communicate final refinements to the top where decisions are made. These decisions are then communicated back to the initiating body. The decision may be nothing more than that nothing can be done at this time, but when the reason is given for this inaction, something has happened. Nothing will go up that is not important; when the best thinking of the staff receives consideration from the head of the agency the intention of that thinking—the development of the agency—is fortified.

The timing of staff meetings is a psychological as well as an administrative problem. Administratively the meetings can be allowed only so much of the agency's precious time, less when staff is in short supply. Psychologically they are timed to relieve stress as much as to achieve staff development purposes. In a busy social agency, physical and mental energies are expended up to the limits of endurance. Staff meetings can be restorative and invigorating when they are spaced at intervals which the agency and the staff find suitable. Once a month, or once every two weeks, seem maximum and minimum intervals to maintain interest and to accomplish the studies undertaken. Emergency meetings can always be called to deal with unexpected problems and the agency is wise when it insists that staff meetings occur without fail—that is, in spite of emergencies—at the time appointed. The administration will determine their length, which should have an ultimate boundary of not more than two hours; after that, restlessness is likely to set in.

The use of staff meetings for group supervision presents problems. Developing techniques in this connection suggest that group supervision is most successful when the staff members are fairly equal in training and experience. The subject discussed is usually one person's work with one or more of the cases he is serving. Criticism voiced or implied by their contemporaries is tolerable and even welcome to many, but criticism by others having less experience may prove intolerable. The leader has much prior work to do to determine what he wishes to accomplish in the use of these cases for teaching. The fear of causing distress may make him apprehensive, and this apprehension will show even though he appears to control it.

For the in-service trained people among the staff, group supervision seems to have many positive virtues, but in this use of the device, direct teaching of principles rather than of the nuances of skill and relationship would appear its logical intention. The time may come, however, if staff meetings are successful, when they will create the kind of freedom in which the staff share their experiences spontaneously with each other. The limits of time demand that the experience to be shared be one from which others may learn, and one about which many are similarly concerned. By and large, group supervision may not lie within the bounds or be the intention of staff meetings in the majority of agencies. This does not mean that group supervision is undesirable. It merely suggests that it is as yet unattainable in the present circumstances of many agencies.

The planning and execution of meetings of the whole staff of large agencies resemble the planning and execution of a conference on social work. There the resemblance ends, however, for this meeting, as all staff meetings, focuses solely upon the agency's work. Institutes or short refresher courses may be a part of this staff conference, but they, too, are conducted in relation to the agency's functions and purposes. These larger meetings, like the smaller ones, are conclusive in that the findings are gathered up and considered by the administration. The administration is present always and from the discussion obtains its own "sense of agency" and responds to the sober, conscientious thought of its staff with an added respect and appreciation. These are morale building as much as staff development affairs; yet without morale, in which mutual confidence is a key element, staff development will not take place.

The rules of staff meetings pertain to large and small meetings. They are obvious to those who have taken the trouble to learn how meetings of any kind should be conducted. Though a standard work on rules of order may not be faithfully followed in this family conclave, the disciplines which rules imply should, nevertheless, be felt. The following rules are intended to illustrate rather than dictate the disciplines of staff meetings.

The agenda is prepared in advance. It contains items left over from or arising out of the last meeting which that meeting has agreed require subsequent discussion. It contains items suggested by the staff.

This makes necessary some device for receiving those suggestions: a committee to plan agendas, or a permanent chairman or secretary.

The agenda is circulated or posted in advance so that all who will attend can think about each item and have something to contribute to the discussion.

The agenda is studied most carefully by the chairman. He budgets the time each item can be given.

The supervisor acts as chairman. The reason for this is that the office of chairman is one carrying authority and this meeting is one which is authorized by the agency. There may be virtue in rotating the chair for purposes of providing experience in controlling and directing a meeting, but the supervisor retains his role as shadow chairman or impartial adjudicator.

The chairman involves everyone in the discussion by calling for opinions and comments. He sums these up, asks for agreement and concludes the discussion. If he is aware of the educational intent of staff meetings, he does not permit irrelevancies, whispered asides, "other-whereness," or trivial impasses to intrude.

The chairman creates the atmosphere of the meeting by his natural-ness and ease of manner. This does not mean that sort of over-done relaxed manner which has a debilitating effect upon others. Of all people, the chairman must be alert. His ease of manner is shown by his ability to meet the gaze of everyone, to modulate his voice to claim attention, to speak without stumbling, to listen and to accord value to what is said. He will inspire laughter and respond to it with enjoyment.

The secretary's office may, with benefit, rotate among the staff. Minutes are brief and confined to the matters on which conclusions are reached or which are deferred for later discussion. These are the findings which will be handed on for further exploration and eventual consideration by the administration.

The staff meeting holds one of the greatest potentials for staff development. The writer commends the subject as worthy of separate experiment and study by all agencies, some of whom would surely be inspired to share their findings through publication channels open to the profession.

## ORIENTATION

The agency's in-service training programme introduces the un-qualified appointees to the practices of the agency; the orientation pro-gramme does the same for the professionally prepared social worker.

The qualified appointees have an understanding of professional practice which needs to be integrated with the practices of this agency in which they have sought employment. These graduates from a school of social work should be accorded the regard and respect which education traditionally inspires. This is not for the purpose of puffing them up by polite patronage but for the purpose of admitting them in a dignified way into the all-important field of practice. The agency assumes that they are willing and able to identify themselves with it to achieve its objectives. At the same time, the agency shows them that, in spite of the difficulties, it has made and is making advances toward attaining standards of service which comply with the community's expectations of results and with the profession's aspirations toward refining methods. This two-part approach to the newly appointed qualified staff creates the atmosphere in which the formalities of reception and introduction will have the best and most expeditious effects.

In large agencies, especially those in which operations are decentralized, there are two kinds of reception and introduction. The first of these is a series of meetings, arranged continuously over a period of some days, with those who head separate parts of the total programme of the agency. In these meetings, broad definitions of legalities and policies are presented and questions invited. The detailed definitions will follow in the second phase of orientation when they are learned by being applied. These first meetings accomplish two further purposes. One is that those who head parts of the work are met and their points of view, their professional acumen and personal qualities communicated by their words, manner and appearance; the other is that the physical setting in which central planning goes on is seen and appreciated for its efficiency, activity and purpose.

Besides broad definitions, the qualified workers, in contrast to the in-service trained people, are ready to receive facts about the agency's history. This history deals with origins and development in terms of the people who were responsible for them. It deals with the problems the agency has faced, is facing and will face. If it is told frankly and honestly, it will incite the admiration of this new group and make them more eager to contribute to the agency's growth. That growth will be commensurate with their own. The programme of staff development is reviewed with them, the longest time being spent on the matter of evaluations. In all that is said, the fact will be made plain that it is up to them to use the agency's provisions for the cultivation of skills. The view will be expressed also that their eagerness to grow toward professional maturity will assure the best use of these devices. On all that is said, the new staff member comments and asks questions.

The second phase of the new staff member's orientation takes place in the office in and from which he will serve the clients for whom the agency makes him responsible. Here the agency's eagerness to see results from this qualified person's work needs to be tempered. He cannot, by the very nature of the casework process, proceed with complete sureness of touch in the first few months of his practice. Much is said today when there is a crisis in the supply of qualified social workers of the wisdom of internship. The crisis itself makes it doubtful that such a plan could be implemented, at least in public welfare agencies where case-loads are large. Nevertheless in all agencies the initial pace of the newly graduated social worker must be slow. The mechanics of the work, the management of time and case-load, the study of records, the developing of relationships and of familiarity with community resources, the adjustment to supervisors and to the world of work, all require time. It cannot, however, take too long. Agencies cannot tolerate dragging feet. Within four months the pace should quicken, in six be at a comfortable stride and from then on grow firmer each time a step is taken.

Experienced, qualified social workers appointed by the agency also need orientation of course. The cordiality and interest accorded any new staff member—the unqualified, the qualified but not experienced, the qualified and experienced, unqualified but experienced—start that person's development auspiciously and with a pleasurable anticipation of the hard but fruitful work ahead of him.

## THE AGENCY'S LIBRARY

The agency's library is a medium of staff development when it is used by the staff. Although the agency may assume that the members of its staff, like all educated people, number reading among their habits, unfortunately there is no guarantee that books bought by the agency will be read. The habit of reading is one which can easily becomed dulled if not lost merely because social workers are so busy doing things that they have little time or energy left for it. However, the agency's library is not, therefore, a useless adornment. Like the agency itself, it needs to be well administered to achieve its purpose.

The purpose of an agency library is, of course, to help the staff to increase their competence. In a library knowledge resides. In an agency library, knowledge of the work of that agency resides. Books are bought which serve the agency, and in this context the agency is its staff. There will be books which will be assigned to the in-service

trained staff as part of the agency's training plan, to deepen understanding of specific aspects of the work. There will be books which
serve the newly graduated social worker to extend his knowledge of
the specific work of the agency which employs him. There will be
books for the experienced trained social worker, increasing his knowledge beyond the immediate boundaries of this agency. There will be
books for the supervisors, and for the administrators. There will be
reference books such as dictionaries, statistical year books, government
documents and reports. And there will be standard works on the
heart of the professional task—man's conduct and society's make-up—
which, in proportion to their education, training and experience, will
deepen the staff's comprehension of human behaviour.

In the acquisition of such books, the application of a principle
pertaining to staff development will pay dividends. The whole staff
should participate by recommending books they think will be of value
to the rest of the staff. A simple form circulated to the staff every three
or four months asking for their suggestions reminds them they should
be keeping in touch with current literature, and at the same time
strongly implies that the agency library is their library. Not everyone
will send suggestions. Those who do are remembered for their interest,
and when the book is acquired, can be asked to review it to show its
applicability to the everyday task.

Another major aspect of a library's administration is that the staff
must know what the library contains. This poses the problem of classification and cataloguing, and as few social workers have a librarian's
training, the task is often baffling. It repays the effort, however, to
learn the rudiments of this skill, and help from librarians will be
cheerfully given if asked for. Perhaps a social agency's library classification system will turn out to be a hybrid of the classic Dewey
system, but the important thing is that it be set up so that subjects
can be easily found when needed, and the books accounted for.

A second step in this classification and cataloguing procedure
requires patient attention, but is of immeasurable value. This is the
classification of the articles appearing in professional periodicals. As
in all professions, these journals contain current additions to the
literature, and the professional social worker regards their advent
monthly or quarterly as a small or large excitement depending upon
his degree of intellectual and professional curiosity. The agency library
should supply each unit or district office with subscriptions to the
major magazines, so that this current material will keep alive the
staff's interest in current professional thought. The back issues of the
journals, however, contain a wealth of material, much of it devoted

to the constant truths underlying professional principle. Much of this is classic writing, too, legacies which profit the spirit as well as the mind. The task of going back and back into the old numbers is an enormous one, but, guided by bibliographies and reading lists garnered from the literature, it is as fascinating a task as it is invaluable.

A sample index to a library catalogue along with classified reading list from the periodicals is found in Appendix IX. Needless to say, each district office of the agency has a copy of the catalogue, and equally obvious, new pages containing the latest titles are added to it annually.

The agency which has a news bulletin can use its pages to publish lists of new acquisitions to the library and reviews prepared by the staff. If there is no such bulletin a monthly or bi-monthly list of reading prepared and circulated to the whole staff helps to ensure the use of the library—or a proper return on the agency's investment of money in the library. This is a duty of the Staff Development Division if such exists, or of consultants if they exist, or of the administrator. If thumb-nail reviews of articles can be included so much the better.[1] This might be a task for a volunteer, one who was once a social worker employed in this agency. (The Social Welfare Branch employs for this job—on an hourly paid basis—one of its former social workers whose permanent home is now in the Polio Ward of a hospital.) However it is done, there is a necessity to keep the staff not only informed of all that is and has been published on the subjects in which their work engrosses them, but also awake to the values of reading.

The question now arises, in view of the comments made earlier in this section, as to when that reading is to be done. During the in-service training period, reading is done in office hours, for what is read is assigned for a purpose and is followed by discussion. Similarly, specific reading which throws light on specific problems being encountered in any social worker's case-load can be permitted if not encouraged during the day, the self-discipline of the social worker being exercised to make this reading count. The place in which the books are housed should if possible have tables, chairs and adequate lighting to make it a quiet retreat in lunch hours. The skilful reader can obtain much from a twenty-minute reading period every day or every other day. Otherwise, reading is a professional duty undertaken on one's own time. Books are taken away from the library, are properly marked out and returned within a time specified by library rules. To encourage

---

[1]The best example known to the writer of the organization and value of such a library bulletin is the State of Colorado's *Library Counsellor*, prepared monthly by Melbourne Davidson, Librarian in the Department of Public Welfare, Denver.

this practice, if encouragement is needed, half an hour at staff meeting could well be devoted to a discussion of budgeting a part of one's leisure time to reading, a minimum, say, of an hour each week, and thereafter, each staff meeting could devote five minutes to a constant agenda item: "What are you reading?"

Much more could probably be said about libraries. Reading is a highly personal habit, and counselling people in respect of what they should read could seem to be an invasion of personal preferences. Appeal to the sense of professional duty is not always fruitful, nor is persuasion. Rather, the cultivation of a reading staff, one that is alert, interested and responsive to the written thoughts of others, is best done by example. Again it is the administrators and the supervisors who set the example. Their attitude to reading pervades the agency. Their talk is interlarded with references to what they have just finished reading or are now reading. They show their pleasure in reading, part of which is their criticism of what they have read. No matter what is written, the art of reading includes the employment of critical faculties. Much that is written will serve the single purpose of arousing thought on current issues. The value of reading increases with the discussion and further thought it gives rise to. Any staff will respond to the patterns of thought they see in their leaders, reading among them. The agency library will have lots of traffic when administrators and supervisors use it, talk about it, take keen pleasure in it. It is not an adornment, a library. It is an agency utility and an indispensable ingredient of staff development, for its use obeys the first maxim of adult education: it is self-motivated.

## Agency Bulletins

Only large agencies, perhaps, can afford a house organ, but the returns on that investment are great. A staff bulletin, whoever edits it (and the Staff Development Division should) emanates from the administrator's office. Little goes into it that does not reflect the administration's viewpoint and attitude. This makes it a reflection of the agency's spirit as well as of its purpose, and the staff, in taking pride in what is reflected, reaffirms its loyalty to this agency and to its aims.

To be sure, the news of people and events which most staff bulletins provide may be the columns which claim first interest. This is all to the good, for the agency "family" is like any other family, held together by relationships and interest in what is happening to its members.

There can be an intimacy about reporting these things which conveys something of the affectionate regard and of the lively delight one has in writing to one's family or friends. When staff people are scattered over a large area, the agency's bulletin will provide the feeling of being recognized and appreciated.

Beyond this, there is another invaluable purpose to be served by a staff publication. Like the agency library, it is the staff's. They contribute to it. This is a crying need. One of the last pieces of writing of the late Dorothy Hutchinson, who contributed so much to the enduring literature of the profession in her too-short life-time, was an appeal[2] for more writing from the practitioner. Here is an admirable way to develop the talent of writing, an admirable way to crystallize the meaning of the social worker's own services, an admirable way therefore to learn by sharing what one knows. This writing, moreover, will be read and its lessons learned, because it is of the work in which all in this agency are engaged.

A staff bulletin, very definitely, is a medium of staff development. It is also a medium for the development of the profession, for it reveals the proof of the profession's efficacy, the results of professional methods in the arena of the agency.

### CONFERENCES

From time to time, one hears criticism of the number of conferences organized for social workers, usually on the ground that they are not very productive. Such criticism is not valid when an agency develops a clear-cut policy in regard to attendance, and when attendance carries with it some clear-cut intention.

The agency must determine how many people each year may attend these several conferences, and on what basis—as a delegate with expenses paid, as a delegate with time-off with pay, or a combination of both. Decisions as to who should go to which conferences are made usually on a rotating basis, so that all members of staff at all levels will eventually have this opportunity. A few if not all such decisions should be made on a basis of the evaluation of any staff member's precise needs, as conferences usually provide learning experiences of an intensive sort. The knowledge that the agency has such policies in itself gives the staff the assurance that the agency is not aloof to the primary value of conferences: the sharing of experience in an atmosphere of dedication to the cause of human welfare.

[2]"Hidden Talent," by Dorothy Hutchinson, *Canadian Welfare*, November 1, 1955.

The agency delegate, indeed anyone who attends a conference, observes the disciplines which surround this privilege. He prepares for the experience, marking which sessions he will attend, giving prior thought to the subjects, having questions ready to ask. During the conference he will associate with his colleagues and in conversation learn from their experience. After the conference he will prepare a critical report for his agency, which will be published in the staff bulletin if one exists, or which will be circulated, or discussed in staff meeting. No conference ever fails, if these disciplines are observed, to profit the agency as well as the delegate. Conferences are seriously planned, and they have equally serious results.

### Educational Leaves

The matter of providing leave-of-absence for further academic study probably should be counted among the agency's personnel practices rather than among staff development media. It falls in the latter niche largely by reason of its relation to in-service training, supervision and evaluations.

A policy in respect of systematic leaves for in-service trained personnel, discussed earlier in this book, is a major administrative matter in that the numbers who may be given this privilege depend upon finding adequate replacements for those away. This usually means that the cycle of agency training of new unqualified people begins again, with resulting hesitation in the progress towards maintaining standards. The number of absences have, in short, to be decided upon on the basis of what absence of personnel the agency can stand at any point without being too severely shaken.

The matter of providing stipends in the forms of bursaries, or leave with full or part pay, is another matter which will vary from agency to agency. The manpower shortage in general, the fact that loss of earning power as much as current expense is involved for the staff person who takes leave to study, suggest the wisdom of providing as much financial help as possible. The example of the United States Department of Health, Education and Welfare, in making federal money available to states for the purpose of training in various important parts of that nation's comprehensive public welfare programme, is one all nations could emulate with benefit. Local governments, community organizations, private foundations need perhaps only to know better all that is involved in order to contribute to the education of the social worker.

The money question is one that is not easy to solve and around it there hovers a kind of desperation. The in-service trained staff, the people on whom a good part of the future stability and development of the agency depends, should perhaps be planned for first. The next most important group—perhaps it is the first in agencies which have few trained social workers—is the agency's corps of supervisors and members of staff who are potential supervisors. Their education will strengthen any agency, and if it is obtained after a period of practice it will pay double dividends. Here and there in this book, there have been allusions to the social worker's "field" of practice. At the time a promotion to the position of supervisor is reached, the social worker pauses to reflect upon his future. By that time he should know where his major interests lie. He may not stay in one agency for the rest of his career, but he will stay in the particular field of activity this agency has helped him determine is his. He will plot his further education then to develop his knowledge and skill in this direction. He will be helped to make his decision and to plan his educational directions in the evaluation process. Any investment of money in the education of this social worker is thus an investment in this agency and the field it serves.

To conclude, education for social work is three-dimensional, involving the social worker, the agency and the school or profession. None can be omitted when the agency grants leave of absence, with or without financial aid, to its staff. In deciding who shall be given this privilege, the administrator takes into account the social worker's gain to himself, the agency's gain, and the gain to come to the profession. The school's co-operation in determining agency gains as well as the individual student's gain is an increasing necessity in these years of crisis. Education for social work and staff development are the warp and woof of the durable material schools produce and agencies purchase and use to the advantage of society.

# X. Alternatives and Adaptations

THE PLAN OF TRAINING and of staff development discussed in preceding chapters was evolved during a full ten-year period and it can be safely predicted that it will never cease to be under critical scrutiny by all who are concerned with preparing staff for the work. Nevertheless, working from the principles and methods on which this plan is based, many variations are possible. They are discussed now in order to reveal how the plan can be adapted to a variety of settings and for people other than the new unprepared recruits.

The foundations of the plan are the simple ones of "learning about the work by talking about it," "learning the work by doing it," "learning by talking about it after a period of doing it," "learning by continuing supervision and evaluation." Each of these requires a formulation of a "content" suited to the nature of the work the agency does, a method of teaching suited to the capacities of the people taught and sufficient time to ensure that the pre-determined goal of this elementary education can be achieved.

To interpolate a thought which many school and agency teachers would probably support, there is within the field of social work education a growing need for teacher-training centres. Whether the teachers are to be trained to work in schools or in agencies, such centres would utilize to the full the texts which are available on teaching and, if it could be done, provide supervised practice in teaching. Virginia Robinson, Bertha Reynolds and Charlotte Towle in their respective books, *Supervision in Social Casework, Learning and Teaching in Social Work*, and *The Learner in Education for the Professions*, have given teachers of social work the benefit of their experience and compelling scholarship. Teaching courses would provide a means to absorb and apply this impressive knowledge. People from the field of education could be employed to help in this training; that is, teachers of social work would learn the unique skills of teaching, and how to measure the results of learning. This is not to suggest that teachers in schools of social work today do not have this knowledge and skill. Rather the thought being advanced is that teaching is a specialized field within social work practice, and its importance demands opportunities for this specialization to be well learned.

Besides knowledge of his speciality, the teacher has a duty to be attuned to the wholeness of his profession and seek to clarify the meaning and relatedness of the parts. He must exemplify the elasticity of mind which permits integration and abhors indoctrination. His principal duty as a teacher is to cause his students to think so that they may arrive at the place where what is taught becomes their own conviction. From every source available, the teacher constantly seeks to enrich his store of knowledge, to seize upon those matters both positive and negative which bear upon and affect the lives of men, to transfer such breadth of comprehension as he can achieve to the growing minds of those he teaches. In his relationships with those he teaches, he displays the humanity, the objectivity, the non-judgmental attitude, the impulse to help others, which will awaken the minds of his pupils to the fidelities and the felicities of his calling. If these qualities are his goal, it may matter little, perhaps, how the teaching is done. The goal is probably never wholly reached, but it would be nearer if, at intervals, teachers could sit down together and talk of teaching.

Many variations on the training plan outlined in this book are possible. Some that are reviewed in the following pages are taken from the writer's experience, others are from the experiments being tried and closely observed in other fields, including the training of volunteers. Others are no more than suggestions, which may be within the bounds of possibility. Specifically, these variations concern the training of staff members who have had a long experience without prior training in the agency; of newly promoted supervisors and administrators; of the staffs of institutions and clerical people. The suggestions apply to training schemes within larger urban centres where like services are given by more than one agency and where the teaching resources of schools of social work may be partially employed. This section also deals briefly with the work-study schemes developed in a few areas in the United States, venturing one or two comments with respect to the agency's responsibilities in such schemes.

## TRAINING OF EXPERIENCED "UNTRAINED" STAFF

The word "untrained" in the heading above is placed within inverted commas to single out and then reduce to proper proportions any opprobrium some people may attach to the word. Statistics prove that these untrained people form the bulk of the staff in the majority of public social agencies. That these social agencies are achieving results from the efforts of their staffs should commend to the world the work of this large number of people. The majority of these workers without formal training have moreover, intuitively grasped and personally subscribe to the basic tenets of the profession of social work. Those tenets are not alone held by trained social workers. The untrained worker regrets his lack of professional preparation as much as the agency does. More than the agency may anticipate, he will respond when training opportunities are provided for him on the job. There could be no better way for an agency to acknowledge the value of these people and to pay the debt owing them than by providing these opportunities.

To be sure, among those who have been performing without any sort of formal training will be a few who will initially resist the idea that training is necessary and among these may be a few who are in administrative posts in the separate departments or offices of the agency. When the chief administrator decides to provide training for the untrained, experienced staff, these sub-administrators are the group to begin with. They know all about the authority an agency must exert over the operation of its services. They "issue instructions," or convey instruction which emanates from above every day. To "take instruction" even when they are not fully convinced it is needed, and to submit to the wisdom of a higher authority in respect of their own and their staffs' training on the job, is surely not out of keeping with their own authoritative functions and experience.

This authoritative approach to learning, however, must meet the obvious argument that no adult can be forced to learn. Forcing, in fact, merely stiffens any opposition to learning and closes the mind around pet theories which may badly need changing. The point in introducing this apparently dictatorial note at all is for the sake of senior administrators who, although convinced that some form of training is necessary for their untrained, experienced staff, hesitate to institute a training plan in face of the opposition they foresee from their first lieutenants. The chief administrator must make this decision just as he makes other decisions and must see that it is carried out. There is a way around the expected resistance to this "order." The decision to initiate such a training plan is no less firm when it is accompanied by an appeal for help from the sub-administrators in planning the content of the training for their untrained staff. It helps to prove the value of providing training for administrators themselves when they are requested to be guinea pigs for the plan being evolved for their untrained staff and asked to adjudicate on that plan's effectiveness. Captivated by this appeal, by its experimental nature, by its solicitation for help, they will not hesitate to obey the order to appear on a certain date. Scepticism will be reduced by the way the teaching is done and will be replaced with enthusiasm and a new purpose if it is done well. But the order must be given; the decision must be made. Few chief or sub-administrators would deny the wisdom and necessity of training the staff so that they will know what they are doing and how they can do better. The wisdom of this is as great as the unwisdom of emphasizing training to the extent that no work gets done.

The teaching which introduced the in-service training programme in the Social Welfare Branch in 1942 began in just that way. A decision was made and a simple and direct order issued. It was issued at the dictate of an administrator who was not a professionally trained social worker, but who was quick and wise in his appreciation of his staff's need for training. He was following a tradition established by others who had preceded him; he needed no convincing about the soundness of that tradition. The "order" went something like this: "All Regional Administrators will arrange their work to permit their absence for three weeks for the purpose of training themselves for newly added services. Following this period of three weeks, plans are being laid for all experienced personnel to have similar training. You will be notified in due course as to the length of time this staff training will take, and which of your staff will receive this training and at what specific time." Certainly nothing could be more direct and, for many people, directness has its own appeal. The regional administrators of that day obeyed. They were themselves refreshed and reassured by the respect accorded them during the training period and have never, since, failed to support the idea and the need for staff development. They now initiate much of it. They have written it into their own job description.

That question embodies a teaching principle which needs to be applied in this training of experienced people. It is the same principle, really, as that applied in the training of inexperienced untrained people described earlier, the principle of beginning where the people who are to be taught "are" in their knowledge of the work. This relates to another principle which can be seen operating in all agency training schemes: the emergence and grasp of theory from an analysis of practice. In the course which education for social work usually takes, practice is the great unknown on which theory is tried.

Thus the training plan for experienced people begins with what they know. They know procedures backwards and forwards; they know the agency "language"; they know community resources at least from a surface viewpoint; they know their clients, perhaps only superficially, perhaps without thought of the causes of their behaviour (which some of these workers might condemn), perhaps with pity, perhaps with regard to their feelings, usually with honest effort to improve the lot in life of the "less fortunate."

The conjectural phrases in the last sentence imply the fore-knowledge the teacher needs to have about the work of his group. It may be gained by study of written evaluations if they exist, or a study of case records, or be unfolded in the first few days of the training sessions. Thus arises another useful, if not necessary, guiding principle in respect of any agency training plan or of its larger staff development programme. Those taught are known to the teacher; the programme is devised to meet the precise needs of the staff at large. The training plan evolved for them is a part of the total plan of staff development. The plan is arrived at after an assessment of their precise needs.

Training plans for experienced untrained staff members can begin after the fashion of Part III of the plan described in chapter VI. A little longer time, however, needs to be budgeted for achieving the group entity or feeling and spirit, without which thinking or learning would be sporadic if not at cross-purposes with the intention of this training. The time allotted for this can be loosely planned. It should certainly review the work each is doing in the same detail and for the same purpose as the first day of the concluding group sessions for the neophytes. To take as much as two days to do this provides time for another thing to happen which will release tensions and bring about freedom of expression and group sanctions on what is thought and said—that is, the testing of the teacher. Case "stories" can be told, the teacher guiding the telling with adroit questions and unfaltering interest. "What was your most interesting case?" The stories will, doubtless, be those where the workers have seen good results for their efforts. The teacher never fails to commend the good in what is told. There will be some, nevertheless, who will test the teacher's sincerity and his acceptance of the experienced worker's value to the agency. For example, in the writer's experience, one case story, told in robust fashion by an older male worker, ended with the proud comment: "I sent that guy to jail for six months." The teacher quietly asked: "And did that do any good?" Quickly, and somewhat sheepishly, the worker replied: "No, none at all." Everyone laughed, including the story-teller, and laughter is a great help in establishing the right spirit. The group's response was immediate: punishment doesn't work . . . what does? The teaching which is possible in reply to that question is obvious. It is better when the group is led to reason out the reply themselves. Their questions are further answered as the whole plan of training unfolds.

Besides this testing of the teacher, another purpose is served by taking time—the creation of patterns of group thinking, talking and feeling. There will be one or two in this group who suffer pangs of imagined inferiority and who will show their suffering by vaguely directed antagonism toward the "in" group among the staff—the shapeless "they," who may be any who know more or who are in authority over them. Antagonisms are the more pronounced if training is unwillingly endured. They tend to evaporate when they are talked about. Let the complaints, the criticisms, the carping, the real or fancied injustices come out freely; in fact, make opportunities for this to happen. The more forcefully they are expressed the better. Some of them will be justifiable, unfortunately, and there is wisdom in admitting it. "The only thing the matter with social work is the social worker, which can be said of any profession, but, more often than not, what is "the matter" with him is the relatively simple phenomenon of growing pains. Certainly he should know more about theory than you do as yet. You know more of the pain and pleasure of practice. Can you share what you know with him and ask him to share what he knows  with you?" The triteness in that statement (probably never made) is obvious. It was composed merely to show that, although criticisms are accepted, they are not left dangling, as the plaintiff probably is as much to blame, if blame is involved at all, as the defendant. All that he will learn will confirm the lesson implied: each contributes to the maximum of his own abilities; each has an obligation to develop his abilities to their maximum.

The plan for this group might be set up in this fashion:

*Mornings.* "Clinics" on established policies, alternated with field trips to give a below-the-surface understanding of resources. Again this clinical examination of policies and procedures gives account of their derivations and subsequent changes.

*Afternoons.* Discussions on professional practices. These, as for the untrained staff, are perhaps focused best when based on outlines of casework principles and normal behaviour and supported by case studies, none of which are from the case-loads of these workers but rather from the work of trained people, and all of which are disguised.

The time allowed for training could scarcely be less than four weeks in a multiple-service agency. In a single-service agency, it could perhaps be two weeks. This, however, is only the beginning of a training plan for the experienced worker. A second experience of this kind is essential as is some carry-over of what is learned into the day-to-day work. The carry-over may include besides supervision, a reading and essay-writing project, like that for the new people, using cases each will select from his own case-load for illustration. The second period to follow may be shorter and planned entirely around their own cases which they prepare for discussion, and around this self-study. An interval of two months is long enough and not too long for this application of casework method and this study to be done. While it is being done, this worker's supervisor, knowing what he was taught in the group sessions, continues to help him to take a deeper look at the cases he carries for the sake of developing his skill in defining the problems which the agency can help the clients to solve. The materials on behaviour and casework are reviewed in the supervisory period. An emphasis is given to examining relationships, of reaching for understanding of unconscious motivations, of accepting the client—understanding while not condoning social or anti-social conduct. The concluding sessions of the training plan can profitably discuss these matters again. The evaluation interviews will mark changes which have taken place in attitude and feelings. The changes are likely to be quite startling and one of them may well be a crystallization of intent to obtain professional training. If that be not possible, then the agency is at least sure that the staff development media it provides to keep the light of learning lit will be used effectively and pleasurably by these people.

## TRAINING OF SUPERVISORS

Specific training for newly appointed supervisors was mentioned in the last chapter and deferred for closer examination here. Unlike the learning experiences provided through staff development media for those supervisors who have been longer on the job, these new people are not as able to think out and plan the kind of study they should have to prepare themselves for supervision. The plan is worked out for them with the help of their former supervisors and closest administrator. If those planning the training can come together with the agency teacher, so much the better. If not, written evaluations, plus definite recommendations as to the content of the plan of training, must suffice. This latter help bases planning not on guess-work, but on observation of performance. It is better if the performance observed has had a specific relation to the skills required in supervision.

For example, the administrative duties a supervisor must assume are so exacting that they must be thoroughly understood. This, in supervision, is more than a mastery of the administrative motions. It includes an understanding of, and respect for, the authority implicit in the administrative controls a supervisor must exercise over the work of his staff. It includes a similar understanding of and respect for those who delegate authority to him. The new supervisor's ability to exercise authority and to be governed by it must, therefore, be observed and evaluated.

Another facet of the supervisor's work is teaching. His ability in this direction will show itself in many ways before he becomes a supervisor. His judgment and his own attitude to learning are signs of it. His abilities to define and evaluate, to relate, to integrate, to transfer the knowledge he possesses are others. Good judgment, clear˙ articulation, lucid thinking, poise and humour also indicate the future teacher.

These administrative and teaching skills are the more clearly observed and evaluated when they are consciously tested. The potential supervisor should have opportunity to assume, in his second or third year of practice, certain delegated administrative and teaching responsibilities. He knows why he is being given these duties and is, therefore, willing to assume them. They are given to him one by one. Successful in assuming one such responsibility (which includes exercising authority over other members of staff), he will then hand it back to the supervisor or another social worker and take on other duties. This can go on until he has mastered all the operative tasks of agency administration and felt the meaning of being in authority over others. To try out his teaching ability, he can share in teaching some aspects of the work to a newly arrived social worker. If he is willing, he could supervise a social worker who is in training.

Thus the training plan for new supervisors begins with an evaluation of experience, and the candidate for a vacancy in the supervisory ranks has some visible proof to offer as to his competence. If there is more than one candidate for the position, the administration will doubtless select the one whose professional knowledge has been effectively used in practice, whose administrative skills have been tested, whose talent in teaching has been revealed and whose ability as a leader has been shown by the way he exercised his delegated authority.

The refinement of teaching skills, the ability to inspire self-learning by use of dialectic methods, to transmit knowledge directly when it is expedient that this be done, to relate the particular instance to the appropriate generalization, to draw inferences and deductions—all these often have to be taught directly. If the new supervisor has, himself, had a good supervisor and has used his knowledge well, he will be well on the way to understanding these skills and techniques. The need to develop the skills of teaching is probably common to all supervisors, regardless of the length of their experience. This new supervisor will be helped to learn the refinements of teaching when sharing in the constant staff development plan the agency provides annually for all its supervisors and which were described in the last chapter in some detail.

There is an initial step the agency should take to help this social worker to walk around the desk and sit down in the supervisor's chair. This is to give him an opportunity to talk about his new functions with senior administrative and consultative people with whom he will, from now on, be working closely. A minimum of two weeks should be allowed for this. It is not "a course" in supervision; neither is it merely random conversation. It is planned, again by the training supervisor, to have sequential form, and the new supervisor takes part in the planning that is done for him. There will be certain matters which the administration will want to include without fail: a review, preferably an historical one, of the entire agency to ensure that this new supervisor sees the work of the agency in perspective: whence it came, where it is, whither it is going. There will be certain parts of the administrative processes which will be relatively unfamiliar; for example, those having to do with personnel practices and with the authority delegated to the supervisor in respect of vouchering for money, ordering office supplies, and so on. These unfamiliar items will be arranged in the time plan for him rather than by him.

His own part in the planning will be his appraisal of the more professional parts of the work with which he still feels uncertain. Some time will be devoted to those administrative parts of the work which he wants to know more about: for example, the legalities which surround the adoption of children, or the correct procedures to be followed in courts of law, or the finer points of eligibility for maintenance and medical care. He will prepare for these sessions by having direct questions ready to ask those in top administrative ranks. They are the "clinic" sessions of Part III of the in-service training plan only sharpened to a much finer point.

The questions in his mind about the skills of supervision he asks the senior supervisor. The Training Supervisor may be the person to help answer these questions if the agency does not have a casework consultant. If he has none, then the consultant must formulate them for him. This is an initial facing of, and talking about, the everyday relationships on which the success of supervision depends. The subject is a vast one and months could be spent in talking about it. The importance of limiting this first examination to a few reassuring essentials is obvious. Whom will you supervise and what are the strengths of these people? How will you plan your week to make sure you give the members of your staff the time appropriate to their particular needs? How will you keep track of the total performance of the staff? Will you read every record or rely upon the staff to bring you the cases they want help with? These are among the techniques rather than the skills of supervision, of course, but techniques, perhaps, need to be ingrained before skills begin to emerge. They give the new supervisor an immediate goal, the attainment of which gives him greater confidence.

Reading courses can be prescribed by the training supervisor, for this new supervisor can learn by reading and must, indeed, set an example which will inspire his staff to use this medium of learning. The records of previous institutes in supervision planned by the agency make the best reading in early stages, as these courses relate the principles of supervision to the work of this agency. Moreover, they were recorded by the training supervisor with just this purpose in mind. When these records are digested, further reading will be forthcoming from the agency library, especially around parts of supervision which demand special skill—evaluations, for example. This latter medium of staff development will also be discussed with the training supervisor during this orientation period, as will all the other facets of the programme, for upon its intelligent use by the supervisor depends much of its success.

One further thing of value is achieved by this period of initial training, or orientation, of the new supervisor. In the past, he has identified himself with his colleagues, all of whom are on the same level operationally as he, although differing in experience. This is not a "bloc" pitted against anyone or anything; rather it is a desirable, often quite tight, relationship in which friendship, easy give and take, social equality and mutual support predominate. The new supervisor must move out of the security this relationship affords him and into a rather lonely position. His excursion for two weeks among the administrative and consultative staff, especially if they have this in mind as an objective, will give him an identification with a new set of people. He will gather, subtly but surely, that they consider him as one of their group. He will stretch up to meet their acceptance of him as one of the planners, assessors and leaders of the agency and—depending upon the effectiveness and quality of the services given—of the community and the profession. When he meets with the other supervisors in the annual institute, in supervisors' staff meetings or on committees, he will find and benefit from the comfort of his identification with those who are at his level of leadership. Meanwhile, he is readier than he would otherwise have been, because of the solicitude and direct help he has had from his agency in becoming a supervisor.

## "TRAINING" ADMINISTRATORS

The agency's training plan for newly appointed administrators, those who have had no administrative experience beyond that included in their everyday work, can follow the same general outline as that for supervisors, the emphasis being, however, upon the special functions of the administrator. The "special functions" of the administrator are, of course, legion. There is literally nothing about the agency he should not know. His orientation will, therefore, seek to establish in his mind the limits of his authority rather than attempt to enumerate and review the extent of his activities. He will have already shown that he has the qualities of personality and character required of those who assume such positions of authority. This new administrator may, in fact, be leaving a supervisor's desk where he has shown skill and interest in the organization of his own office and in the work of those he has supervised, as well as maintaining an easy although dignified relationship with his staff. These are among the talents which, unique to the individual, are assessed in selecting a new administrator.

The skills of administration are built upon these innate qualities as much as upon a mastery of the detail of administration. The new administrator, during his planned orientation period, may want to acquire a complete knowledge of that detail for the sake of the security it will give him. That security will be false unless he has an understanding of the human element in which he will work. Besides the leadership he will give his staff by the integrity of his conduct, he will be doubly effective in his work when he comprehends that authority exerted and details executed are a means to an end, never the end itself. The objective of all administration is to convey and to facilitate the conveyance of the agency's purpose in being. Those who will talk with him during his orientation, or during agency training for administration, will not fail to make this objective clear.

The training prescribed for experienced administrators will take a different form. The desirability of testing out on them, when it is first introduced, the plan and content of training for the experienced, untrained staff has been mentioned in a previous section of this chapter. Whether this is done or not, the administrators should be given the opportunity from time to time to sit down together, sleeves rolled up as in any workshop, with a leader from within or outside the agency, or both, to consider in the abstract the quality of the agency's administration. It will never be totally abstract, for principles, theories and hypotheses will be related at once to practice, affirming what is good, leading to changes in what may be bad. It will never be totally impersonal, for much of the quality of administration is measured in human terms. Self-evaluation will be one by-product.

This sort of discussion among highly experienced people has a deeper significance than that of developing a greater self-awareness, or that of refining administrative practices. It approaches and may arrive at a spiritual level, beyond cogent thought or speech, in which this company of people renew their dedication to the cause they serve, or find that dedication for the first time. This will seldom, if ever, be spoken of, but it will be observable and, in the aftermath, transmissible in the mysterious ways in which things of the spirit are communicated.

The planning of special training events, as suggested above, takes into full account and generously uses the breadth of experience of people operating at this level in the agency. It is not direct teaching in the sense that it is a training plan or a course in administration. It is rather a distinctive kind of learning experience which has a content determined by an assessment, by the administrators themselves as much as by their chief, of common errors or faults in their own administrative practice; the plan they help to evolve is fashioned to give preponderant attention to desirable and accepted principles of practice. By means of that standard, shortcomings can be seen and accounted for and self-effort extended to overcome them. The effect of such effort will show up in the work through the normal channels of communication that exist between this group and the top level of administration. The latter watches for and evaluates any change which takes place and completes the evaluation by means of periodic interviews with each administrator.

## TRAINING CLERICAL STAFF

The members of the clerical staff have, of course, already been trained for their jobs. The training to be discussed now concerns the part the secretaries, stenographers, filing clerks, accountants, typists, and others play in achieving the smooth running of the office and in creating an atmosphere worthy of its purpose. These people are indispensable, of course, but more than that they are, or become, a part of the dynamic entity an agency is. They are capable of great devotion and their devotion will be the better employed when they know to what object it is being directed.

Promotion of those with skill and talent is carried out using the same evaluatory process as for professional promotions. Training in the specific parts of the new job may be given by a social worker, supervisor or administrator, or by the senior clerk in charge of the office. Except for the interview with the supervisor or administrator, which should be arranged at the time promotion is effected, the teaching involved in helping the person promoted to learn his new job deals only with mechanics and can be quite quickly accomplished.

Time and the many duties of the clerical staff do not permit long periods to be devoted to special training efforts. Nor are such long periods necessary. It is, however, quite possible to budget an hour at the end of one day every two months or so to give all the clerical workers a chance to hear and talk about the over-all work of the agency. Seniority in service, or in grades occupied and salaries earned, does give rise almost inevitably, and not undesirably, to cliques among the clerical workers. At the first gathering, it is well to respect this small social phenomenon and ask the most experienced person to call the meeting to order and to be conspicuously active in the discussion to follow. Encouragement given by the leader of the group to the newest workers to take part in the talk, his tacit recognition of the value of each one to the agency, will tend to build easy steps to connect the terraces the people in this group naturally landscape for themselves.

The content of these discussions needs careful planning, should have a sequence of simple and singly achieved objectives and should be capable of evaluation. All should be filled with lively illustration, and should appeal to the kindness of heart and goodness of intent which social work epitomizes. Moral lessons can be freely drawn. Thus the administrator does not lecture from a graph on the wall which reveals the structure of the agency, or its statistics, or expenditures. He takes a case example, a hypothetical one no doubt (although it need not be as confidentiality is one of the things he will teach), and follows its course from the moment the client arrived in the office to the day services were terminated. The supervisor does not talk about the virtues or faults of social work but about Johnny J. whom the whole agency, including the clerical staff, helped to regain his family and home. The social worker does not talk about the villain of the work—Time—but traces the way in which the orderliness of filing, the speed and efficiency of the clerical staff, helped to bring services quickly to bear when a life was threatened by illness.

The group can draw its own conclusions when the story is finished and the question is asked: "What can we gather from that story?" The answers will be a revelation and, from the quality of some of them, an evaluation is made which is added to the personal record for future use.

Occasionally one of the sections of the clerical group will meet alone. This will be necessary when a new procedure is introduced, say on filing methods, which has to be learned by the people concerned. Or the clerical supervisors may be called together to discuss how to evaluate the work of juniors, or how to deal with small misdemeanours. If the agency is decentralized, the people concerned in all adjacent offices will come together in the main office. They are being taught, to be sure, which is economical and efficient, but in being granted time and help in learning how to do their work better, they are also being considered. Such consideration will be repaid in kind.

The desirability of the clerical staff organizing itself into committees for preparing such a programme of studies is perhaps to be questioned. A social agency can become overly organized rather easily and too much time can be used in keeping these committees alive and properly functioning. It is not a part of the duty of the clerical staff to learn how to use the committee process and the democratic process is not ill served when the administration determines what will be taught. The fact that any teaching is provided at all suggests the agency's regard for its clerical staff and, from the first few planned sessions of teaching, there are ways of determining the needs and wants of this staff. Without a meeting, the supervisor of the agency, or the clerical supervisor, can collect the ideas of the workers. Stenographers have many an informal meeting in their coffee-breaks and lunch hours in which ideas, often of much value, germinate. Formal organization of committees is, thus, not a necessity.

### TRAINING OF INSTITUTIONAL STAFFS

In an institution in which people of any age receive care and treatment, whether voluntarily or under compulsion, each member of the staff, no matter how casual his position, is a member of a team, with a part to play in achieving the purposes of treatment. All those employed should be made aware of this and from that awareness become resolved to learn, if they do not already know, how to fulfil these terms of their employment. Those who already know are obviously the professional staff employed. Those who do not know are likely to be the staff who maintain order, supervise during unplanned leisure periods of the day, do the ordering of provisions, prepare and serve meals, garden, maintain the building and generally provide the degree of home-likeness which an institution seeks to achieve. Each of these people meets and gets to know, sometimes very well indeed, the people who are being cared for and treated. They are, in turn, known and sometimes known best, by these people. They can have a profound effect upon the course of treatment prescribed by the professional members of the team. They can be trained on the job to make this a positive effect.

It can be assumed that institutional directors are able to take the same pains in selecting those who will staff the order and management part of the work as in selecting professional staff. In recruiting for some of these jobs, some of the criteria reviewed in chapter III might be applicable. Maturity and simple out-going kindness of heart are surely a necessity, the latter ensuring an acceptance and natural sympathy for those to be cared for and the former suggesting sanity and an ability to develop on the job.

The administrative problem of manipulating work-shifts to make time for training is not a small one, but it is not insuperable. Some sacrifices will have to be made, no doubt, by those who are to be trained in giving some overtime to this while away from their normal duties. Some extra help may have to be hired while training is going on. The importance of giving a block of time to this training, at intervals spaced over a year or two, or three, is considerable. It is proof of the administration's regard for the importance of training to which the staff will respond earnestly.

The principal elements of the training plan previously discussed in this book apply here as well. On the teaching principle of beginning "where these people are" in their experience and knowledge, there is wisdom in beginning with a group comprised of those having the longest experience, as this group will have a wisdom developed out of experience which will be of greater value if recognized and consciously used. A few in this group may have defects of personality which affect their own performance and cause difficulty of a kind not easy to isolate or to take direct action to overcome. The observations made for purposes of evaluation, as well as the effect of the group's acceptance of the subject-matter taught, may help these few to change and, if not, obstruction will be the more marked so that it can then be dealt with. The "authority" of staff development, mentioned already several times, is sufficient in itself to lead to termination of employment.

Two rather significant points which should be mentioned concern not merely the more experienced of the "operations" staff of an institution but also all who work in these vital positions. One is that, because these people are not professionally trained, because they work hard for their wages and because there are relatively few people who seek work in an institution caring for people, the training planned for them could loom in their minds merely as an opportunity to win promotion. The second is that the evaluations, implicit in any agency training plan, could seem to some a threat to employment. Either promotion or dismissal could, of course, be the result of training, but such negative attitudes on the part of the trainees will take something away from the intent of the teaching and could make learning merely a parroting of the leader.

The way in which the training is introduced, in fact the way in which it is announced, can inspire sincerity of effort to fulfil its objectives. Its announced purpose is to build a staff made up of workers who, as they work in their separate positions yet together as a team, bend their energies to help the people in their care to regain social good health. It is intended to fulfil another primary goal of any agency training, that is, the achievement of the objectives of the agency. It will help to impress the non-professional staff with the importance of training if they see the professional staff is learning, too. Staff development for the professional workers can include learning about the operative work of all departments, not merely to know what is done, how and under what conditions, but also to discover and appreciate the influence of the people who man these humbler tasks upon the individuals the professional person treats. The wise warden of Provincial Gaols in British Columbia, Warden Hugh Christie, himself a professionally qualified social worker, insists that the social workers he employs spend time in each of the units of the prison before taking up their professional duties. Among other things, they take on guard duty. The understanding that the professional person thus gains of the responsibilities and sensibilities of the non-professional workers gives him an identification with the total operation.

These responsibilities and sensibilities are the stuff of the training planned for non-professional staff. Taking the more experienced people together, at the start at any rate, will help to reveal flaws in the plan. It will bring forth feelings about the work which can be incorporated into subsequent courses in a natural way. Listening to these men and women talk about their experience will be inspiring and many an idea will come to light which can be put to good use by the administration. Above all else, the experienced person will sense the human value of his work by reason of the recognition he is given for what he contributes, which will make him more willing to learn both the limits and the extent of the work he is employed to do.

These training plans should be planned consecutively for newly employed staff in the three-part orientation-practice-consolidation sequences described in this book and should, without fail, be continued through the use of staff development media, chiefly supervision. The supervision implied here is not the same as for the person thrust into a professional position, nor is it merely seeing that the work gets done. It is, rather, the consistent use of the team approach. Here in the institution is a man or woman, boy or girl, who has a special need to identify with a warm, responsible person who does not wear a white coat, make notes in a book, or sit behind a desk. Here is a friendly, now—since his training—more understanding gardener who is as devoted to people as to his plants. This boy likes this gardener better than the football coach. Let the gardener share what he learns about the boy with the professional staff; let him know a little more about the boy's problem so that he can help carry out the treatment more intelligently. This is the "supervision" implied; perhaps it need not be called by any formal word but merely be the sensible practice of putting the training to responsible use.

## Training Volunteers

The work the volunteer is enlisted to do determines the content and extent of the training he will be given. It is conceivable, though not within the writer's direct experience, that some volunteers, having a desire to serve their fellow-man, needing no salary and possessing the qualities requisite to social work practice, could do the same kind of work and at the same level of performance as is done by the in-service trained staff. Doubtless this service would not be on a full-time basis but, whether full-time or for short periods—when vacancies are not filled immediately or when illness occurs among the paid staff—the same dependability and consistency will be demanded from the volunteer as from the paid staff. With that provision met, the training of this volunteer obviously should be the same as for the agency-trained staff.

When the work the volunteer is to do does not directly touch the client, or, if it does, not in the way or with the intent of treatment, the desirability of providing some form of training is still evident. "Training" may be too ostentatious a word for what an agency can do to prepare its volunteers. Perhaps the word "interpretation" would be better as it implies an understanding of what the professional people do without suggesting that the volunteer will be expected to do the same things in the same way. The professional person, on the other hand, does not do and often cannot do what the volunteer does. The professional person has to understand this and accord this often vital auxiliary person the dignity of his service. With such mutual understanding and respect, a partnership exists which achieves the results intended.

The volunteers, for instance, who work within hospitals and institutions have a job to do today which was only barely touched by the good people in the past who performed the kindly deed of "visiting the sick." That gentle service will always go on in hospitals for the acutely ill, but a new dimension is added in the volunteer services now developing in hospitals treating crippled children, chronic diseases, mental deficiency, mental illness and the infirmities of age. Here the volunteer is a new arm of treatment. He is "the people," the neighbour and friend who extends to the patient the ordinary everyday graces of human relationships, who makes him feel that "people care about me," that he is not merely a "case" but still a part of the world outside. No matter how conscientiously the professional people apply their conviction that it is the whole person and not the disease that is to be treated, their time and the science of their work does not often permit communication of the ordinary, the usual, the everyday flavours of life. The hospital or the institution is not ordinary, usual and everyday. It is grossly artificial. Yet it can become "usual" and supplant the ordinary all too easily for some. Institutional life is, for them, a protection and an easy retreat into dependency. The new volunteer brings the community the patient has left into the institution and gives visible evidence of the joys of independence.

The newness of this service excites the greatest interest among professional people. To the initial training given these volunteers, it would seem wise, after three to six months of operation, that they devote a period of time, planned for the purpose, to talk about what they have done, about their feelings, about their observations, queries, points of difficulty and achievements. This would make opportunity for the evaluation process to take place, not just of the volunteers—whose powers of self-evaluation will be, if they have been successful, well exerted—but also of the programme itself. Again the volunteers whose interests have been involved will be eminently able to do this in a constructively critical way.

There are many other forms of voluntary service in use in many communities and only waiting to be put to use in others. There are committees of all kinds all the time everywhere. Many of them are indispensable and prove their value as being beyond price. Others seem to get nowhere, their members become frustrated, withdraw, and are lost to the cause of social welfare forever. Schools of social work or the agency might well give a course to all students of social work on the conduct of committee meetings. The agency's obligation when it does set up a committee is to choose its chairman with care, clearly define the terms of reference, that is, state explicitly what this committee is to do, set a time limit for its activity, ask for interim reports, and then act upon its findings. A community council could endear itself to member agencies by setting up a short "school for committee chairmen." It could perhaps be followed up by practice and evaluated.

All training or interpretation programmes instituted for the volunteer social worker should make the volunteer feel that he is a useful, needed part of the total service. He will feel this way if he knows what the agency does and why and how and if he knows precisely what his own part of the service is. He will be doubly useful, and doubly gratified by his service, when the agency plans time to hear from him after he has been on the job awhile, at this time helping him further to comprehend his own and total agency efforts, and listening intently to his ideas about the agency's services.

### Training "Co-operatives"

The possibility of a number of like agencies undertaking co-operative training plans for the people without professional qualifications appeals to the writer as being possible and productive. The plan described in earlier chapters of this book has, in fact, proved of considerable value to a few local voluntary agencies in the city of Vancouver over the years, who have arranged for their professionally untrained people to take part in it. It has, indeed, been an advantage to the sponsoring public welfare agency to have these people with us, for the "oneness" of the common task and the close relationship between private and public agencies which can and does, here, exist, can be the more emphatically impressed upon both sets of beginners. More than that, the inspiration behind the organization of voluntary agencies, their democratic roots, their functions of refining and demonstrating methods—in short, the debt owing to the voluntary agency by communities, governments and professions—can be acknowledged to the growing pride of the visiting trainees.

The above arrangement has its limited uses quite obviously. The voluntary agencies participating in the public welfare in-service training plan have been those which are responsible for administering the Province's child welfare legislation within city boundaries. The things taught about legislation of all kinds, and about the application of elementary casework principles and knowledge in agency practice, could nevertheless serve voluntary agencies as they do the public agency as a start in the educational process. Some of the subjects taught seem remote from the voluntary agencies' practices, yet what social worker does not need to know the resources available to all families in the community? The fathers of some children, at least, may be eligible for Old Age Assistance.

The possibility of community councils, or associations of like agencies, combining forces to plan and conduct in-service training seems worthwhile in the light of the above experience. Training is either important or unimportant, and where there is a convinced will, there invariably follows the contriving of a way. All the steps outlined in chapters 2 and 3 of this book seem adaptable to community planning. Firm policies in respect of: costs; who shall teach with what objectives; under what conditions or guarantees of continuing employment the people who are trained will be working; when and after the training takes place; who is recruited, who is retained and who is rejected; all these require setting up in advance. Policies must exist, but they can always be redefined. The important thing is to stand not upon the order of doing this, but do it. The planning for it is the first step.

### AGENCY-SCHOOL TRAINING SCHEMES

The whole content and tenor of this book to the contrary, the writer is convinced that agency training for agency practice is an expediency. There are few, if any, jobs in social agencies which do not, for their proper discharge, require professional preparation. It is only the present and continuing crisis in the supply of professional workers that makes agency training a necessity. This crisis also seems to make necessary a compromise with respect to the skilled use of such qualified personnel as are employed, which means separating off some agency functions to be carried out by them and leaving others to the less qualified. Expediency and compromise are scarcely the ideal; they are condoned only when they are consciously adopted as such and do not become standard practices.

The "educational plan," discussed in chapter I of this book, and so following, was clearly created as an expediency. That it seeks to make the best of that state of affairs is as clear. The end of the plan is the achievement of an education in a school of social work. Its beginning and middle reaches are designed to start that education. The professional safeguards around the plan are the recruiting and evaluatory methods employed. The development of the total staff, with special emphasis upon the supervisors, makes as sure as human frailties permit that the standards of the agency will not, in this period of crisis, distintegrate or degenerate. Experience proves that this plan works.

Two further thoughts arise. One is that the agencies which have seen the wisdom of developing such comprehensive plans as this and others like it have had their efforts recognized, not only by the agency, but also by the people who have gone through these primary grades of education for social work. Their special need, educationally, is for knowledge. These agencies ask the schools to admit them for purposes of academic study of a field in which they have found their feet in practice. It is now their heads they wish to find. Shortly, there will be enough of them to make special treatment of them possible. Such special treatment will, unquestionably, require the setting up of courses which satisfy their hunger for knowledge. This would mean more time in classrooms and in reading than in field-work. If the orthodox methods of teaching social work cannot be altered, then let the agency-trained and experienced student start further along in the course than at the very beginning. Let him have some credit for his experience. He is needed back urgently. The time saved alone would be worth the effort. The agency's evaluations will ensure that the school is not making a mistake. This is said more to suggest than to demand. The forcefulness of the words seeks only to place these propositions on the discussion table. Agency need of qualified staff is the sole justification for that discussion.

The second and final thought is this: other ways out of the crisis than those suggested in this book can be developed. In localities where there are schools of social work, extra-mural courses are picking up some of the slack. In certain parts of the world work-study programmes have developed which admirably hasten the achievement of professional preparation. Government training grants, especially in the United States, give impetus to the movement to overtake the serious shortages of trained people. Paid field-work in some places creates inducements to qualify properly before venturing to practice. In these experiments, the schools are actively serving the agencies' needs as well as the students' and the professions'. But let them not have to do what the agencies should do for themselves, lest the fatigue of the school faculty detract from their normal functions.

All of these, and other ways around and through the dilemma, are laudable, not only because they produce greater numbers of social workers, but also because where these efforts are made, schools and agencies are working together on the problem. Neither is in isolation from the other. Neither is intimidated by the other. They are pooling their thought and their resources for the cause each serves. This is the saving grace of these difficult times.

# APPENDIXES

# Appendix I

## TEACHING NOTES, PART I, OF THE
## IN-SERVICE TRAINING PLAN

The following is a detailed outline of the subject-matter contained within the separate "sequences" listed in chapter v, page 82. The material is arranged horizontally in weekly intervals of time. Rearrangement in a vertical way would reveal the progression of study from day to day, and a time graph of the total four weeks would show the close inter-relation of the separate subjects, lines flowing horizontally, vertically and obliquely to form a fabric rather than a chain.

The teacher as well as time controls the extent to which each of these subjects can be pursued. The purpose of each subject is therefore stated in the outline below, revealing that every topic is immediately related to the work of the agency.

The teaching devices employed are also listed. Though these are varied, all are preceded and followed by discussion of the lessons learned (see chapters iv and v).

### FIRST WEEK

SEQUENCE A: THE DERIVATION AND NATURE OF "SOCIAL PROBLEMS"
(8:30—10:00 A.M.)

*Purpose*

This sequence accounts for the existence of social work. It examines some of the aspects of present-day society which affect individual conduct and family life. The discussion reveals the extent or limits of the knowledge each trainee has of these things, his opinions about them, and his own biases or prejudices. The accent is upon the fairness and liberality of democratic concepts; the philosophic as well as the socio-economic components in man's relations to society; the values of life.

*Period I* (Monday)

In this period the plan of training is introduced and explained; preconceived ideas about social work and the motivations for entering this field are discussed; titles and terms are defined.

*Method.* Free discussion, prompted by the teacher's postulations and questions, each person in the group being called upon to say something, each comment further elucidated by the teacher or the person speaking at the teacher's request. All questions are answered.

*Period II* (Tuesday): *The Evaluation of Western Society and Culture*

(*a*) Brief historical review of philanthropy.

(*b*) Effects of wars and threat of war on manners, morals and conduct.

(*c*) Problems and benefits created by economic conditions.

(*d*) Problems and benefits created by scientific and technological advances.

(*e*) Problems and benefits of increased leisure.

(*f*) Problems and benefits concerned with population, communications, education.

(*g*) The authority of the law.

(*h*) Problems of conflicting ideologies.

*Method.* The group is asked to give their opinions about the problems and benefits of the social order as these seem to bear upon social work. The topics listed above are not, therefore, necessarily discussed in that order. The teacher moves to suggest a topic if the group hesitates to do so. This is the dialectic method. Time dictates that the topics be introduced, briefly examined and left. Allusions to them are frequent in other sequences. Reading is prescribed in these fields of inquiry.

*Period III* (Wednesday): *Particular Problems Examined*

(*a*) Unemployment.

(*b*) Our aging population.

(*c*) Illness and physical handicap.

(*d*) Insufficient and bad housing.

(*e*) Depressed communities and underprivileged families (i.e. poverty).

(*f*) Crime and juvenile delinquency.

(*g*) Mental illness and mental deficiency.

(*h*) Drug addiction and alcoholism.

(*i*) Prostitution.

*Method.* Here besides expressing opinions and preconceived ideas of these problems, the group looks up various references to obtain an idea of their extent and gravity. The references used are the *Canada Year Books*; the *Social Work Year Books*; annual reports of various departments of government; monthly statistical letters and so on. This establishes the importance of speaking from the authority of facts rather than impressions. Discussion is focused on cause and effect.

*Period IV* (Thursday): *Problems Created by Faulty Relationships*

(*a*) The significance of the family; cultural contrasts; the family today in Canadian culture.

(*b*) Family "problem" or breakdown; desertion, divorce, separation; the "common-law family"; indifference to or ignorance of parental responsibilities.

(*c*) Grandparents.

(*d*) School, church and community influences upon the family and relationships.

(*e*) The family is the focus of the practice of social casework.

*Method.* Chiefly dialectic. The teacher is vigilant in observing reticences, feelings and cynicism as these may reflect personal experiences. The focus is upon the family problems the Social Welfare Branch attempts to treat, and the discussion is illustrated by examples drawn from the teacher's experience in the agency.

*Period V* (Friday): *The Meaning of Democracy*

(a) The meaning of "freedom."
(b) The rights, privileges and responsibilities of citizenship.
(c) The meaning of "self-determination."
(d) The principles of social work embraces these concepts.

*Method.* The "Four Freedoms"; the Charter of the United Nations; the International Declaration of Human Rights; the organization of the U.N. to effect these objectives for all mankind, form the base of this discussion. The week's discussion thus ends on a positive note, though not ignoring the difficulties which exist in the realization of these lofty aims.

SEQUENCE B: THE PHILOSOPHY, PURPOSE AND ORGANIZATION OF SOCIAL WELFARE AND SOCIAL SECURITY MEASURES OF THE CANADIAN AND PROVINCIAL GOVERNMENTS
(10:15—12:00)

*Purpose*

To establish what Canada and B.C. have done to meet the problems discussed in the preceding period. Precise teaching of the parts of the federal social security programme which bear upon the work of the agency takes place in this period the next week.

*Period I: British Columbia's Social Welfare Services*

(a) Philosophy and purpose.
(b) Constitutional and legal responsibilities as outlined in the British North America Act; Provincial Municipalities Act, and Provincial Interpretation Act.

*Method.* Discussion based on outline of British Columbia's public welfare programme (see Appendix II), a copy of which each has before him.

*Period II: Concepts underlying the Social Security Legislation of the Government of Canada.*

(a) Definition of terms: social security; social welfare; administration.
(b) Social work convictions re social security.
(c) The arguments against social security.
(d) The present components of social security in Canada: Unemployment Insurance, Family Allowances, Old Age Security, Blind Persons' Allowances, Disabled Persons' Allowances.

*Method.* Discussion is based on the outline of Canada's social security measures which each has before him (see Appendix III).

*Period III: Other Established and Developing Federal Programmes*

(a) The developing rehabilitation programme.
(b) Health insurance.
(c) Indian Affairs, citizenship and immigration.
(d) Penitentiaries.
(e) Health Services.
(f) Social Research.

*Method.* As for Period II, with the introduction of annual reports and other literature which is left on the table for leisure-time examination.

*Period IV: Provincial Social Legislation*

(*a*) The "family" implications of the legislation administered by the Social Welfare Branch.

(*b*) The Health Branch.

(*c*) The Hospital Insurance Service.

(*d*) Provincial Mental Health Services.

(*e*) Provincial Probation Services, Provincial Prison, Young Offenders Unit, New Haven.

(*f*) Workmen's Compensation.

(*g*) Bureau of Economics and Statistics.

(*h*) Provincial Library.

(*i*) Civil Defence.

*Method.* Further discussion of outline of B.C.'s public welfare programme, with notes added to opposite pages.

*Period V: The Local Community's Responsibilities in Social Welfare*

(*a*) The history and growth of voluntary agencies and their influence upon public welfare.

(*b*) The major private agencies in B.C.: casework; group work; health; community organization.

(*c*) Community organization in smaller urban and rural areas.

(*d*) The schools and churches; service clubs; fraternal orders; institutes.

*Method.* Overnight reading assignment of Marjorie J. Smith's *People, Problems and Professional Services* (Canadian Welfare Council (reprint), Ottawa, 1953) starts this discussion. Examination of *Manual of Health, Welfare and Recreational Services of Greater Vancouver* (Vancouver Community Chest and Council, 1952, out of print) further brings this discussion to life. Joanna Colcord's *Your Community* (Russell Sage Foundation) is referred to also.

SEQUENCE C–I: AN EXAMINATION OF "NORMAL" BEHAVIOUR
(1:30–3:00 P.M.)

*Purpose*

To establish criteria of normal behaviour against which deductions may be made with respect to serious deviations from this norm. The deductive reasoning implicit in social diagnosis is thus illustrated.

*Period I: Motivations of Human Behaviour and Social Controls of Behaviour*

(*a*) Instinctive drives—as determined by psychology: the instinct to survive; the instinct toward self-fulfilment (ego-maximation); the instinct toward procreation; the instinct to conform.

(*b*) Social controls—as determined by social anthropology, philosophy, religious doctrine, law: The natural moral laws—governing force, sex, wealth, integrity, and thought as defined by anthropology; religious doctrines in relation to the moral laws; cultural sanctions, taboos, mores; the laws of the state; family patterns, traditions, teaching; community influences; changes in manners and morals which give rise to conflict and insecurity.

*Method.* This is a lecture-discussion and notes are taken. It follows a discussion of an extension of the ideas contained in the definition of "normal behaviour" in the outline on normality and maturity, a copy of which each has before him (see Appendix IV). Points (*a*) and (*b*) above are referred to again and again in this and other periods.

*Period II: Generally Accepted Concepts of Normalcy*

(*a*) Economic normalcy.
(*b*) Environmental normalcy.
(*c*) Physical normalcy.

*Method.* The paragraphs devoted to these subjects in the "Normality and Maturity" outline are focused on the work of the social worker in discussion of questions such as these: "Is it natural to want to work?" "Are the majority of people working in jobs to which they are suited or are wages the major consideration?" "Should wives work?" "Is credit buying good or evil?" "Why do some people get heavily in debt?" "How does one learn to be provident?" "What is the significance of good housekeeping?" and so on. Everyone has something to say revealing his attitudes. The teacher states the social worker's way of thinking about these questions, and cites resources and policies in use within the Branch with respect to them.

*Period III: The Handicapped and the Aged Can Live Economically, Environ-
        mentally and Physically Normal Lives If. . . .*

*Method.* Film showings: *Everybody's Handicapped* and *Date of Birth*, productions of the National Film Board of Canada in co-operation with the Federal Department of Labour (black and white, 20 minutes). Introduction of these films highlights their purpose, and alerts the group to watch for significant points made in the commentary. Each is asked to have at least one question or comment to contribute to the discussion to follow.

*Period IV and V: Maturity Defined*

(*a*) Maturity of action.
(*b*) Maturity of experience.
(*c*) Maturity of responsibility.
(*d*) Maturity of realism.
(*e*) Maturity in object relationships.

*Method.* Discussion based on Normality and Maturity outline. The case to be discussed in the next period will illustrate these points, thus showing how the social worker arrives at an understanding of the degree of maturity and normalcy possessed by their clients.

*Reading assignment.* Reading at home is assigned of chapters ɪ and ɪɪ, *Common Human Needs*, by Charlotte Towle (American Association of Social Workers, New York, 1952). Notes are submitted on this reading. Week-end assignment: reading of chapter ɪɪɪ, *Common Human Needs*; *Interview-ing*, chapters ɪ, ɪɪ and ɪɪɪ, by Annette Garrett (Family Service Association of America, New York, 1953).

SEQUENCE D–I: CASEWORK—AN INTRODUCTION
(3:15—4:45)

*Purpose*

To define the caseworker's approach, manner, and way of thinking about the people he serves; to bring practice to life by a study of case records. The principal focus in this sequence is on the casework method.

*Period I:What is Social Casework?*

(a)  Definitions of social casework.
(b)  Assumptions underlying its practice.
(c)  The logic of social casework.
*Method.* Discussion based on outline of principles of social casework which each has before him (see Appendix V).

*Period II: The Casework Process*

(a)  The art of casework: the client-worker relationship.
(b)  The scientific method: gathering accurate data; study of this data against criteria of normalcy and maturity; the social diagnosis or assessment of the problem; treatment planning; a treatment goal.
(c)  Study of the face sheet of several Branch records.
*Method.* Discussion based on the section of the casework outline dealing with "Process." Examination of actual case records, in which confidentiality is discussed and filing procedures are taught incidentally to the main purpose of this exercise: the social worker's interpretation of identifying information as recorded on the face sheet. This partially satisfies the group's curiosity about the people and the problems they will meet in their work. The teacher alerts the group to the significance of obvious deviations and discrepancies, and to "danger signals" which have to be proved unbased in fact.

*Period III: Study of the Record*

(a)  The purpose of recording; the physical make-up of the Branch record; the names of its parts.
(b)  The social data in the eligibility study is a family history and at the same time satisfies legal requirements.
(c)  Reading of the record to answer the questions: what was the problem, how was it treated, with what results?
*Method.* Lecture with respect to points (a) and (b); silent reading of the same record each examined the day before; a concluding round-the-room reply to the questions posed before reading began—"this is the way to summarize essential points for discussion with your supervisor."

*Period IV: Group Study of a Case*

To establish:
(a)  The evidence to prove and confirm eligibility (an interim and partial social diagnosis) and chronological narrative recording.
(b)  The deviations from the normal.
(c)  The evidence of maturity.
(d)  The social worker's activity in this case.
(e)  The quality of the relationship between the social worker and client.
*Method.* The eligibility evidence is reviewed for the diagnosis it provides of the family's circumstances; the legal implications are deferred until the

Social Assistance Act is studied. The group experiments with deductive reasoning, using as generalizations the criteria contained in the "Normality and Maturity" outline. It sees the principle of self-determination at work. It is led to see the emotional implications of the situation, and in view of the maturity of the clients, their ability to face this crisis. The group formulates a social diagnosis (which is not in the record) and a plan of treatment. The desire to "do something for" these people is discussed, and the effect upon the social worker of the "power" he therefore is exerting (even kindness) is talked about.

*Period V: Film Showings*

(a) *The Roots of Happiness*, Mental Health Film Board, U.S.A. (23 minutes, black and white).

(b) *Friend at the Door*, National Film Board of Canada, 1950 (27 minutes, black and white), a documentary film on the work of the Social Welfare Branch.

*Method.* Introduction of films; questions and comments discussed following the showing.

## SECOND WEEK

### SEQUENCE E–I: BRITISH COLUMBIA'S SOCIAL LEGISLATION
(8:30—10:00)

*Purpose*

A study of the social legislation administered by the Social Welfare Branch to reveal the legal basis of the services given; to trace origins and establish its "true intent, spirit and meaning"; to emphasize the necessity of adhering to the letter as well as to the spirit of the law; to explain the processes involved in amending laws; inculcating a respect for the "limitations of the law." Specifically, to teach the methods employed (legalities, policies and procedures) in bringing the benefits and protection of the law to those who need it.

*Period I: The Social Assistance Act*

(a) The formalities of the law: title, chapter, by whom enacted, date of enactment etc.

(b) The definition clause: "social assistance" is financial aid; aid in kind; aid to municipalities, organizations, persons; counselling (casework) services; health services; vocational training and retraining; generally any aid to relieve destitution and suffering.

(c) The voting of money—"funds appropriated by the Legislative Assembly"; the "Vote Number" in vouchering and accounting.

*Method.* Each clause, many separate phrases and words within each clause or section of the Act are discussed to learn their meaning and implications for administration purposes. Each person in the group has a copy of the Act in front of him.

*Period II: The Social Assistance Act (Mothers' Allowances Act; Federal Public Assistance Act, 1956)*

At least two periods are devoted to a study of this Act, and often three. This is the "parent" Act of the Branch, and is short enough to permit exhaustive review. The new formula of federal sharing of costs of social assistance is here reviewed. The Mothers' Allowance Act is contrasted with the Social Assistance Act.

*Period III: The Regulations to the Social Assistance Act*

(a) Definitions clause.

(b) The duties of the Director and social workers.

(c) The eligibility requirements: residence; personal property; school attendance of children.

(d) The duties of municipalities.

(e) The duties of recipients.

(f) The powers of the Director.

*Method.* The Regulations are read and discussed, with special emphasis upon the relationship between the municipalities of B.C. and the Social Welfare Branch. The importance of the municipality, its sources of revenue, the services it gives, its closeness to its people, are emphasized.

*Period IV: The Old Age Assistance Act; the Provincial Supplementary Assistance for Old Age Security Pensioners; the Blind Persons Allowance Act; the Disabled Persons Allowance Act*

(a) The Federal Acts and the Provincial "Enabling" Acts.

(b) The eligibility factors of each Act.

(c) The method of administration.

*Method.* These Acts are examined, but not read in detail. The group prepares, at the teacher's direction, a chart of the principal eligibility factors to reveal similarities and differences. The reasons for the strictness of the Federal Means Test is explained. The administrative duties of the Provinces are reviewed. Contrasts are drawn between the means tests of the Federal Acts and of the Provincial Social Assistance Act. The difficulties created by too many "categories" of assistance are discussed.

*Period V*

Teaching continues with special reference to the relation of the Disabled Persons Act and the provincial rehabilitation programme.

SEQUENCE F–I: THE ADMINISTRATION OF SOCIAL ASSISTANCE
(10:15—12:00)

*Purpose*

To familiarize the trainees with the administrative process; to teach the use of application and other forms; to acquaint the trainees with the Policy Manual of the Branch and to use it in relation to the Acts studied in the previous period.

*Period I: The Administrative Process in Proving Eligibility*

*Method.* Using a specific record, an application form is filled out as a group exercise. Skills in interviewing are discussed before this begins. The feelings of the applicant are discussed. The social worker's manner and attitude, his sensitivity to probable feelings, his assumption of the client's honesty, his "standing over on the client's side," etc., are all visualized. The interpretation of the Act and of the agency's policies are mentioned to be referred to again in other sessions when the acts are better known. The Declaration is interpreted as a serious part of the application process.

*Period II: The Administrative Process (continued)*

(a) The social investigation leads to a social diagnosis of the situation.

(b) The plan of treatment is determined by a tentative social diagnosis of the client's abilities and disabilities, based on the social worker's deductions based on observations and factual evidence.

*Method.* Comparison of the eligibility study in the specific record with the eligibility outline found in the Policy Manual; with the section of the "Casework" outline (studied the previous afternoon) which reviews the social worker's method of defining the problem and understanding the client, which is thus seen to be similar to the purpose of the eligibility study contained in the policy manual.

*Period III: The Medical Services Provided Recipients of Social Assistance*

(a) The agreement with the B.C. College of Physicians and Surgeons regarding medical attention given by the local doctor.

(b) The Provincial Pharmacy and the local druggist.

(c) The functions of the Medical Services Division with respect to extraordinary expenditures for medical diagnosis or treatment.

(d) The forms involved.

*Method.* The tedium is reduced by inviting the Medical Social Work Consultant to attend this session or the Medical Director, who is a doctor. Either may bring that morning's mail to illustrate their functions.

*Period IV: Applications for Old Age Assistance*

(a) The "application-investigation" process is reviewed.

(b) The application form is filled out.

(c) The "social investigation" form is also completed.

*Method.* Using a specific case record, the teacher becomes the client, and each member of the group takes a turn at asking for information to be entered on the form. The "client" asks questions which have to be looked up in the Policy Manual.

*Period V: The Social History is a Part of the Disabled Persons' Allowance Application*

(a) Study of a sample history.

(b) The social worker's casework services in relation to mentally deficient applicants, the chairfast and bedridden, etc.

(c) Occupational and diversional therapy.

*Method.* Oral review of such a history; discussion of the challenge to the caseworker of working toward the rehabilitation of the "totally and permanently disabled"; and preparation for the afternoon visits to the Western Society for Rehabilitation; to the Canadian Arthritis and Rheumatism Society; to the Cerebral Palsy Association.

### SEQUENCE C–II: THE DEVELOPMENT OF PERSONALITY
### (1:30—3:00)

*Purpose*

To establish the significance of parent-child relationships; to trace the stages of social maturation of the child; to introduce the stages of emotional maturation as defined in the psychodynamic psychology; to define emotional maturity; to consider the significance of the emotions and ways taken to deal with them in every day conduct.

### Period I: The Pre-School Years

(a) Discussion of home reading assignment: chapter III of *Common Human Needs*, by Charlotte Towle.

(b) Film showings: *Terrible Two's and Trusting Three's*; *Frustrating Fours and Fascinating Fives* (Crawley Film Studio Productions, Ottawa, 20 minutes, colour).

*Method.* Discussion of the points made in Miss Towle's book; seeing these points in two charming films.

### Period II: The School Aged Child and the Adolescent

(a) Further discussion of Miss Towle's chapter.

(b) Film showings: *Sociable Six to Noisy Nine; The Adolescent* (Crawley Film Studio Productions, Ottawa, 20 minutes, colour).

*Method.* As in Period I.

### Period III: The Psychodynamic Theories of Emotional Development

(a) The pleasure principle.

(b) The reality principle.

(c) Frustration.

(d) The ego.

*Method.* These concepts are introduced by the teacher, that is, reviewed orally and discussed. The point is made that this serves merely to define terms, and the group is admonished to defer acceptance of these ideas until further study and considerable testing can be given them. These ideas are not unknown to the majority as a rule; most literate people today know Freudian theories rudimentally at least. The child welfare laws and practices discussed in the next week provide opportunities to seen how these theories apply. The point is carefully made that this is psychological theory and not therefore to be mistaken for the psychiatric method of psychoanalysis.

### Period IV: The Meaning of Emotions

(a) Discussion of chapter III of *Interviewing* by Annette Garrett.

(b) Application of these ideas to the cases studied thus far.

*Method.* Discussion which is focused upon the questions and comments brought by the group as a result of their reading. This is a synthesizing session. Assignment of chapter IV: *Common Human Needs.*

### Period V: Visits to Outside Agencies (mentioned in Period V, Sequence F-I).

To hear about and observe the treatment afforded to physically handicapped people by these agencies.

*Method.* Appointments were made weeks before, and the purpose of the visit explained to the directors of each agency. The group is prepared to ask specific questions, and especially to be observant of the patients they see, and sensitive to their probable embarrassment in being observed. Friendly chats with any who seem to welcome them are advocated. This gives the teacher an opportunity to observe the trainees' ease of manner in speaking to people who may be like his clients, and to assess his sympathetic objectivity.

SEQUENCE D–2: CASEWORK METHOD—A SCIENCE AND AN ART

*Purpose*                    (3:15—4:45)

To illustrate further the diagnostic thinking involved in casework; to examine further the casework relationship; to reveal the importance of knowing resources; to relate the casework practice to agency practice—by definition of "environmental modification" and "psychological support."

*Period I: Method in the Casework Process*

(a) Establishing a bridge of communication or rapport between client and social worker.

(b) "Defining the problem" and "understanding the client" are the two interrelated purposes of the social diagnosis.

*Method.* Oral review and discussion of the above points as contained in the casework outline.

*Period II: A Sample Case*

(a) Study of the eligibility factors and the emergence of a plan of treatment in the first or application interview.

(b) The normality and maturity displayed by the client.

(c) The social worker's activities on the client's behalf; the client knows and co-operates in these; the observance of administrative procedures.

(d) The community resources utilized to help the client get on his or her feet.

(e) The summary recording used by the social worker.

*Method.* Oral review of a sample case, each having a copy before him. The points are made in the order listed above, commented upon, and finally summarized by the group. This case is a clear example of environmental modification and psychological support.

*Period III: A Sample Case*—Old Age Assistance

(a) The special needs of the aged.

(b) The findings and use of resources within the community.

(c) The social worker's activities on behalf of the client.

(d) The definitions of "environmental and supportive" casework.

*Method.* Oral review of the sample case, copies before everyone, preceded by a general discussion of the special needs of the aged. Reading is assigned to be done at home of selected articles from the literature. The original record is produced to learn the format of Old Age records. The abbreviated narrative reveals many nuances which are suggestive of the social worker's feelings toward the client.

The outline of casework principles furnishes definitions of casework practiced at the levels of environmental modification and psychological support. The cases studied to date illustrate them. These definitions also define the generalized practices of this agency.

*Period IV: Visit to Boarding Home for the Aged*

This visit is arranged by the Inspector of Welfare Institutions. It is a "friendly visit" to the old people living there; tea is served. The teacher has the opportunity of observing the trainees' ease of manner, ease of speech and general deportment.

*Period V: Visits to Other Agencies*

## THIRD WEEK

SEQUENCE E–2: BRITISH COLUMBIA'S CHILD WELFARE LAWS AND PRACTICES
(8:30—10:00)

*Purpose*

To familiarize the trainees with the principal terms of the child welfare legislation and the courts of jurisdiction involved; to examine major policies in respect of these laws as found in the policy manual.

*Period I: The Protection of Children Act*

(a) General discussion on the question: "When, if ever, should children be separated from their own families?"

(b) Origins of this law and historical development of its implementation.

(c) The importance of preventive casework which precedes the use of the Act; the "approach" to parents who are reported to be neglecting their children; the use of authority.

(d) The decision to lay charges under this Act is based on a clear social diagnosis, which must satisfy the Superintendent of Child Welfare before authority to apprehend is granted.

(e) Reasons for apprehension provided in the Act and the evidence required to obtain an Order of Committal.

*Method.* Discussion of (a) brings out pre-conceived ideas and attitudes towards parents who fail in their responsibilities. This discussion permits the teacher to present the social worker's way of thinking and acting in such situations, with illustrations drawn from experience. Sections 1 to 7 are then reviewed by reading them aloud and discussing each in turn. Case discussions later in the day and week will further emphasize the care exercised in making decisions to apprehend children.

*Period II: The Placement of Children*

(a) The social worker's relationship to the child during the separation process.

(b) The selection of the foster home is made before his apprehension.

(c) The child moves slowly from a receiving home to a foster or adopting home, if resources and time permit.

(d) The foster parents are prepared to receive the child.

(e) The social worker helps foster parents and child to understand each other.

(f) The business arrangements required.

*Method.* This is a lecture-discussion, with examples drawn from the agency's practice. The Policy Manual is consulted for examples of foster home studies and for the administrative procedures involved. The forms used in the latter are examined. Reading assigned: "British Columbia's Adoption Services," by Ruby McKay, Superintendent of Child Welfare (unpublished).

*Period III: The Adoption Act*

(a) The motives for adoption of children.

(b) Legal implications of adoption; review of Act's principal terms.

(c) The adoption home study.

*Method.* As for Period I.

*Period IV: The Children of Unmarried Parents Act*

(*a*) Is the child born out of wedlock at a disadvantage in life?

(*b*) The social worker's focus is the child's welfare and the effort is to help the mother plan realistically for the child's and her own future.

(*c*) The social worker's activities with the unmarried mother begin with concern for her immediate well-being. The social worker is her friend.

(*d*) The unmarried father reveals a sense of responsibility when he admits paternity and voluntarily agrees to support the child.

(*e*) Court action under this Act is a last resort.

*Method.* Lecture-discussion to reveal preconceived ideas and attitudes to this problem followed by a review of the principal terms of the Act, with references made to the Policy Manual to see how it is implemented.

*Period V: The Juvenile Delinquents Act, Juvenile Courts Act, and Boys' and Girls' Industrial School Acts*

(*a*) Is juvenile delinquency a child behaviour problem?

(*b*) The ordeal before the child who is apprehended by the police.

(*c*) The social worker's or probation officer's functions in relation to the court hearing.

(*d*) The decisions the judge may make.

(*e*) The co-operative work when the child is committed to either school, between the school social workers and the field social workers to plan for the child's return to better circumstances.

*Method.* Lecture-discussion, with emphasis upon the child's feelings when apprehended by the police and throughout the court proceedings. The values of probation services are contrasted with institutional treatment. The programmes of the schools are reviewed in preparation of a visit that day to one of them.

SEQUENCE F–2: THE ADMINISTRATION OF THE SOCIAL WELFARE BRANCH
(10:15—12:00)

*Purpose*

To familiarize the trainee with the way things get done, are taken care of, are communicated; to define administrative terms.

*Period I: The Structure of the Social Welfare Branch*

(*a*) The Minister's functions in relation to the Executive Council and in relation to the staff.

(*b*) The general administration of the Branch.

(*c*) The divisions of the Branch.

(*d*) The regions of the Branch.

(*e*) The district and municipal offices.

*Method.* Examination of a structural chart of the Branch. A copy is provided for each trainee on which he writes the names and titles of each administrator, given a thumb-nail verbal portrait of each as this is happening. The lines of communication are pencilled in, the trainee finds his own place on this chart.

*Period II: Office Procedures—Record Management and Filing*

(*a*) The parts of the record; the card index; the administrative necessity of keeping Face Sheets up to date.

(b) The Office Manual.

(c) The filing procedures with special reference to the B.F. '(Bring Forward) system.

(d) The use of the B.F. system in case-load management.

*Method.* The office consultant takes this session, illustrating from a demonstration unit set up for the purpose: that is, filing cabinet, filing materials, cards, etc.

*Period III: Office Procedures—Statistics*

(a) The purpose of statistics; their use by the social worker, supervisor, administrator and general administration.

(b) The daily work sheet.

(c) The relation of the index cards (kept in the social worker's desks) to case count.

(d) The statistical report.

*Method.* The research consultant takes this session, illustrating from samples (copies for each trainee) of one social worker's actual day-to-day activity as recorded on the daily work sheet; from a set of corresponding cards and by completing a statistical form on the basis of this material.

*Period IV: Accounting Procedures*

(a) The total budget of the Branch and how it is estimated and the moneys obtained.

(b) The process of vouchering.

(c) The accounting procedures.

*Method.* The Branch accountant takes this session, limiting his teaching to broad headings, by use of the Accounting Manual, copy of which each trainee has before him.

*Period V: Personnel Practices*

(a) Salaries, increments, superannuation.

(b) Holidays, sick leave, educational leave, retirement.

(c) The Staff Association and employee medical services.

(d) Evaluations.

(e) Staff development.

*Method.* Sections (a), (b) and (c) are quite quickly disposed of, and the matter of evaluations discussed in detail. The outlines used in the training period—one for each of its three parts—is reviewed, each trainee having a copy before him.

SEQUENCE C–3: AN EXAMINATION OF ABNORMAL BEHAVIOUR
(1:30—3:00)

*Purpose*

To review commonly known deviations from the normal and to define and teach correct terms.

*Period I: Lack of Development*

(a) Immature behaviour.

(b) Delinquency.

(c) Mental deficiency.

(*d*) Film showing: *The Feelings of Hostility* (N.F.B. production, black and white, 20 minutes).

*Method.* Discussion of these sections of "Normality and Maturity" outline, followed by introduction of the film to be shown. This film provides a discussion summary by a psychiatrist.

*Period II: Distortion or Deviation*

(*a.*) Definition of medical terms, with emphasis upon the need for medical or psychiatric diagnosis before applying them in casework.

(*b*) Film showing: *Breakdown* (N.F.B. production, black and white, 3 minutes).

*Method.* As for Period I.

*Period III: Review of the Social History Prepared for the Psychiatrist*

(*a*) The casework implications of this history.

(*b*) The statement of the problem.

(*c*) The child's development.

(*d*) The parents' histories.

(*e*) The caseworker's conclusions.

*Method.* The social history contained in a sample case is studied after review of the outline of this history found in the Policy Manual.

*Period IV: The Care of the Senile Aged*

Visit to the Home for the Aged, a unit of the Provincial Mental Health Services.

*Period V: The Institutional Treatment of Juvenile Delinquency*

Visit to the Girls' Industrial School, the Superintendent, after a tour through the building, leading a discussion on the prevention of juvenile delinquency, the after-care of the delinquent girl, and the field staff's responsibilities in working with the girl's family while she is in the institution.

### SEQUENCE D–3: CASEWORK IN CHILD WELFARE
### (3:30—4:45)

*Period I: "Lucy"*

A study of a case record taken from *Social Service Review*, September 1948, "Maintaining Foster Homes through Casework Skills."

*Method.* The group is left for 25 minutes to read this case silently, preparing notes for the last hour's discussion. The discussion earlier in the day is illustrated and in the skilful casework this case shows, the trainees see with what care, as learners, they must proceed in the Branch's foster home programme.

Assignment of reading: *Interviewing*, chapter IV.

*Period II: The "Donald" Case*

A study of an adoption application, in which the casework method, process recording, and changing diagnoses as the clients become better known are clearly revealed.

*Method.* Oral reading and group comment on the casework knowledge and skills the case illustrates.

*Period III: The "Donald" Case Completed*

*Period IV: Visit to the Home for the Aged*

*Period V: Visit to the Girls' Industrial School*

## FOURTH WEEK

### Sequence G: Provincial and Local Resources
(8:30—10:00)

*Purpose*

To familiarize the trainees with the major resources used in the care and treatment of people who are unable to find or provide such care and treatment themselves.

*Period I: The Welfare Institutions of the Province*

Study of the Welfare Institutions Licensing Act, with special reference to the duties of the social workers in the licensing and inspection of boarding homes for the aged (private or public), of maternity homes, hostels, boarding homes for children, of pre-school education, of summer camps.

*Method.* A discussion of the feelings of old people when they can no longer care for themselves, followed by a review of the Act, Regulations and policies carried out as for other acts described previously.

*Period II: Health Resources*

(*a*) Provincial Health Branch: divisions of T.B. and V.D. control; public health units; school health services; sanitary engineering; education.

(*b*) Provincial infirmaries (chronic disease).

(*c*) General and private hospitals.

(*d*) Children's Health Centre; Crippled Children's Hospital; Crippled Children's Registry.

(*e*) Junior Red Cross services.

(*f*) Voluntary health agencies.

*Method.* Brief descriptions of each, following the resources listed in the Policy Manual.

*Period III: Local Resources*

(*a*) Voluntary agencies.

(*b*) Recreational services and youth organizations.

(*c*) The churches, schools and service clubs.

(*d*) The Women's Institute; women's service clubs.

(*e*) The clergyman, teacher, doctor, lawyer.

(*f*) The police, probation officer, magistrates.

(*g*) The municipal clerk.

(*h*) The district agriculturist.

*Method.* Lists are made as the group tells of the people he thinks he will meet in his work.

*Period IV: The Provincial Social Worker and Community Organization and Community Interpretation*

(*a*) Time does not permit the social worker to play an active part in developing community services, though he may act in an advisory capacity.

(*b*) Interpretive speeches must have the Regional Administrator's sanction. The film *Friend at the Door* is the best means of describing the agency's work.

(*c*) The communities of B.C. offer the social worker opportunities for social contacts of an enjoyable kind.

*Method.* This period further serves to prepare the group for the "feel" of rural life, and permits free questioning about the communities in which each will work.

*Period V: Assignment of Essay Topics*

(*a*) Purposes of the essays as an exercise in learning from the literature and in applying this to the work done by the trainee in the subject or category he selects to study and write on.

(*b*) Use of the essays as discussion material in the second group sessions.

(*c*) Review of the topics (one for each category of the generalized service) followed by selection of topics.

*Method.* Discussion of the above points and listing of the topics selected. The reading prescribed (books, pamphlets, periodicals) and the essay outline is sent six weeks later, with a dead-line for its completion and submission. Two months is usually provided for the study and writing to be done.

SEQUENCE F–3 LETTER-WRITING; INTER-OFFICE MEMORANDA; TELEGRAMS
(10:15 – 12:00)

*Purpose*

To teach skills of letter writing and to discover special difficulties this presents.

*Period I: Letter-Writing*

(*a*) The rules of letter-writing.
(*b*) The letter of inquiry.
(*c*) The letter in reply to an inquiry.
(*d*) The letter to the client.

*Method.* After a review of "rules of letter-writing" found in the casework outline, letter-head is distributed, and letters composed around hypothetical situations pertaining to (*b*), (*c*) and (*d*) above. If there are nine people in the group, three take (*b*), three (*c*) and three (*d*). The letters are read aloud for group criticism.

Evaluation interviews begin in this period when the letters are being drafted.

*Period II: Inter-Office Memoranda*

(*a*) The purpose and format of the memo.
(*b*) The memo to a division.
(*c*) The memo to another district office.
(*d*) Intra-office memos: dated, timed, signed.

*Method.* After a discussion of purposes, memos are composed around hypothetical situations, and later read aloud and criticized.
Evaluation interviews continue.

*Period III: Telegrams and Long-Distance Telephone Calls*

(*a*) When to telegraph and when to telephone.

(*b*) Wording telegrams.

(*c*) The telegraphed and telephoned message is confirmed, by letter or memorandum.

(*d*) Emergencies involving the need to telegraph or telephone are cleared first with supervisor and administrator.

*Method.* Composition of several telegrams relating to hypothetical emergency situations addressed to the Medical Services Division and the the Child Welfare Division. These are later criticized by the group.
Evaluation interviews continue.

*Period IV: Evaluation of the Orientation Period*

(*a*) Review of the sequences of study.

(*b*) Composition of critical comments on each sequence and a summary of the values the members of the group found in the whole.

*Method.* After explanation of the purpose and uses of their own evaluation of the study undertaken, the group is left to write their comments. These are not discussed, but left with the teacher for study.

*Period V: Conclusions*

(*a*) Review of separate "categories" of the generalized services of the Social Welfare Branch.

(*b*) Review of the definitions and statement of functions of social case-work.

(*c*) "The Ideal Qualities of the Social Worker," Georges-Henri Levesque, o.p. (published in *British Columbia Welfare,* October 1952).

This session is the last, and concludes with great friendliness; all know each other very well indeed and with mutually held respect and liking.

SEQUENCE C–4: INTERVIEWING, RECORDING, THE LITERATURE OF SOCIAL WORK AND ASSOCIATIONS OF AGENCIES AND SOCIAL WORKERS
(1:30—3:00)

*Purpose*

To gather up the many things said and read about interviewing skills and recording techniques; to encourage a thoughtful use of the Branch library.

*Period I: The Techniques of Interviewing*

(*a*) Questioning.

(*b*) Listening.

(*c*) Talking.

(*d*) Observation.

(*e*) Leadership and Direction.

*Method.* The group has read Miss Garrett's book on interviewing in its leisure time; the chapter on "Techniques of Interviewing" is now reviewed in conjunction with this section of the casework outline.

*Period II: The Techniques of Recording*

(*a*) The kinds of records in use in the Social Welfare Branch.

(*b*) The guides to recording found in the Policy Manual.

(*c*) The general content of the record.

(*d*) The purposes of the record.

(*e*) Suggestions for good recording.

*Method.* Review of sections of the casework outline devoted to recording.

*Period III: The Literature of Social Work*

(*a*) The principal publishers and publications.

(*b*) The writers social workers always read.

(*c*) The Branch library catalogue.

(*d*) Prescribed "general reading" for the next year.

*Method.* The examination of books, pamphlets and periodicals—handling and leafing through them—is followed by an examination of the library catalogue. This is an indexed reading list as much as a list of the books, pamphlets, periodicals and documents in the library. Advice is given on how to use it to plan a reading course, or to obtain literature on specific problems. A mimeographed list of reading suggested for the next year is distributed. How to get the material is explained.

*Period IV: The Associations of Agencies and Social Workers*

(*a*) The Canadian Welfare Council has individual as well as agency memberships. Its purposes and services are reviewed.

(b) The Canadian Association of Social Workers—in-service trained people are not as yet eligible for membership.

(*c*) The Canadian Conference of Social Work.

(*d*) The International Conference on Social Work.

(*e*) The American Public Welfare Association and its Regional Conference organization.

(*f*) Other American agency associations.

(*g*) The National Conference on Social Welfare.

(*h*) The Council on Social Work Education.

*Method.* The people who direct these associations as well as the association itself are described to implant the values of their leadership.

*Period V*

The sessions have ended at 12 noon on this last day.

SEQUENCE H: WHAT HAPPENS NEXT?
(3:15—4:45)

*Purpose*

To make the office to which each trainee is going come to life.

*Period I: The Flow of Work and Dictation*

(*a*) The weekly office schedule: time is allotted for interviewing; travelling to interview clients in their homes; dictation; conferences with the supervisor; staff meeting; intake.

(*b*) Emergencies may upset the schedule.

(c) The stenographer is a person. The dictaphone is a machine.

(d) Getting ready to dictate; accepting constructive criticism of dictation.

## Period II: The Conference with the Supervisor

(a) The supervisor is the teacher and the administrator.

(b) Preparing for conferences with the supervisor.

(c) The supervisor's judgment and his direction of casework prevail until the trainee is ready to assume some duties independently. This latter will not happen in the next four months.

(d) The supervisor's responsibilities in caseload management and administration.

(e) The relationship with the supervisor is conducive to learning.

*Method.* The teacher explains that the supervisor will take over the teaching in the next four months. Questions are many and frank, and all are answered.

## Period III: On Being a Professional Person

(a) Deportment and manners in and out of office time.

(b) Professional ethics.

*Method.* Frank discussion of the social worker as a community or public "servant." Leisure-time activities; the friends one makes; dress and manners make their impression upon the community. The social worker is, however, a person having the right to follow his own inclinations in his leisure time. The Code of Ethics devised by the professional association is reviewed.

## Period IV: Introductions and the Tools Required

(a) Report to the District Supervisor at 8:30 on Monday morning.

(b) Introductions will be made to the staff, and a familiarization tour of the office conducted.

(c) Settling in: check for all the tools needed.

(d) The study of the case records B.F.'d: preparing notes to discuss with the Supervisor at the time of the first conference.

(e) Planning to meet your first client the next day.

(f) Care of office car; mileage and car expense reports; social worker's expense accounts.

# Appendix II

### PURPOSE, PHILOSOPHY AND ORGANIZATION

Provincial public welfare services are organized for the purpose of administering a province's social legislation. That legislation may be regarded as an expression of the citizens' concern for those persons who suffer from social disabilities which affect them adversely, and which, unless treated, could have equally detrimental effects upon their families and ultimately the community.

### Social Legislation is Remedial

All Provincial statutes in British Columbia, according to the "Interpretation Act", are "to be deemed remedial." Hence, in administering social legislation, the Social Welfare Branch has as its objective not merely the relief of suffering, but also provision of social treatment to effect a cure of the causes of that suffering. The efforts of the Social Welfare Branch, in other words, are those of restoring persons to a status of self-direction and self-dependence in so far as the nature or curability of their disabilities permit; the provision of opportunities for purposeful living, even for those who must remain economically or physically dependent, and the protection of children and adults who are in particular need of such protection.

### Professionally Trained Social Workers are Employed

Social treatment can only be given effectively, it is obvious, by a staff which has appropriate training. Hence the Social Welfare Branch employs persons who have had an education in professional social work. Recognizing the infinite wisdom and skill, as well as knowledge, required to do the exacting work entailed in the social treatment of socially disabled persons, qualified supervisors have been appointed to guide the social workers so that they may develop to the maximum of their abilities. In this way the standards of service the Branch gives are constantly improving, to the greatest possible benefit of the people served.

Because there has been a shortage of professionally trained social workers in Canada, the Branch has augmented its staff by recruiting carefully selected persons to whom it has given in-service training. The ratio, however, of professionally trained to in-service trained staff has been kept evenly balanced. Continuing supervision ensures the development of the knowledge and skills of the in-service trained staff, who are encouraged in every way to obtain training as soon as is feasible from a school of social work.

*This Service Covers the Whole Province*

Provincial social legislation is designed to meet the needs of people wherever they may live in the province. Hence district offices are to be found in all the major centres of the province, the social workers posted to these offices covering the surrounding rural territory. The topography and fluctuating industrial development of the province have created many small isolated communities and homesteads, but, though travel conditions are often rigorous, these people are served when needs arise.

*The Social Workers are General Practitioners*

To effect the greatest economies in administration, the social workers serving the rural areas give a generalized service. Like the country doctor they are general practitioners. This generalized practice is also sound professional practice, for a variety of problems may exist within one family, and the family is the focus of treatment. The principles and methods of social casework, which are based on theories of family inter-relationships, are thus well employed.

*The "Divisions" Give Specialized Consultation and Services*

Specialized social welfare services are provided, however, within provincial institutions, hospitals and clinics, such as the Industrial Schools, T.B. Hospitals. While the social workers in these settings work with the client, the social worker in the locality from which the client comes works with his family. An integration of service is effected through correspondence between the field and division, and planning for the rehabilitation of the client is co-operatively undertaken.

Moreover, the senior supervisors in these settings offer expert consultation services to the generalized worker in the District Office, when treatment depends upon the latter having a more comprehensive understanding of an unusually difficult situation. A Medical Social Work Consultant, who works closely with the Medical Director, offers similar consultation regarding serious health conditions which have given rise to, or are aggravated by psychological pressures.

Certain divisions, the senior officials of which are named in the legislation as responsible for the administration of certain Acts, maintain administrative controls over the province-wide service these Acts provide in two ways; through written policies provided in manual form and constantly under revision; through the services of three field consultants who act as liaison between these divisions and the field. Both the divisional heads (and their staffs), and the field consultants give consultation services to the district supervisors.

*The Service is Decentralized*

The district offices of the Branch are grouped geographically into six regions. Each region is under the jurisdiction of a regional administrator, who has delegated authority to authorize expenditures when need is proven. This authority is further delegated to the district supervisors, who, acting upon well-established, well-controlled policies, authorize normal forms of expenditure, obtaining sanction for extraordinary expenditure from the regional administrator. This greatly facilitates the granting of benefits in the local areas.

*Municipalities are Concerned in Social Welfare*

Believing implicitly in the principles of local government, the Social Welfare Branch encourages the active participation of the Municipalities in these social welfare services. Municipalities of over 10,000 must, in fact, establish their own social welfare administrations. Except in Vancouver and Victoria, where a network of long-established private agencies give family and child welfare services (leaving the granting of financial assistance to the city-administered agencies), all other large municipalities give the generalized services of the Social Welfare Branch. Because they do this, the provincial supervisors give supervision to their staffs. Because these municipalities are administering provincial legislation, the Social Welfare Branch provides half the staff required to give these services within municipal boundaries.

Smaller municipalities may elect to have their own social welfare administrator to give the service all municipalities are required to give, under the Municipalities Act, to their "sick and destitute." When they do, and only five do so, the Social Welfare Branch pays half the salary of that official, who also is supervised by the district supervisor from the nearest provincial office.

The remaining municipalities, the majority of them, "buy" the services of the social workers in the provincial offices, at the rate of 15 cents per capita of population per annum. In this instance, as indeed in all the others, the closest liaison is maintained with municipal officials, and often councils, in order that they may authorize expenditure when it is needed, and may be kept fully informed of the social needs of their citizens.

A further stimulation to effecting uniformly high standards of service to people who live within municipal boundaries is provided by the sharing of the costs of welfare benefits. This arrangement provides that the Social Welfare Branch reimburse the municipalities 80 per cent of the costs to them of social assistance grants, medical costs (the province pays the whole cost of hospital insurance premiums), foster home care, and boarding and nursing home care.

*Conclusion*

To sum up, the social legislation of the province provides financial aid as needed and services for the rehabilitation of those who suffer from social disabilities, and for the protection and enhancement of life for those who cannot become self-dependent. The methods used in effecting these ends are those of the profession of social work, its philosophy and goals being compatible with those of the Branch.

Through staff development devices, clearly stated administrative policies and controls, through supervision and consultation, through co-operative sharing of the work and costs with Municipalities, the standards of service are safeguarded and continually rising. The objective of all that is involved in administration is that of helping people to the place where they want, are able, and have the opportunities, to help themselves.

# Appendix III

## PRÉCIS: SOCIAL SECURITY IN CANADA

### CONSTITUTIONAL AUTHORITY

The British North America Act, or the Canadian Constitution, sets out the specific areas of governmental responsibility over which the Government of Canada shall have jurisdiction, and, as specifically, those areas over which the governments of the provinces shall have jurisdiction. Sections 91 and 92 of the B.N.A. Act list these separate areas.

As far as "social security" and "social welfare" are concerned—both of which are mid-twentieth century developments undreamed of by the Fathers of Confederation—the B.N.A. Act gives only very scant general recognition to governmental responsibility in this area. Section 92, sub-section 6, allocates to the provinces responsibility for the "Establishment, maintenance and management of public reformatory prisons, hospitals, asylums, charities and eleemosynary institutions." Modern provincial social welfare legislation falls within the "class of subject" enumerated in that sub-section.

Thus, constitutionally, the Government of Canada has no definite responsibility for services to individuals in time of economic or social need. Various devices, including amendments to the constitution, have had to be employed to permit the federal government to assume responsibility for the social security programmes thus far instituted.

### SOCIAL SECURITY MEASURES

(a) *Old Age and Blind Pensions Act.* Passed in 1927, this Act provided that a proportion of the costs of benefits would be assumed by the federal government from general revenue. To make use of the federal share or to enter into such a financial contract with the federal government, the provinces had first to pass "enabling legislation." This legislation provided for the setting up and maintaining of an administrative office by the province, and adherence to the terms of the federal legislation. Federal government audit of all accounts in respect of benefits determined the right of the province to collect back the federal share.

This device, a federal act implemented through a provincial enabling act, is an example of a way out of the constitutional restriction on the federal government to participate in social security programmes.

British Columbia passed its enabling legislation in 1927 some weeks before the federal act had been proclaimed. The first recipient was a resident of Port Alberni, B.C.

(b) *Unemployment Insurance Act.* Passed in 1941, this Act put into effect the principal recommendation of the Royal Commission set up in

1938 to study Dominion-provincial relations. This Commission (the Rowell-Sirois Commission), dealt exhaustively with the tangled financial affairs of the three areas of government caused by the economic depression of the 1930's. Contributory unemployment insurance was its major recommendation and the only one to be fully implemented by legislation.

The Unemployment Insurance Act was passed in 1941 after appropriate amendment to the B.N.A. Act had been made to permit federal entry into this area of governmental service. It is administered directly by the Department of Labour of the federal government on a nation-wide basis, with offices located in strategic centres within each province.

Under the Act, contributions are collected from employees and employers in approximately equal amounts, and out of general revenue the federal government contributes an amount equal to one-fifth of these combined contributions. Benefits are paid out of the Unemployment Insurance Fund on a ratio roughly equivalent to one day's benefit for each five days of recorded contribution.

Besides the provisions of benefits to those rendered unemployed through no fault of their own, the Act provided for the establishment of the National Employment Service. Designed to help an unemployed person obtain other suitable employment, the N.E.S. has attempted in its Special Placement Division to find employment for the handicapped persons, a service seldom directly related to unemployment insurance. Vocational counselling to the extent of making satisfactory job placements is a recognized function of the N.E.S. officers. Vocational institutes or schools are established in various centres in Canada, capital and maintenance costs being shared among the three levels of government.

(c) *Family Allowance Act*. Passed in 1944, this Act instituted a measure conceived pa tly to maintain consumer purchasing power, partly to bridge the gap betwe·n a rigid wage structure and the needs of larger and smaller families, and ɩ artly to assure more equal opportunities for all Canada's children. Benefits vary from $5 to 8 per child according to age, there is no means test or ɔntribution, the funds coming out of general tax revenue. The annual cost, ; at 1956, was $366.5 million.

(d) *Departmen of National Health and Welfare Act*. Instituted in 1944, this new departmen is charged specifically with developing plans and undertakings designed to ɩ romote the health and social well-being of the Canadian people. Its creation marked the acceptance of federal responsibility for services hitherto considered the sole prerogative of the provinces.

Under a Cabinet Minister, two Deputy Ministers are respectively responsible for national developments in health and welfare. A Research Division fulfils the function of providing necessary data on which existing and subsequent developments can be improved and instituted.

(e) *Department of Veterans' Affairs*. Created in 1944, this department drew together existing veterans' legislation and implemented Canada's Veterans' Charter. These measures for ex-servicemen and women included discharge gratuities, re-establishment credits, land settlement, university and vocational training, special life insurance, medical and hospital treatment, rehabilitation and job-finding services, military pensions, unemployment insurance and cash allowance (W.V.A.) to the needy.

(f) *National Health Programme*. Begun in 1948, this programme is characterized as a "fundamental prerequisite of a nationwide system of health insurance." This plan provided for a series of grants to the provinces to improve, strengthen and extend existing health services and facilities. Grants-in-aid, involving provincial matching funds, were provided for cancer programmes and all types of hospital construction; a full-cost grant for a comprehensive survey of existing services and future needs in health, and continuing full-cost annual grants for research and personnel training of all types.

The next step in this scheme will be the launching of a Hospital Insurance scheme. Enabling legislation will be required by the provinces in order to obtain federal moneys voted for this purpose by virtue of a Federal Act.

(g) *Old Age Security Act, 1951 and Old Age Assistance Act, 1951.* The passage of these two acts did away with the former Old Age Pensions Act. O.A.A. continues for 65- to 69-year-old persons on a means test basis, the terms of which are similar to the former O.A.P. Act. The O.A.S. scheme, however, is unique in the world. This "universal" pension is free of means test, is payable to all persons over 70, subject only to a twenty-year residence qualification. Non-contributory, the costs of this scheme were met by imposing an additional 2 per cent corporation tax, an additional 2 per cent income tax (with a ceiling of $60 per year) and an increase in the general sales tax from 8 to 10 per cent.

Two principles are thus involved: "pay-as-you-go" financing, and universality of benefit. The latter relieves the programme of any stigma of "charity" and makes it a purely economic device. Because it is a strictly monetary benefit, the social needs other than financial still remain the responsibility of the provinces and their local areas to meet.

The B.N.A. Act was amended to make possible the passage of the Old Age Security Act. It is administered by the Department of National Health and Welfare, in regional offices in each province. As the administrative machinery required is similar to that of family allowances, the Regional Family Allowance Division is now known as the Family Allowance and Old Age Security Division, the regional directors of the former administering both programmes.

(h) *Blind Persons Act.* Passed by the Federal House in 1951, this Act required provincial enabling legislation. Previously provisions for the blind were included in the Old Age Pension Act. The means test is set forth in the Regulations to the Federal Act but is administered by the provinces. The eligibility requirements beyond medical proof of blindness, include proof of age (18 or over); proof of residence in Canada (10 years); proof of means—calculated on a more generous basis than for O.A.A.

(i) *Disabled Persons Act.* Passed in 1954 and requiring provincial enabling legislation this programme became effective in B.C. in April 1955. It provides allowances (shared 50–50 from provincial and federal revenues) to persons who are eligible in regard to age (18 and over); residence in Canada (10 years); means. A principal eligibility requirement is, however, medical and social proof that the person is "totally and permanently disabled," the meaning of this term being tempered by subsequent definition.

In the first year of operation, 15,441 persons were granted this allowance in Canada.

(*j*) *Unemployment Assistance Act.* Passed in 1956, this federal Act, (requiring provincial enabling legislation) provides money and administrative machinery for federal sharing in the costs of assistance granted to both unemployed and unemployable persons who meet provincial eligibility requirements. The Province of B.C. has a slightly different agreement with the federal government, but in general terms, it stipulates that the federal government will share 50 per cent of the costs of benefits when the numbers receiving them rise above .45 per cent of the population.

(*k*) *Other Federal Services.* (1) Penitentiaries. Reforms in penitentiary administration include provision for trained personnel for classification and remission services. (2) Indian Affairs. Social services for the native population of Canada are gradually being provided. (3) Citizenship and Immigration. Liaison officers perform many services directly to the new Canadian, by consultative work with community organizations and by educational efforts. (4) Rehabilitation. Consultation in regard to Provincial Rehabilitation Services is provided by the Civilian Rehabilitation Board, Federal Department of Labour.

# Appendix IV

## PRÉCIS: NORMALITY AND MATURITY*

The caseworker is in daily contact with human problems—disorganization, maladjustment, abnormality, immaturity, deviation from the normal. It is pertinent that the caseworker have a knowledge of what normality is in order to have a balanced approach to human beings who are for some reason far from even a relative "normal" in their behaviour and attitudes.

### DEFINITION

"Normal" behaviour, or normal reactions to life situations, has been defined as a "composite of generally recognized and accepted desirable standards of living, which society upholds and which have been laid down in the mores and laws."

### GENERAL CONCEPTS OF THE NORMAL

A person may be said to be normal who fills an average niche in society, is *useful* to himself and society, can *adjust* to changing situations, and keep a *balance* under ordinary conditions and the usual situations of stress and strain.

These concepts may be considered in casework from the economic, environmental, health, psychological and sociological viewpoints. It is to the deviations from these standards of normalcy that the caseworker must be especially sensitive.

(a) *Economic normality* may be judged by: (1) the individual's ability to maintain himself in terms of income and material goods, services and comforts, so as not to require outside help in cash or kind; (2) the fact that the individual maintains employment in a type of work he likes, to which he is adapted, and which pays him a living wage.

(b) *Environmental normality.* What a person does with his economic assets is another indication of a normal adjustment to life. In this area, the caseworker may judge the degree of normality the person has achieved by: (1) ability to budget his accounts and money to meet his obligations; (2) the maintenance of his home, which should be well managed and arranged,

*This précis is a summary of Dr. LeRoy M.A. Maeder's classic paper, "Diagnostic Criteria: A Concept of Normal and Abnormal," first published in *The Family*, 1941, and subsequently republished in *Principles and Techniques in Social Casework: Selected Articles*, ed. Cora Kasius, Family Service Association of America, New York, 1950. Grateful acknowledgment is made to both the author and the publishers for their kind permission to reprint their material in this form.

clean, with an effort made to have an attractive dwelling and grounds; (3) efficiency in his job; (4) use of public and private recreational facilities, in accordance with the customs of the community and his personal preferences; (5) affiliation with a church for religious, social and recreational purposes; (6) balance of the individual's time between work, play or home life, and sleep; (7) use of average educational opportunities, the press, radio, books; (8) utilization of opportunity for group living, which satisfies a basic human need for some association with one's fellows outside the family group; (9) participation in or opinions about community affairs.

(c) *Physical normality.* To be physically normal requires generally that a person have: (1) a generally healthy body, relatively free from painful, disabling, contagious or active social disease, injury or defect which may interfere with earning, enjoyment of life and social functioning; (2) fairly accurate sense organs and balanced perceptions, relatively sound in motor apparatus, skeletal structure and limb, all of which enables him to get about, speak and care for himself adequately; (3) a sensible health régime, which implies (besides a balanced rhythm of eating, sleeping and elimination) an avoidance of excesses, unjustified health risks and undue fatigue.

(d) *Psychological and sociological normality* implies the adjustment and maturity of the person in himself as an individual, and in his relationships with others. "Adjustment" and "maturity" imply that a person is effective in life situations and is capable of making and enjoying group relationships.

To be mature, an individual must be capable of action, have learned by experience, accept responsibility, be governed by realism, and capable of having complete, warm object relationships.

(1) *Maturity in action* is shown in the areas of observation, thought, judgment, speech, sex, work, play and social relationships. Normal action is self-initiated, has a purpose, is properly directed, is controlled when necessary, co-ordinated with the outside world, and continued in order to accomplish an average ambition.

(2) *Maturity of experience* denotes that a person has profited by living through each stage of his development, retained what is of use in his social functioning, and sloughed off childish ways no longer of use to him.

Through experience he thus has good habits, attitudes and ways of thinking and reacting. He will have, too, a clear-cut character, positive cultural traits, and realistic ideals. He will have definite ideas, ambitions, likes and dislikes. He will have a sane attitude towards religion and morals and politics. He will have a realistic attitude towards money, considering it as a medium of exchange, and an important power, neither over- nor under-estimating its significance.

(3) *Maturity of responsibility* is revealed when a person is self-dependent, serious, and able to take responsibility for his own successes and failures. He is his own ultimate authority in the progress of his life, and recognizes prestige as a result of self-accomplishment. He is able, moreover, to give direction and stability to others, and to accept the responsibility of dependence of others upon him.

(4) *Mature realism* enables a person to see the world as it is, and himself as he is. Maturity in this respect enables him to give regard, affection and love where they are merited, and enables him to withdraw his regard when it ceases to be merited. A realistically mature person suffers only from

necessity. He does not love his enemy, but rather protects himself against him. He will experience guilt, remorse and sorrow only when the necessity for these feelings are unavoidable. He may have healthy anxiety reactions to warn him of impending danger, but he is neither hair-triggered nor sluggish in responding to apparent danger. He can foresee obstacles and either overcome them or side-step them.

(5) *Maturity in object relationships* is characterized by a person's ability to relate fully and warmly to another person as a human entity. This is an altruistic relationship having three main elements: *anchorage*—stable, dependable, but not necessarily perpetual security that derives from other persons; *understanding*—knowledge of another person's traits of character and personality which has been gained through observation, conversation, association; *acceptance*—pleasure and value that derive from association with a friend over and above anchorage and understanding. This is based on similar interests, experiences and objectives, and connotes mutual selection and attraction.

(6) *Affectional responses* may be considered as follows: (*a*) purely sensual and sexual impulses, or those nearest to the physiological; (*b*) tender or affectional impulses and responses; (*c*) object relationship; (*d*) sublimated responses, which are intellectual, and associated with cultural interests —work, art, literature, travel. All four of these may be present in the marital relationship. The last three are present in the filio-parental relationship, in sibling relationship, and relationships among women. The last two are usually present in relationships among men.

### CONCEPT OF THE ABNORMAL

Abnormality may be due to lack of development, or to distortion, disorganization or deviations from the normal.

(*a*) *Lack of development.* The manifestations of behaviour due to lack or arrested development may be seen in:

(1) *Immature behaviour* or the failure of the person to develop quantitatively and qualitatively. The main indices of immaturity are inactivity or passivity; dependency; ambivalence and emotionalism; paucity of ideals; pleasure functioning; narcissism; partial object relationships; childish mechanisms.

(2) *Delinquency* or conduct or misconduct so deviant as to come to the notice of persons. Delinquency may be due to immaturity, to mental deficiency, neurosis or a psychosis.

(3) *Mental deficiency*, caused by defect, injury or disease in the prenatal period, at birth, or early in life makes a person so lacking in intellectual capacity as to be unable to take care of himself. He is in need of aid, care, supervision, and protection for fear of exploitation.

(*b*) *Distortion or deviation*

(1) *Neuroses.* In this condition, the personality remains intact, but derives no pleasure and satisfaction from life. The individual is immature, excessively in need of affection, has exaggerated hostility and strivings for power, prestige and possessions. He is deficient in personal relationships, inhibited, evasive and devious in action and thought. He has many mechan-

isms of defence and childish modes of dealing with life situations. He is beset by unrealistic guilt feelings and aggressiveness, and lacks a fine synthesis of all functions.

(2) *Psychosis.* A psychotic person is mentally ill, or mentally disordered. His observations are twisted by illusions and hallucinations. His memory is impaired and distorted, his thought processes are warped, delusional, and he is prone to fantasy. His insight is deeply disturbed. His emotions are out of contact with reality.

The psychotic person is unable to take care of himself, is likely to be dangerous to himself and others, and may be the victim of designing persons. If the mental illness or disorder produces socially incompatible conduct, grave and serious enough to entail social or legal consequences, the condition is *insanity*.

## SUMMARY

Thus the social worker is engrossed with: (1) determination and distinction between normal and abnormal behaviour (2) evolution of the client and his problem—or social disorder; (3) interpretation to the client of his difficulties, when his disturbance is not too deep-seated and in an objective way; (4) re-education of the client and his family in normal and accepted functioning and relationships, to the end that he may lead a personally satisfying and socially useful life.

# Appendix V

## PRÉCIS: SOCIAL CASEWORK*

CONCEPT, FUNCTIONING, METHODS AND PHILOSOPHY OF THE PROFESSION
OF SOCIAL WORK

*What is Social Work?*

Social work is an institution of modern society which has its roots in philanthrophy ("practical benevolence for mankind"). While the traditional idea of ameliorating the social distress of the underprivileged ("relief of the poor") remains, the meaning of "social distress" and "underprivilege" has undergone a change in this century. They are seen as both psychologically and environmentally derived, as having no class distinction, and as affecting adversely not only the family but also the community of which the family is a part.

Social work exists to remedy the causes of social distress and underprivilege wherever they are found for the sake of strengthening and fulfilling the democratic idea of a free society.

*How Does It Function?*

The organization through which social work functions is the social agency. Initially the social agency was set up and maintained solely by the efforts of philanthropic people in the community. These "voluntary" or "private" social agencies exist today in larger urban areas. They are supported by voluntary giving from all the citizens usually through a system of "federated fund raising." This is called by various names: Community Chest; United Appeal, etc. "Councils" of social agencies are a necessary part of these community chests, their purpose being to co-ordinate the efforts of all private agencies to meet old and new social needs. The methods of social work are employed in both fund raising and social planning (see *Manual of Health*, Welfare and Recreation Agencies for Greater Vancouver).

The passage of social legislation, especially since the economic depression of the 1930's, has resulted in the creation of government agencies to administer that legislation. The intention of these laws and the way in which they are administered determines whether government agencies can be called "social agencies" in the meaning social work attaches to the term. When the intention and the method of carrying that intention out are remedial, government agencies are social agencies ("public welfare" agencies).

The developing importance of "mental health" (emotional maturity or

*See chapter v. Case records drawn from the agency's files are studied in conjunction with this discussion material.

224

stability) in medicine in determining causes of illness and in effecting its cure, has resulted in social work becoming an important medium of treating illness. In hospitals and clinics for the acutely and chronically ill, for the physically incapacitated, for the mentally ill and mentally defective, social work is one of the "disciplines" (professionally derived methods) employed in treatment. The total treatment planned by the doctor is therefore "multi-disciplined" (a team effort).

The development in the administration of justice of the concept of the rehabilitation of the "offender" has resulted in social work being introduced as a service to courts and penal institutions. In the courts, probation officers assist the magistrate or judge by providing "pre-sentence reports" (social histories) on the offender. Acting on the basis of these reports and the nature of the offence, the judge may place the offender "on probation" (social work treatment in the community). In prisons, social work is variously used in rehabilitation. Post-prison or "after-care" services are often provided by private agencies.

The development of the idea that acceptable social deportment is learned by pleasurable associations in natural groups within the community, and within institutions, has resulted in social work being employed to develop and direct such groups. Employing recreational devices, social group work is intended to treat deviant conduct, stimulate the desire and provide the opportunities for a fuller life.

The development of social security legislation and of community planning organizations whether governmental or private, has brought social work into the field of social research. The growth of large governmental agencies and of private·agencies has resulted in social work being employed in their administration.

The continuous development of all the above functions of social work is its ethical responsibility. Through appropriate "social action" social work seeks to better existing institutions of society and to create new institutions to meet newly emerging needs.

### What are Its Methods?

Its methods are (1) social casework, (2) social group work, (3) community organization, (4) social research, (5) administration. These are commonly based upon a knowledge of the social sciences: psychology, sociology, economics, social anthropology, political science, social research, etc. Each includes skills and techniques unique to it but not unrelated to the others. All require the exercise of the individual talent of the practitioner; on his knowledge, professional judgment and devotion depend the success of the method he employs. They have evolved in the past 50 years from a combination of academic scholarship and agency practice. The close relationship between the universities' professors of social work, the profession, and the social agencies ensures their constant refinement.

These methods are learned in the schools of social work; it is here that the body of knowledge, the methods, skills and techniques of social work have been co-ordinated and enunciated.

*Reading. Historical Survey of the Evolution of Social Work* by Annette Garrett; *A Belief in People* by Margaret E. Rich.

*What is Its Philosophy?*

The beliefs on which social work is founded are essentially those of democracy. It is assumed that the social work practitioner (the social worker) holds these beliefs as his own; that is, he: (*a*) respects the dignity and intrinsic worth of all people regardless of their differences; (*b*) stands for an orderly society and respects and upholds its just institutions and laws; (*c*) accepts the right of all people, within the bounds of law and society's safety, to self-determination in directing their lives; (*d*) possesses a highly developed balanced social conscience which prompts principled action to ensure social justice for all citizens and the remedy of social suffering wherever it is found.

The ethical implications of holding these beliefs demand that the social worker: (*a*) prepare himself for his profession through appropriate study at a school of social work; (*b*) use every opportunity thereafter to deepen his understanding; (*c*) identify himself with his profession in the effort to refine and improve professional practices; (*d*) assume willingly his obligation to give the service he is employed by his agency to give, and to employ his professional knowledge to the betterment of the agency's standards of service.

*Reading. The Underlying Philosophy of Social Casework* by Gordon Hamilton.

BASIC CONCEPTS, METHOD, SKILLS AND TECHNIQUES OF SOCIAL CASEWORK

*Basic Concepts*

The caseworker works *with* the individual and his family in such a way as to enable him and his family to achieve socially desirable satisfactions in life. Basic to this enabling method are certain psychologically derived beliefs. (*a*) Each individual helped by the caseworker (client) differs from every other individual. The social problem he suffers may be similar to that of others, but its causes differ, its development has differed, his capacity to deal with it will differ. (*b*) Each client has feelings about his problem which must be allayed or understood before he can begin to overcome his problem. (*c*) Each client will have built up ways (defences) of relieving the discomforts of his feelings, which are revealed by his words and behaviour and by his reactions to the caseworker's words and behaviour. (*d*) Each client's problem derives from both subjective (personality) and objective (environmental) factors in varying degrees of intensity and complexity. (*e*) The behaviour of all people is motivated by feelings (the emotions) as much as if not more than by intellect.

These concepts comprise the "approach" of the caseworker to the client. This approach ensures that the client will be met sensitively, that his feelings will be respected and not violated, that he will sense at once the caseworker's concern for him, desire to understand him and to be of help to him.

*Method and Skill*

The caseworker's method of helping is based on scientific knowledge and procedures and is made effective by the relationship he has with his client.

The acquisition of scientific knowledge is a lifelong quest which is best begun in undergraduate years and continued in a school of social work.

The scientific procedures followed by the caseworker are: (*a*) the gathering of accurate social data (facts and clear objective observations) about the client's problem and about his capacities; (b) the study of this social data from criteria (established accepted generalizations) appropriate to the case (this is deductive reasoning); (c) drawing tentative conclusions as a result of this reasoning, or formulating a "social diagnosis," or assessing the problem and the client's capacities; (d) the development of a tentative plan of treatment, in which the client shares, which is within the functions of the social agency to carry out; (e) determining a goal of treatment which when reached will terminate the help given.

The supreme skill in casework is that of the ability of the caseworker to form a relationship with the client. The nature of this relationship consists of the "anchorage, acceptance and understanding" (see Appendix IV) which the client finds in the caseworker, which gives him a sense of worth and the determination to do something about his problem and about himself.

*Techniques of Social Casework*

(a) *"Levels" of casework practice.* The function of the agency will determine to a large extent the level or intensity of the casework performed. The education, training and experience of the caseworker is another determining factor. These terms were devised by an authority on casework practice (Florence Hollis) to define levels: environmental modification; psychological support; clarification; and insight development. The casework performed in this agency encompasses the first two; the first cannot be performed without the second, but the second may be the sole need of a few clients. The third and fourth levels (or techniques) are usually employed in controlled settings (such as institutions, hospitals, clinics) where psychiatric consultation is available and the client can be reached regularly.

*Reading. The Techniques of Casework* by Florence Hollis.

(b) *Interviewing.* A study of the book *Interviewing: Its Principles and Methods,* by Annette Garrett (Family Service Association of America, New York) will be undertaken, the chapter on "Techniques" summarized by the group and discussed.

The interview is the heart of the casework process. It is in the interview that the casework relationship is formed. It is by means of the interview that the environmental help is planned and psychological support necessary to its fulfilment is given.

Beginning in the first interview, the caseworker effects a speaking relationship with the client, a *rapport* which gives the client confidence in him. In doing this, the caseworker's manner will be warm, natural, outgoing and at ease. In this interview, the client states what his problem is, as he sees it. Professional skill is involved here, first in winning the client's confidence for the caseworker and second in focusing upon the problem the client states is his. The caseworker restates the broad aspects of the problem and interprets how the agency can help him to solve it. Certain practical things may have to be done, some by the client, some by the caseworker. The time of the next interview is set and its purpose explained. The keynote of this interview is to give the client some encouragement that he can re-attain his normal situation in life or a satisfying alternative.

In this interview and subsequent interviews this necessary information is obtained: the usual accurate identifying data; the client's major attitudes, aims, ambitions, way of thinking and feeling about people and situations; his general health and that of his family; his progress in school or on the job; his relationships in his family; the major events and relevant persons in his life; his home and social setting; the roots of his problem as well as its manifestations and ramifications.

(c) *Collateral interviewing.* It is frequently necessary to obtain information from and to enlist the co-operative assistance of other agencies, professions, organizations and people in the community. The cardinal principles in collateral interviewing are: it is done with the client's knowledge and consent; it is done in his interests; it carries a professional guarantee that his confidence will not be disclosed beyond the point of necessity.

(d) *Recording.* Recording the interview—and the activities such as collateral interview, case conferences, letters—is an integral part of the casework process. It is also an integral part of agency administration.

The case record follows the scientific process implicit in the casework method. From the facts and observations recorded, conclusions are drawn and recorded; the steps to be taken, that is, the planning, should be put down. Conclusions and planning may change as the casework progresses, and these too are recorded.

Frequently the data is a composite of information obtained on application forms supported by data required to establish eligibility for services or benefits. The caseworker's observations form a part of this study.

Case records are dictated in simple narrative or story form whether formal headings (such as those required in eligibility studies) are used or not. These are the kinds of recording practised in this agency:

(1) *Chronological recording.* Following the record of the in-take interview, entries are made under the date of each interview of activity.

(2) *Summary recording.* Following the diagnostic statement, one entry may summarize activity over a period of time. Care must be exercised to record administrative factors meticulously.

(3) *Process recording.* The interview is recorded in order to reflect the dynamics of the interview. This is not a "total recall," but a careful recording of the caseworker's direction of the interview, his observations, questioning and interpretation. Not all casework is recorded in this way, but it must be done in cases involving child welfare. Part of these records may have to be used as evidence for court purposes.

(4) *Form records.* Forms provide a means of recording in our work with the aged. Diagnostic thinking and casework planning should always be included in the appropriate places on the forms. Narrative chronological entries on separate pages are necessary when problems and activities require it.

*Reading. Principles of Social Case Recording* by Gordon Hamilton, Columbia University Press, New York, 1946; *Plain Words: The A.B.C. of English* by Sir Geoffrey Gower, Her Majesty's Stationery Office, London, 1953.

### ADMINISTRATION, SUPERVISION AND STAFF DEVELOPMENT

*Administration*

The administration of the agency will in part determine the caseworker's orderliness and efficiency in doing his work. Adequate clerical help, rules of office procedure, filing systems, methods of keeping statistics, planned time-schedules, indexed policy manuals, provision of necessary office equipment, all induce order and efficiency.

The management of the case-load, however, is within the caseworker's own prerogative. It involves careful planning of the time to be devoted to each case; establishing—on the basis of social diagnosis—priorities of need for services; organizing case activity geographically; attending to correspondence, legal forms, and recording with business-like dispatch; providing for emergencies in periods of absence; and generally knowing the case-load in total.

The agency's administrators have over-all responsibility in ensuring that the above matters are faithfully carried out.

*Supervision*

The supervisor in a social agency assumes authoritative, consultative and teaching responsibilities. Authority is delegated—within certain limits—in relation to authorizing expenditure of money and overseeing administrative routine, and in relation to decisions in casework planning. Consultation and teaching functions are professional safeguards in relation to casework standards and the development in competence and understanding of the caseworkers. The supervisor shares responsibility with the in-service trainee in the conduct of his casework and teaches directly from the cases he carries.

*Staff Development*

The agency provides the means through which the whole staff may improve the quality of their work. The chief element of this agency's staff development programme are: in-service training; supervision; specialized consultation; institutes and staff conferences; staff meetings and committees; the library, bulletins, circulars; attendance at community, national and international meetings of social workers. The Training Division has responsibility for co-ordinating and implementing many of these devices.

*Public Relations*

Administrators, supervisors and social workers "meet the public" every day. Their deportment is the best assurance of establishing good public relations. Opportunities often arise to address organizations, schools, church and other groups in the community for the purpose of interpreting the agency's functions. (All addresses given must be "passed" by the administrator). Opportunities to sit on community committees also arise when the social worker can often give professional advice. The staff's public relations activities must be determined by the amount of time they consume and by the talent of the worker in this field.

Devices which assist in interpreting the agency and the profession are:

> N.F.B. Film: *A Friend at the Door*
> N.F.B. Film Strip: *Social Work*
> Recruitment Kit
> Pamphlets and Leaflets
> Mimeographed sample addresses to young people
> Social Welfare Branch Exhibit, P. N. Exhibition
> Portable panel exhibit for conventions.

# Appendix VI

## CONCLUDING GROUP SESSIONS*

FIRST WEEK: PRINCIPLES UNDERLYING CASEWORK WITH THE SICK AND
INCAPACITATED; RESOURCES FOR REHABILITATION

*Monday*

A.M. Reports back and review of outline; review of case-load and
compilation of questions for "clinic" sessions

P.M. Management of case-load, in respect of administrative controls and
casework methods
*Consultant*: the training supervisor

*Tuesday*

A.M. *Essay—discussion*: "The Meaning of Illness," Miss A. (in-service
trainee)
*Consultant*: Miss W., Provincial Supervisor of T.B. and V.D.
Social Services

P.M. *Case study*: Casework in a Medical Setting, the "Multi-Disciplined" Approach
*Leader*: Miss W.

*Wednesday*

A.M. *Essay—discussion*: "The Rehabilitation of the Handicapped,"
Mr. B.
*Consultant*: Mr. R., Provincial Rehabilitation Co-ordinator

P.M. *Field trip*: Provincial Infirmary for Chronic Disease
*Conductor*: Mrs. T., R. N., Superintendent of Infirmaries

*Thursday*

A.M. *Clinic*: Resources for Rehabilitation
*Director*: Miss M., Provincial Supervisor of Medical and Rehabilitation Services

A.M. *Field trip*: Workmen's Compensation Board
*Conductor*: Mr. H., W.C.B. Rehabilitation Officer

P.M. *Case discussion*
*Leader*: Miss M.
*Field trip*: Canadian National Institute for the Blind
*Conductor*: Miss K., Chief Social Worker, C.N.I.B.

*Friday*

A.M. *Clinic*: Federal Services for War Veterans
*Director*: Miss S., Supervisor of Social Services, D.V.A.

P.M. *Clinic*: Hospital Clearance,. Private Hospitals and Hospital Insurance

*Part III of the In-Service Training Plan. See chapter VII.

*Director*: Mr. R., Inspector of Hospitals
*Field trip*: B.C. Cancer Institute
*Conductor*: Miss G., Chief Social Worker, B.C.C.I.


SECOND WEEK: FAMILY SERVICES IN THE PUBLIC ASSISTANCE CATEGORIES

*Monday*

A.M. *Essay—discussion*: "Human Needs Met in Normal Family Living,"
Mr. C.
*Consultant*: Miss R., Provincial Supervisor of Family Division
(i.e., Public Assistance to Families)

P.M. *Essay—discussion*: "Family Casework in Social Assistance Administration," Miss D.
*Consultant*: Miss R.

*Tuesday*

A.M. *Clinics*: Social Assistance; Mothers' Allowance; Residence and
& Responsibility Acts; Policies and Procedures

P.M. *Director*: Miss R.

*Wednesday*

A.M. *Essay—discussion*: "The Special Needs of the Aged," Mr. E.
*Consultant*: Mr. L., Provincial Supervisor, Social Services for the
Aged

P.M. *Clinic*: Old Age Assistance Act, Regulations and Policies
*Director*: Mr. Q., Chairman, O.A.A. Board (at O.A.A. offices)

*Thursday*

A.M. *Clinic*: Welfare Institutions Licensing Act
*Director*: Mrs. P., Chief Inspector of Welfare Institutions

P.M. *Field trips*: Boarding Homes and Nursing Homes for the Aged
*Conductor*: Miss P.

*Friday*

A.M. *Field trip*: Home for Senile Aged, Essondale
*Conductor*: Miss T., Provincial Supervisor of Psychiatric Social
Services

P.M. *Clinic*: Administration of the Social Welfare Branch
*Director*: Mr. S., Director of Welfare.
Review and consolidation of week's activities.


THIRD WEEK: CHILD WELFARE IS FAMILY WELFARE

*Monday*

A.M. *Lecture—discussion*: The Symptoms of Behaviour Disorders
Treated by the C.G.C.
*Leader*: Mr. J.
Film showing

P.M. *Clinic*: The Functions of the Provincial Child Guidance Clinic
*Director*: Mr. J., Supervisor, Child Guidance Clinic
Film showing

*Tuesday*

A.M. *Essay—discussion*: "The Social Worker's Role Where a Child is Removed from his Natural Parents," Miss N.
*Consultant*: Mr. Y, Supervisor, Protection Section, Child Welfare Division

P.M. *Clinic*: Protection of Children Act
*Director*: Mr. G.

*Wednesday*

A.M. *Essay—discussion*: "In Quest of Foster Homes," Mr. F.
*Consultant*: Miss T., Supervisor, Foster Home Section, Child Welfare Division

P.M. *Essay—discussion*: "Placing Children in Foster Homes," Mr. G.
*Consultant*: Miss T.

*Thursday*

A.M. *Essay—discussion*: "Steps in the Adoption Process," Miss W.
*Consultant*: Mrs. F., Supervisor, Adoption Placement Section, Child Welfare Division

P.M. *Clinic*: Adoption Act, Policies and Procedures
*Director*: Mrs. F.

*Friday*

A.M. *Essay—discussion*: "Unmarried Parents," Miss J.
*Consultant*: Mrs. M. Supervisor, Unmarried Parents Section, Child Welfare Division

P.M. Summary of Child Welfare Practices in British Columbia
*Leader*: Miss McK., Superintendent of Child Welfare

FOURTH WEEK: BEHAVIOUR DISORDERS REQUIRING AUTHORITATIVE ACTION
AND SPECIALIZED TREATMENT

*Monday*

A.M. *Essay—discussion*: "The Problems of Adolescence," Mr. E.
*Consultant*: Mrs. S., Casework Supervisor, Boys' Training School

P.M. *Field trip*: Boys' Training School
*Conductor*: Mr. S.

*Tuesday*

A.M. *Field trip*: Provincial Gaol
*Lecture—discussion*: "Treatment of the Adult Offender"
*Leader*: Mr. C., Warden, Provincial Gaol

P.M. *Field trip*: The Woodlands School
*Lecture—discussion*: "Care, Education and Rehabilitation of Mentally Defective Children"
*Leader*: Miss H., Supervisor of Social Services, Woodlands School

*Wednesday*

A.M. *Field trip*: Provincial Mental Hospital and Crease Clinic of Psy-
& chological Medicine

P.M. Case presentations (revealing co-ordinated work between Hospital
and Field Social Workers)
*Leader*: Miss T., Provincial Supervisor of Psychiatric Social Work

### SUMMARY AND RE-ORIENTATION TO EVERYDAY PROCEDURES

*Thursday*

A.M. Review of activity to date and evaluation of learning opportunities
provided; individual evaluation interviews commence

P.M. *Quiz*: Accounting Procedures; Office Procedures and Statistics
*Leader*: Mr. McK., Chief Accountant.

*Friday*

A.M. *Review*: Personnel Practices, Miss L., Assistant Director of
Welfare
Discussion of evaluation of the training plan, of staff development
programme and ways to use it effectively

P.M. The afternoon is free to prepare for return to District Offices

# Appendix VII

## PURPOSES AND PRINCIPLES OF EVALUATION*

### PREAMBLE

... The administrative decision to inaugurate regularly conducted evaluations of staff was made shortly after decentralization became effective. A committee was appointed by the Planning Council to study the whole question. Working steadily for many months, this committee drafted material which was circulated to all supervisors for discussion with their staffs. The supervisors' and staffs' suggestions for amendments to this material were in turn discussed thoroughly in committee, and incorporated where it seemed wise. The results were further examined by the Planning Council and submitted by it to the General Administration for final approval and release. In short, every member of staff has in some way contributed to this study. ...

### PURPOSES AND PRINCIPLES OF EVALUATION

#### Evaluations as They Affect the Worker

The primary purpose of the evaluation is to help the social worker improve the quality of his work. The same statement may be made of the purposes of supervision, which comparison illustrates the close identity that exists between supervision and evaluation. Potentially each supervisory conference has within it elements of evaluation, which can be carried over into succeeding conferences and which can be used to advantage by the worker himself in his efforts toward self-evaluation.

The periodic, regularly conducted evaluation interview can thus be regarded as a summation of the more casual evaluation which has taken place continuously. In other words the evaluation serves as a focal point seeking to analyse the worker's total performance, to estimate his development in knowledge and skill, to state his probable potentialities for further professional development and to reveal educational needs which the agency can attempt to meet.

A primary principle of the evaluation is that it should be conducted in relation to the job the worker is expected to do. Hence it is necessary that the worker know, when his employment begins, what his employer requires him to do. He should also be fully aware of what his profession expects of him and have thought of what he is prepared to give of himself to the job. Conversely, he should have the right to state what he expects of his employers in the way of professional development and advancement.

A second principle underlying the evaluation is that the worker should know, again when his employment begins, that he will be evaluated. It follows that the uses to which the evaluation will be put should be care-

*A staff study by the Social Welfare Branch, 1947.

fully stated and fully understood. He should know that his professional attributes are to be judged in the light of the type and depth of his training and experience and not in competition with his co-workers. He should realize, moreover, that the evaluation is one means of assisting him to measure and recognize his own professional growth.

A third principle and one perhaps of greatest importance is that the evaluation is as much the worker's as the supervisor's. The ability to analyse and measure one's own performance and growth depends upon professional objectivity and integrity and upon a real desire to improve one's services to the people. Insight into one's own strengths and weaknesses will be aided by the supervisor's observations, but in the last analysis, the worker himself must evaluate his own performance in the light of his own self-knowledge. Self-knowledge itself is one of the cardinal requirements of social casework. This quality of professional insight does not come suddenly and completely as a rule, but is, too, a matter of growth toward maturity.

A fourth principle, related to the purposes of evaluation for the worker's own use, is that when the evaluation is recorded, the worker's own comments and interpretation should be included. Where there is difference of opinion between worker and supervisor, this is especially necessary. Avenues for further discussion and consideration are well defined where there are outstanding differences of opinion, which should be appropriately and promptly dealt with as much to benefit the supervisor as the worker.

Thus the evaluation would seem to be a definite advantage to the worker in encouraging his self-analysis, in measuring his growth toward greater professional competence, in providing a stimulating incentive in this idea and process of growth, and in giving recognition to his efforts.

*As They Affect the Supervisor*

Supervision in social work has been defined as a teaching process, with the aim of developing more skilled professional performance on the part of the staff. Teaching is in itself a learning process for the supervisor, demanding as it does thorough professional knowledge, administrative skills, and a conscious awareness of the community's needs and of the agency's place in the community. This fact can be considered as a purpose of evaluation for the benefit of the supervisor. Only, however, as he considers how he has helped the worker learn and develop his skills, can the evaluation process be helpful to the supervisor. This implies his ability to be objectively self-critical in defining for himself where his own strengths and weaknesses lie.

The Evaluation of a worker can be a two-way matter, for the worker's criticism of the supervision he has received can be used to advantage by the supervisor. The worker's comments regarding the areas in which he feels he has not obtained adequate help should be incorporated in his evaluation, which in a sense can be construed as an evaluation of the supervisor.

With a definite time set for evaluation interviews, the supervisor should make use of every opportunity in the interim for teaching. Case conferences cannot always be used for teaching purposes at the moment cases are presented, but at a later time, during the hour planned for supervision, practically all cases can be utilized to reteach basic principles of human behaviour and professional principles applied to them. Thus the evaluation would seem to serve as an incentive in making supervision more meaningful.

The evaluation also acquaints the supervisor with the qualifications and skills of a worker transferred to or placed under his supervision. The personnel director should pass on this information when the transfer is made, as it is advisable not to have the recorded evaluation filed in the District Offices.

A principle which may be stated in so far as the supervision is concerned is that the evaluation constitutes a discipline in maintaining proper standards of supervision. As teaching and learning is a two-way process the supervisor thus may grow as much as the worker.

A second principle would seem to be that the supervisor must be free from prejudice and have a relationship with the worker that allows for give and take. Conflicts will not arise if this relationship is sound, and when the worker has confidence in and respect for the supervisor's ability and opinions. These can only be built up through the adequacy of the supervision given the worker.

*As They Affect the Agency*

The evaluation is of importance to the administration and may be used for various purposes. One of these uses is that of administrative planning, as the extension of services to the people must of necessity be geared to the capacities of the personnel employed. Services can only expand as social workers are able to encompass these. Unless the administration is informed of the progress of the staff, wise decisions regarding expansion cannot be made, even though the community itself is pressing for wider services.

As the department grows and services extend, as more qualified staff become available, as the community comes to demand and expect more and better services, the onus is upon the administration to use greater selectivity in employing staff. At the same time, the workers now on the job have the right to expect that their jobs will be secure. A continuous orderly programme of staff development must be considered as a major part of the administration's obligation to the worker, the community and the client. Such a programme can only be effective if the worker's special needs are revealed through careful review of the evaluations.

The evaluation is also indispensable in personnel practices. Placement of staff is an exceedingly important operation in which not only the worker's general qualifications but also his particular interests and qualities are taken into consideration, as well as his stated preferences. Transfers, too, must be given serious thought, as the client, the community and the worker himself must be considered. With more staff available and with proper evaluations, the administration may do a more selective job in placement and transfers which will be satisfying to the worker, the client and the community.

Educational leave, as part of our staff development programme, has become a matter for careful planning. There are many considerations outside the worker's desire for more education—the over-all staff picture, the filling of vacancies created, the timing of leave from the point of view of the worker's usefulness to the community and his clients and so on—but wherever feasible educational leave will be granted. The evaluation will show the workers' need and readiness for wider education and will be added guidance in wise selection from the many applicants for this privilege.

Where termination of employment is considered, the evaluation, in which the worker has shared fully, is the only fair means of both worker and the administration coming to a proper decision. Presumably the worker's personal qualifications have been deemed suitable. Termination of employment then can only be judged on the worker's performance on the job as defined, and thus may be based on objective evidence of which the worker is well aware. Moreover, dismissal should not be considered until every effort has been made to overcome the weaknesses of the worker concerned, which might involve a tranfer, closer supervision, planned training on-the-job, and so on. In such instances, which are happily very few and far between, the evaluation is essential.

Promotions, and recommendations for better salaries, can only be made suitably and equitably when the administration considers that these are warranted. The evaluation should serve this purpose most fairly and effectively.

One principle of evaluation that grows out of this examination of their administrative purposes is that each worker should be judged on his individual merits and not in comparison with or in competition with other staff members. For our own particular purposes, and in conformity with our existing personnel practices within our Branch, the individual professional evaluation should sum up the results of continuous supervision and self-evaluation. This should guarantee effective use of the evaluation by the worker himself, by the supervisor, and by the administration.

A second principle is self-evident—that the record of the evaluation should be limited in its review to the worker, the supervisor and the personnel director. The latter should exercise discretion in its use. This is a highly confidential document and should not be kept in the office, or taken out of the worker's personal file kept by the Branch personnel director.

# Appendix VIII

Below is a sample of the outlines on which essays are written by in-service trainees for discussion in Part III of the In-Service Training Plan.

STEPS IN THE ADOPTION PROCESS

"Each step taken by the social worker in the process of adoption is one of protection of the child."
Develop this statement to include these considerations:

(1) The needs of every child met by his family and the special (psychological) needs of the child to be adopted.

(2) The factors considered by the social worker in approving adoption homes, with special reference to judging the suitability of the adopting parents for parenthood. Are our adoption home studies compatible with the philosophy and thinking discussed in the literature? (i.e., in the reading listed below).

(3) Considerations in selecting the adopting home for *this* child (case illustration, if possible, placement of an older child).

(4) The nature of the relationship established by the social worker with the adopting parents during the adoption process, with special reference to preparing them to receive the child (case illustration, as above).
Conclude with at least two questions for group discussion.

*Reading List*

SENN, MILTON J. E. "What We Know about the Average Child," *Child Welfare*, February 1950.

TOWLE, CHARLOTTE. *Common Human Needs*, chap. III, part II, pp. 37–57.

CLOTHIER, FLORENCE. "The Psychology of the Adopted Child," *Mental Hygiene*, April 1943.

D'ESTRUBE, FRANCETTE. "The Adoption Home Study," unpublished paper read at Regional Staff Meeting, Prince George.

MCKAY, RUBY. "Adoption of Children: A Family Service," *British Columbia's Welfare*, September 1952.

HAMMELL, CHARLOTTE L. "Helping Children Move into Adoptive Homes," *Child Welfare*, January 1949.

RAINER, LOUISE. "Helping the Child and the Adoptive Parents in the Initial Placement," *Child Welfare*, November 1951.

SHAW, JUNE. "Placement and Supervision of Children," *British Columbia's Welfare*, April 1953.

PRICE, MORRIS H. "The Adoptive Parents See a Child!," *Social Service Review*, December 1952.

# Appendix IX

## LIBRARY CATALOGUE OR CLASSIFIED READING LIST*

LIBRARY CATALOGUE

INDEX

*See chapter IX.

239

# Bibliography

BENJAMIN, LISELOTTE. "The Role of Supervision in the Beginning Social Worker's Experience in Public Assistance," *Public Welfare* (June-July 1950).

Canadian Welfare Council. "In-Service Training: Public Programmes." Prepared by the Committee on Personnel in Social Work. Ottawa, 1956 (mimeo.).

—— "Methods of Training Social Workers." Prepared by the Committee in Personnel in Social Work. Ottawa, 1956 (mimeo.).

—— "Staff Development Series": 1, "A Programme of Staff Development"; 2, "Orientation"; 3, "Staff Meetings"; 4, "Supervision."

Canadian Association of Social Workers. "Social Work Education." A Summary of Local Workshop Reports. Ottawa, 1954.

CASSATT, ANNA A. "Some Considerations in the Orientation of the Inexperienced Worker who is Untrained," *Public Welfare* (November 1944).

Department of Health, Education and Welfare, Bureau of Public Assistance, Washington, D.C. "Current Practices in Staff Training Series":
1. "Selected Materials Developed by Two State Public Welfare Agencies in Orientation of Visitors."
2. "An Institute for County Executive Directors as a Tool in Staff Development."
3. "The Staff Development Programme" (Texas).
4. "Individual and Group Conferences as Methods of Supervision" (New York).
5. "Staff Development through Administrative Process" (Montana).
6. "The Staff Meeting as a Means of Improving Administration" (Arkansas).
7. "Staff and Student Training."
8. "Process in the Development and Teaching of a Policy on Case Recording."
9. "Staff Participation in the Evaluation of a Policy on Case Recording."

—— "The Orientation Period for Public Assistance Staffs as Part of a Total Staff Development Programme."

—— "Supervision as an Administrative Process Contributing to Staff Development."

—— "The Work of the Full-Time Training Supervisor in State Public Assistance Agencies."

Family Service Association of America. "Development of Staff through Supervision." New York, 1942.

—— "Supervisory Techniques in Public Assistance Agencies." New York, 1946.

—— "Techniques of Student and Staff Supervision." New York, 1950.

LEHMAN and GINSBERG. "In-Service Training in Military Social Work," *Family* (April 1946).

MEEKER, BEN S. "In-Service Training for Probation Officers," *Year Book, National Probation and Parole Association*, 1952.

REYNOLDS, BERTHA. "Learning and Teaching in the Practice of Social Casework." New York, 1942.

SCHWEINITZ, KARL DE. *People and Process in Social Security*. American Council of Education, 1948.

TOWLE, CHARLOTTE. "The Distinctive Attributes of Education for Social Work," *Social Work Journal* (April 1952).

TROUT, BESSIE E. "In-Service Training as a Programme for Staff Development," *Social Welfare Bulletin* (October 1941).

United Nations, Department of Social Affairs. *In-Service Training in Social Welfare*. New York, 1952.

# Index